CROSSWORDS WORD SEARCHES
LOGIC PUZZLES & SURPRISES!

mind STRETCHERS

CITRON EDITION

EDITED BY STANLEY NEWMAN

Reader's Digest

The Reader's Digest Association, Inc.
Pleasantville, NY / Montreal

Project Staff

EDITORS
Neil Wertheimer, Sandy Fein

PUZZLE EDITOR
Stanley Newman

PRINCIPAL PUZZLE AUTHORS
George Bredehorn, Stanley
Newman, Dave Phillips,
Peter Ritmeester

SERIES ART DIRECTOR
Rich Kershner

DESIGNERS
Tara Long, Erick Swindell

ILLUSTRATIONS
©Norm Bendel

COPY EDITOR
Leda Scheintaub

PROOFREADER
Adam Cohen

Reader's Digest Home & Health Books

VP, EDITOR IN CHIEF
Neil Wertheimer

CREATIVE DIRECTOR
Michele Laseau

EXECUTIVE MANAGING EDITOR
Donna Ruvituso

**ASSOCIATE DIRECTOR,
NORTH AMERICA PREPRESS**
Douglas A. Croll

MANUFACTURING MANAGER
John L. Cassidy

MARKETING DIRECTOR
Dawn Nelson

The Reader's Digest Association, Inc.

**PRESIDENT AND
CHIEF EXECUTIVE OFFICER**
Mary G. Berner

**PRESIDENT, HOME & GARDEN
AND HEALTH & WELLNESS**
Alyce C. Alston

SVP, CHIEF MARKETING OFFICER
Amy J. Radin

**PRESIDENT, GLOBAL CONSUMER
MARKETING AND CEO, DIRECT
HOLDINGS**
Dawn M. Zier

ISBN 978-1-60652-989-8

Address any comments about *Mind Stretchers, Citron Edition* to:

The Reader's Digest Association, Inc.
Editor in Chief, Books
Reader's Digest Road
Pleasantville, NY 10570-7000

To order copies of this or other editions of the *Mind Stretchers* book series,
call 1-800-846-2100.

Visit our online store at **rdstore.com**

For many more fun games and puzzles, visit www.rd.com/games.

Printed in the United States of America

1 3 5 7 9 10 8 6 4 2

US 4967/L-13

Contents

Dear Puzzler,

Long before the term FAQs (short for "frequently asked questions") became well-known in the Internet Age, I was assembling my own mental list of the questions most frequently asked of me as a long-time author and editor of crossword puzzles, as well as the author of dozens of puzzle books. Here, then, are answers to questions that might come up if we found ourselves together in the same room.

How did you get started in crosswords?
I've been solving crosswords since childhood, and started solving the New York Times crosswords regularly in high school. My entry in the crossword business came about as a direct result of winning three crossword tournaments in 1982, including the first U.S. Open Crossword Championship. The next year, I started up a crossword newsletter, for which I served as editor, publisher, and one of the regular puzzle authors.

What does a crossword editor do?
Generally speaking, crossword editors receive submissions from puzzle authors, decide which puzzles to accept for publication, and make adjustments to accepted puzzles to adjust the difficulty level, change unwanted answer words, etc.

When you're making a crossword, which comes first, the clues or the answers?
The crossword diagram with the answers is always created first, then the clues are written. If you're wondering why the answers are never written first, try making your own 3x3 crossword by writing the answers first. Then it'll be clear!

Do you know Will Shortz?
I've known the New York Times' puzzle editor for nearly 30 years, since long before he got his current job. Will is the person most responsible for my puzzle career, since he ran all the crossword tournaments I won in 1982 (see above). We still see each other several times each year, and travel together as part of the U.S. delegation to the annual World Puzzle Championship.

Now I've got a question for you: How do like Mind Stretchers? Your comments on any aspect of this or any other edition of Mind Stretchers are most welcome. You can reach me by regular mail at the address below, or by e-mail at mindstretchers@readersdigest.com.

Best wishes for happy and satisfying solving!

Stanley Newman
Mind Stretchers Puzzle Editor

Mind Stretchers
c/o Reader's Digest
1 Reader's Digest Rd.
Pleasantville, NY 10570-7000

(Please enclose a self-addressed stamped envelope if you'd like a reply.)

■ Foreword

Meet the Puzzles!

Mind Stretchers is filled with a delightful mix of classic and new puzzle types. To help you get started, here are instructions, tips, and examples for each.

WORD GAMES

Crossword Puzzles

Edited by Stanley Newman

Crosswords are arguably America's most popular puzzles. As presented in this book, the one- and two-star puzzles test your ability to solve straightforward clues to everyday words. "More-star" puzzles have a somewhat broader vocabulary, but most of the added challenge in these comes from less obvious and trickier clues. These days, you'll be glad to know, uninteresting obscurities such as "Genus of fruit flies" and "Famed seventeenth-century soprano" don't appear in crosswords anymore.

Our 60 crosswords were authored by more than a dozen different puzzle makers, all nationally known for their skill and creativity.

Clueless Crosswords

by George Bredehorn

A unique crossword variation invented by George, these 7-by-7 grids primarily test your vocabulary and reasoning skills. There is one simple task: Complete the crossword with common uncapitalized seven-letter words, based entirely on the letters already filled in for you.

Hints: *Focusing on the last letter of a word, when given, often helps. For example, a last letter of G often suggests that IN are the previous two letters. When the solutions aren't coming quickly, focus on the shared spaces that are blank—you can often figure out whether it has to be a vowel or a consonant, helping you solve both words that cross it.*

Split Decisions

by George Bredehorn

Crossword puzzle lovers also enjoy this variation. Once again, no clues are provided except within the diagram. Each answer consists of two words whose spellings are the same, except for two consecutive letters. For each pair of words, the two sets of different letters are already filled in for you. All answers are common words; no phrases or hyphenated or capitalized words are used. Certain missing words may have more than one possible solution, but there is only one solution for each word that will correctly link up with all the other words.

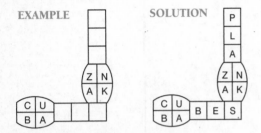

EXAMPLE   SOLUTION

Hints: *Start with the shorter (three- and four-letter) words, because there will be fewer possibilities that spell words. In each puzzle, there will always be a few such word pairs that have only one solution. You may have to search a little to find them, since they may be anywhere in the grid, but it's always a good idea to fill in the answers to these first.*

Triad Split Decisions
by George Bredehorn
This puzzle is solved the same way as Split Decisions, except you are given three letters for each word instead of two.

EXAMPLE   SOLUTION

Word Searches

Kids love 'em, and so do grownups, making word searches perhaps the most widely appealing puzzle type. In a word search, the challenge is to find hidden words within a grid of letters. In the typical puzzle, words can be found in vertical columns, horizontal rows, or along diagonals, with the letters of the words running either forward or backward. Usually, a list of words to search for is given to you. But

ANSWERS!

Answers to all the puzzles are found beginning on page 233, and are organized by the page number on which the puzzle appears.

to make word searches harder, puzzle writers sometimes just point you in the right direction, such as telling you to find 25 foods. Other twists include allowing words to take right turns, or leaving letters out of the grid.

Hints: *One of the most reliable and efficient searching methods is to scan each row from top to bottom for the first letter of the word. So if you are looking for "violin" you would look for the letter "v." When you find one, look at all the letters that surround it for the second letter of the word (in this case, "i"). Each time you find a correct two-letter combination (in this case, "vi"), you then scan either for the correct three-letter combination ("vio") or the whole word.*

NUMBER GAMES

Sudoku

by Conceptis Ltd.
Sudoku puzzles have become massively popular in the past few years, thanks to their simplicity and test of pure reasoning. The basic Sudoku puzzle is a 9-by-9 square grid, split into 9 square regions, each containing 9 cells. Each puzzle starts off with roughly 20 to 35 of the squares filled in with the numbers 1 to 9. There is just one rule: Fill in the rest of the squares

EXAMPLE

8	4					7	1	
3			7	1	8			9
		5	9		3	6		
	9	7	8		1	2	3	
	6						9	
	3	1	2		9	7	6	
		4	3		2	9		
1			5	9	4			6
9	8						5	3

SOLUTION

8	4	9	6	2	5	3	7	1
3	2	6	7	1	8	5	4	9
7	1	5	9	4	3	6	8	2
5	9	7	8	6	1	2	3	4
2	6	8	4	3	7	1	9	5
4	3	1	2	5	9	7	6	8
6	5	4	3	8	2	9	1	7
1	7	3	5	9	4	8	2	6
9	8	2	1	7	6	4	5	3

with the numbers 1 to 9 so that no number appears twice in any row, column, or region.

Hints: Use the numbers provided to rule out where else the same number can appear. For example, if there is a 1 in a cell, a 1 cannot appear in the same row, column, or region. By scanning all the cells that the various 1 values rule out, you often can find where the remaining 1 values must go.

Hyper-Sudoku

by Peter Ritmeester

Peter is the inventor of this unique Sudoku variation. In addition to the numbers 1 to 9 appearing in each row and column, Hyper-Sudoku also has four 3-by-3 regions to work with, indicated by gray shading.

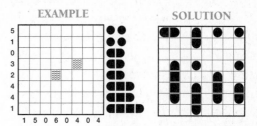

EXAMPLE   SOLUTION

Find the Ships

by Conceptis Ltd.

If you love playing the board game Battleship, you'll enjoy this pencil-and-paper variation! In each puzzle, a group of ships of varying sizes is provided on the right. Your job: Properly place the ships in the grid. A handful of ship "parts" are put on the board to get you started. The placement rules:

1. Ships must be oriented horizontally or vertically. No diagonals!

2. A ship can't go in a square with wavy lines; that indicates water.

3. The numbers on the left and bottom of the grid tell you how many squares in that row or column contain part of ships.

4. No two ships can touch each other, even diagonally.

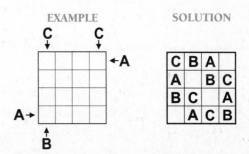

EXAMPLE   SOLUTION

Hints: The solving process involves both finding those squares where a ship must go and eliminating those squares where a ship cannot go. The numbers provided should give you a head start with the latter, the number 0 clearly implying that every square in that row or column can be eliminated. If you know that a square will be occupied by a ship, but don't yet know what kind of ship, mark that square, then cross out all the squares that are diagonal to it—all of these must contain water.

ABC

by Peter Ritmeester

This innovative new puzzle challenges your logic much in the way a Sudoku puzzle does. Each row and column in an ABC puzzle contains exactly one A, one B, and one C, plus one blank (or two, in harder puzzles). Your task is to figure out where the three letters go in each row. The clues outside the puzzle frame tell you the first letter encountered when moving in the direction of an arrow.

EXAMPLE   SOLUTION

Hints: *If a clue says a letter is first in a row or column, don't assume that it must go in the first square. It could go in either of the first two squares (or first three, in the harder puzzles). A good way to start is to look for where column and row clues intersect (for example, when two clues look like they are pointing at the same square). These intersecting clues often give you the most information about where the first letter of a row or column must go. At times, it's also possible to figure out where a certain letter goes by eliminating every other square as a possibility for that letter in a particular row or column.*

Fences

by Conceptis Ltd.

Lovers of mazes will enjoy these challenges. Connect the dots with vertical or horizontal lines, so that a single loop is formed with no crossings or branches. Each number indicates how many lines surround it; squares with no number may be surrounded by any number of lines.

EXAMPLE   SOLUTION

Hints: *Don't try to solve the puzzle by making one continuous line—instead, fill in the links (that is, spaces between two dots) you are certain about, and then figure out how to connect those links. To start the puzzle, mark off any links that can't be connected. That would include all four links around each 0. Another good starting step is to look for any 3 values next or adjacent to a 0; solving those links is easy. In time, you will see that rules and patterns emerge, particularly in the puzzle corners, and when two numbers are adjacent to each other.*

Number-Out

by Conceptis Ltd.

This innovative new puzzle challenges your logic in much the same way a Sudoku puzzle does. Your task is to shade squares so that no number appears in any row or column more than once. Shaded squares may not touch each other horizontally or vertically, and all unshaded squares must form a single continuous area.

EXAMPLE   SOLUTION

Hints: *First look for all the numbers that are unduplicated in their row and column. Those squares will never be shaded, so we suggest that you circle them as a reminder to yourself. When there are three of the same number consecutively in a row or column, the one in the middle must always be unshaded, so you can shade the other two. Also, any square that is between a pair of the same numbers must always be unshaded. Once a square is shaded, you know that the squares adjacent to it, both horizontally and vertically, must be unshaded.*

Star Search

by Peter Ritmeester

Another fun game in the same style of Minesweeper. Your task: find the stars that are hidden among the blank squares. The numbered squares indicate how many stars are hidden in squares adjacent to them (including diagonally). There is never more than one star in any square.

EXAMPLE   SOLUTION

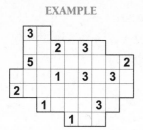

Hint: If, for example, a 3 is surrounded by four empty squares, but two of those squares are adjacent to the same square with a 1, the other two empty squares around the 3 must contain stars.

123

by Peter Ritmeester

Each grid in this puzzle has pieces that look like dominoes. You must fill in the blank squares so that each "domino" contains one each of the numbers 1, 2, and 3, according to these two rules:

EXAMPLE   SOLUTION

1. No two adjacent squares, horizontally or vertically, can have the same number.

2. Each completed row and column of the diagram will have an equal number of 1s, 2s, and 3s.

Hints: Look first for any blank square that is adjacent to two different numbers. By rule 1 above, the "missing" number of 1-2-3 must go in that blank square. Rule 2 becomes important to use later in the solving process. For example, knowing that a 9-by-9 diagram must have three 1s, three 2s, and three 3s in each row and column allows you to use the process of elimination to deduce what blank squares in nearly filled rows and columns must be.

VISUAL PUZZLES

Throughout *Mind Stretchers* you will find unique mazes, visual conundrums, and other colorful challenges, each developed by maze master Dave Phillips. Each comes under a new name and has unique instructions. Our best advice? Patience and perseverance. Your eyes will need time to unravel the visual secrets.

In addition, you will also discover these visual puzzles:

Line Drawings

by George Bredehorn

George loves to create never-before-seen puzzle types, and here is another unique Bredehorn game. Each Line Drawing puzzle is different in its design, but the task is the same: Figure out where to place the prescribed number of lines to partition the space in the instructed way.

Hint: Use a pencil and a straightedge as you work. Some lines come very close to the items within the region, so being straight and accurate with your line-drawing is crucial.

One-Way Streets

by Peter Ritmeester

Another fun variation on the maze. The diagram represents a pattern of streets. A and B are parking spaces, and the black squares are stores. Find a route that starts at A, passes through all the stores exactly once, and ends at B. (Harder puzzles use P's to indicate parking spaces instead of A's and B's, and don't tell you the starting and ending places.) Arrows indicate one-way traffic for that block only. No

EXAMPLE   SOLUTION

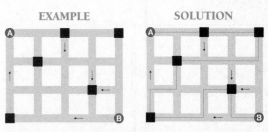

block or intersection may be entered more than once.

Hints: *The particular arrangement of stores and arrows will always limit the possibilities for the first store passed through from the starting point A and the last store passed through before reaching ending point B. So try to work both from the start and the end of the route. Also, the placement of an arrow on a block doesn't necessarily mean that your route will pass through that block. You can also use arrows to eliminate blocks where your path will not go.*

BRAIN TEASERS

To round out the more involved puzzles are more than 150 short brain teasers, most written by our puzzle editor, Stanley Newman. Stan is famous in the puzzle world for his inventive brain games. An example of how to solve each puzzle appears in the puzzle's first occurrence (the page number is noted below). You'll find the following types scattered throughout the pages.

* Invented by and cowritten with George Bredehorn

** By George Bredehorn

But wait...there's more!

At the top of many of the pages in this book are additional brain teasers, organized into three categories:

• **QUICK!**: These tests challenge your ability to instantly calculate numbers or recall well-known facts.

• **DO YOU KNOW** ...: These more demanding questions probe the depth of your knowledge of facts and trivia.

• **HAVE YOU** ... and **DO YOU** ...: These reminders reveal the many things you can do each day to benefit your brain.

For the record, we have deliberately left out answers to the **QUICK!** and **DO YOU KNOW** ... features. Our hope is that if you don't know an answer, you'll be intrigued enough to open a book or search the Internet for it!

■ Meet the Authors

STANLEY NEWMAN (puzzle editor and author) is crossword editor for *Newsday,* the major newspaper of Long Island, New York. He is the author/editor of over 125 books, including the autobiography and instructional manual *Cruciverbalism* and the best-selling *Million Word Crossword Dictionary.* Winner of the First U.S. Open Crossword Championship in 1982, he holds the world's record for the fastest completion of a *New York Times* crossword— 2 minutes, 14 seconds. Stan operates the website www.StanXwords.com and also conducts an annual Crossword University skill-building program on a luxury-liner cruise.

GEORGE BREDEHORN is a retired elementary school teacher from Wantagh, New York. His variety word games have appeared in the *New York Times* and many puzzle magazines. Every week for the past 20 years, he and his wife, Dorothy, have hosted a group of Long Island puzzlers who play some of the 80-plus games that George has invented.

CONCEPTIS (www.conceptispuzzles.com) is a leading supplier of logic puzzles to printed, electronic, and other gaming media all over the world. On average, ten million Conceptis puzzles are printed in newspapers, magazines and books each day, while millions more are played online and on mobile phones each month.

DAVE PHILLIPS has designed puzzles for books, magazines, newspapers, PC games, and advertising for more than 30 years. In addition, Dave is a renowned creator of walk-through mazes. Each year his corn-maze designs challenge visitors with miles of paths woven into works of art. Dave is also codeveloper of eBrainyGames.com, a website that features puzzles and games for sale.

PETER RITMEESTER is chief executive officer of PZZL.com, which produces many varieties of puzzles for newspapers and websites worldwide. Peter is also general secretary of the World Puzzle Federation. The federation organizes the annual World Puzzle Championship, which includes difficult versions of many of the types of logic puzzles that Peter has created for *Mind Stretchers.*

■ Master Class: **Crosswords**

How to Write Crossword Clues

It's been said that the talented professionals who create crossword puzzles need to be "masters of arts" as well as "masters of science." With more than 3,000 of my own crosswords published (I lost count of the exact number years ago), I can humbly agree.

Just think for a moment about the parts of a crossword puzzle and the different skills required for them. Devising a workable theme and theme answers is mostly artistic, I think, with just a bit of science thrown in—thinking of answers with symmetric lengths to fit in a standard diagram. Working out a diagram pattern to accommodate your theme answers is clearly a scientific skill, with fairly strict rules that must be followed. Fitting the remaining answer words into your diagram is clearly a mostly analytical task, with creativity coming into play as you select the best word to fit in a given space.

As you'll see shortly, the last step in creating a crossword, the writing of the clues, has both scientific and creative elements to it. In this Master Class, I'll introduce you to each of these elements, and share with you with the fundamentals of how good crossword-clue writing is done.

The Cardinal Principles

While specific puzzle editors' requirements vary somewhat, there is general agreement about these qualities that crossword clues must have:

Accuracy Is Job One

That accuracy is the single most important rule of crossword-clue writing should come as no surprise. Every clue in a puzzle must accurately define or describe its answer. If, for example, the answer is a plural noun, the clue must indicate that a plural is called for. Clues containing factual information must be correct in every detail. As a rule of thumb, any lowercase puzzle answer and its clue should be able to be used interchangeably in a sentence.

Variety

In the early years of crossword history (the 1910s through the 1930s), virtually all puzzle answers were single, uncapitalized words, and only "dictionary-style" definitions were allowed for them. These days, editors encourage puzzle authors to liven up the language of their clues, using colloquial terms, factual references, etc. That variety certainly spices up crossword solving in a way that I think makes for a more entertaining experience.

Balance

Puzzle authors must always take care that their clue lists don't have "too much" or "too many" of anything. A crossword intended for a general audience shouldn't have more than one clue about baseball, or opera, or literature, or TV sitcoms, to name just a few topical areas. Likewise, there should be a balance in a puzzle's factual clues between academic subjects (geography, science, etc.) and "pop culture" subjects (current events, films, etc.).

Fairness

Crossword-clue writers must always play fair with the solver. Contemporary editors won't allow dictionary words to be defined with rarely seen synonyms, such as "Transude" for SEEP, because most solvers won't know the word, and would most likely have to consult a dictionary to understand it. Similarly, factual clues shouldn't require you to know something that's just not worth knowing. There happens to be a town in Utah called Loa, whose current population is about 500. Although editors and solvers would certainly welcome a new alternative to the clue "Mauna __," a clue about Loa, Utah, just wouldn't be fair.

Of course, this doesn't mean clues can't be tricky, or even intentionally misleading, as many clues for tougher crosswords are.

Brevity

Whether they're printed in books or newspapers, crosswords are allocated a fixed, fairly limited space. That's why most crossword clues have no more than three words.

Types of Clues

If, like most *Mind Stretchers* readers, you've solved many crosswords over the years, you'll certainly be familiar with the various types of clues. As a would-be puzzle author, however, you always need to be aware of all the tools in the toolbox available to you, and, as previously discussed, vary their use as much as possible within a particular puzzle. Listed below are most of the major clue categories, with examples of each.

Some of My Clue Requirements

These are taken from the editorial guidelines that I provide to puzzle authors who inquire about submitting puzzles to me. Most other editors have similar guidelines.

- No references to anything unpleasant or controversial

- No unusual or obscure words in clues

- One-word clues shouldn't be used for more than 10% of the puzzle (this helps to keep the clue language lively)

- Define common dictionary words with contemporary idioms where possible

- Wherever possible, use clues that provide interesting information about frequently seen answers (such as ERIE being the shallowest of the Great Lakes)

Straight Definition

Clues like these read as if they've come directly from a dictionary, with no embellishment.

"Donate" – GIVE
"Depose from an office" – OUST

By Example

A little harder than definition clues, these require you recognize the particular category of a word or words.

"Sycamore or spruce" – TREE
"The Nile, for instance" – RIVER

Abbreviation

May be tipped off either by a tag at the end (like "Abbr." or "in brief"), or an abbreviation in the clue. This style may also be used for shortened forms of a word that aren't abbreviations, such as DOC and STAT.

"Nov. follower" – DEC
"Timetable info, for short" – ETA

Comparative/Superlative Adjective

Almost always clued either with "More/Less" or "Most/Least" as the first word.

"More sensible" – SANER
"Least ordinary" – ODDEST

Foreign Word

Clues for foreign words frequently use alliterative references to people or places associated with foreign languages.

"Hernando's house" – CASA
"Gold, in Guatemala" – ORO

Fill-in-the Blank

Used most often to clue multi-word partial phrases, these often have a parenthetical explanation at the end.

"From __ Z (completely)" – A TO
"Wise __ owl" – AS AN

Referential

When two answers in a puzzle are closely related, you'll often see clues that refer to each other. From the mail I receive, I know that many solvers aren't overly fond of referentials. That's why I try to use them sparingly.

"With 23 Across, *M*A*S*H* star" – ALAN (with ALDA at 23 Across)
"Brand of 14 Down" – OREO (with "Sweet treat" – COOKIE at 14 Down)

Colloquial/Slang

While they may not necessarily be found in the dictionary, informal synonyms like these make a crossword more fun to solve.

"Keep out of sight" – HIDE
"Chow down" – EAT

Evocative

Clues that paint a word picture are among my favorites to think up, as well as encounter in the crosswords that I solve. They're a great change of pace that, while not usually very difficult, require a different kind of thinking to figure out.

"Bachelor's last words" – I DO
"Makeshift swing" – TIRE

One frequently used evocative device is the word "Like" at the start of the clue to indicate an adjective that is an appropriate descriptor of the word or words that follow.

"Like loose-leaf paper" – LINED
"Like an omelet" – EGGY

Another is a word like "concern" or "bane" at the end of a clue that usually starts with an occupation, which gets solvers to think about what they know about that occupation.

"Pilot's concern" – FOG
"Librarian's bane" – NOISE

Half/Part

Clues that start with words like "Half" or "Part" may be literal or figurative.

"Part of a shirt" – ARM
"Half of L.A." – LOS (as in "Los Angeles")

Partner

The relationship here may also be either real or figurative.

"Currier's partner" – IVES
"Bill's partner" – COO (as in "bill and coo")

Qualifiers

Use clues followed by words like "sometimes," "usually," and "perhaps," or with "as" in the middle, to indicate that the clue is not really synonymous with the answer, but is correct under certain conditions.

"Farmer, at times" – HOER
"Improve, as wine" – AGE

Kin

Clues that end with "relative," "kin," or "cousin" usually indicate relationships that are more figurative than familial.

"Bassoon kin" – OBOE
"Button relative" – VELCRO

Start/End

Words of this nature are used in place of "prefix" and "suffix" to indicate parts of words.

"Ending for press" – URE
"Freeze beginner" – ANTI

Wordplay

They may involve puns or rhymes, and are a fun variation that is intended to bring smiles to solvers.

"Do the Wright thing" – FLY
"Air pair" – THE WRIGHT BROTHERS

Brand Names

Once a crossword taboo, well-known brand names are crossword regulars today. But most editors prefer that a brand-name answer be clued using the name of a competitor, so as not to appear to be showing favoritism toward any particular product.

"Hertz rival" – AVIS
"Paper Mate competitor" – BIC

Preposition Addition

Prepositions are often used in clues either to provide the solver with a little extra hint to the answer, or for precision in defining phrases that include a preposition.

"Depend (on)" – RELY (This indicates that "Depend on" is synonymous with "rely on")
"Misbehave, with 'up'" – ACT ("Act up" means "misbehave")

Difficulty Levels of Clues

In general, crossword editors require the level of clues to be on a par with the difficulty of the theme. If your theme is very straightforward and will be easy for solvers to figure out, most (if not all) of the clues should likewise be easy. With more subtle or trickier themes, editors will expect most of your clues to be a little tougher.

What's an easy clue? One that points the solver directly and unambiguously to the answer. In other words, a clue that most will know the answer to, for which there will ideally be only one possible answer with the given number of letters.

Let's say you want to write a very easy clue for the word PURR, and think of "Cat's sound." Well, that's pretty easy all right, but not as easy as it can be. Why? Because MEOW might also be a perfectly reasonable answer as well. So, to make your clue very easy, you'd need to alter your clue so that PURR will be the only answer—in other words, to eliminate MEOW as a possibility. "Happy cat's sound" would do it, for instance.

More difficult clues don't "point right at" the answer as easier ones do, of course. As a clue writer, you have two basic tools at your disposal to make your clues harder: ambiguity and trickiness. "House pet's sound" as a clue for MEOW is clearly tougher than "Cat's sound" because the type of pet isn't stated. Keeping our clues in the veterinary vein, if you wanted to write a tricky clue for the word BARK, your first step would be to find a word related to your answer that has a common but unrelated additional meaning. One such word is "Boxer," which can be a dog breed or an occupation. Then, word your clue in such a way that it appears to refer to the unrelated meaning rather than the actual one. You might therefore come up with something like "Boxer's complaint."

No matter what the intended difficulty level of the clue you're writing, you must always examine your clue from the solver's standpoint, to be as sure as you can that the clue is really at the level you want it to be. Two ways you might do this:

- Examine all your clues after you've written them, covering up the answers

- Have a puzzle-fan friend or relative do the same

The latter is highly recommended for beginners, for whom getting a "second opinion" is a very good idea.

Additional Resources

Unfortunately, there is no book currently in print that covers crossword clue writing. The out-of-print *Random House Puzzlemaker's Handbook*, originally published in 1995 and written by my colleagues Mel Rosen and Stan Kurzban, is an excellent resource for beginners that can still be found at used book stores and online booksellers, as well as at local libraries.

For would-be clue writers with Internet access, the Web site www.cruciverb.com, the "Crossword Community Center," is a must. It has much useful information for beginners.

With every edition of *Mind Stretchers*, you've got 60 "lessons" in clue writing available to you. To take advantage of them, review the clues of each puzzle after you complete it, noting the star rating at the top first. Based on what you've learned in this section, ascertain each clue's difficulty level, noting the different devices the puzzle authors utilize for various levels. You should find, of course, that as the puzzles' star ratings increase, the puzzles have a lower percentage of easy clues.

Final Words

If this Master Class has given you the inspiration to try creating your own cross-words, I wish you the best of luck. Even if not, I hope you've gained a greater insight into the puzzle-writing process that will boost your solving skill and give you a greater appreciation for all that puzzle authors do to make your time spent with crosswords both fun and challenging.

—Stanley Newman

★ Off-White by Gail Grabowski

ACROSS

1 Makes a trade
6 Ginger cookie
10 Lobster relative
14 Attacked
15 Army-medal recipient
16 Competition on foot
17 Place removed from reality
19 The Emerald Isle
20 For each
21 Most August babies
22 Wall Street employee
24 Regret one's wrongdoings
26 *The King and I* setting
27 Language ending
28 Toy auto
31 Soft drink
34 Eagle's claw
36 Pull along
38 Sonny's partner, once
39 Backtalk
40 Author __ Stanley Gardner
41 Sledding site
42 Copy-machine powder
44 Sporting sword
45 Tune from the past
47 TV commercials
49 Spot of land in the sea
50 Nasty smiles
53 Snow-removing tool
56 Religious group
57 Chimp or gorilla
59 Old answering-machine insert
60 Foolish
63 "__ the Rainbow"
64 College grad
65 Informal language
66 Farm enclosures

67 Soldiers in gray
68 Not on time

DOWN

1 Ocean vessel
2 Be undecided
3 Dote on
4 Golfer's goal
5 Fashions
6 Take, as a photo
7 Six o'clock broadcast
8 "__ you sure?"
9 Meal serving
10 Bagel filling
11 Surprise attack
12 Land measure

13 Keg contents
18 Religious doctrine
23 Tattletale
25 Certain oyster hunters
26 Mountain incline
28 Injured-arm support
29 50-and-over org.
30 Regulation
31 K-8 facility: Abbr.
32 Cleveland's state
33 Wooded valley
35 Single-handedly
37 Director Spike
42 Turnpike barrier

43 Salad-dressing flavor
46 Compass pt. opposite NNW
48 Really dislike
50 Appears
51 Air-traffic controller's device
52 Lighten one's purse
53 "Cut it out!"
54 Possess
55 Ready for customers
56 Rudely ignore
58 Nervous
61 Guadalajara "Rah!"
62 Birmingham's state: Abbr.

★ Minty

Which peppermint stick was laid down in the middle of the pile, having the same number of peppermint sticks below it as above it?

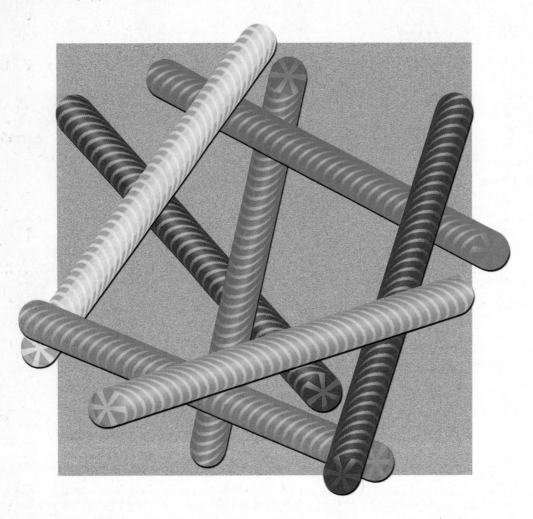

CENTURY MARKS

Inserting plus signs and minus signs, as many as necessary, in between the nine digits below, create a series of additions and subtractions whose final answer is 100. Any digits without a sign between them are to be grouped together as a single number.
Example: 4 7 - 5 + 2 2 + 8 - 1 + 2 9 = 100

| 5 | 2 | 1 | 2 | 1 | 3 | 9 | 4 | 6 | = | 100 |

★ Stress-Free

Find these calming things that are hidden in the diagram, either across, down, or diagonally. Individual words of all multiple-word answers are hidden separately. Ignore words contained within parentheses.

```
J  A  C  U  Z  Z  I  D  E  P  D  O  W  N  E
G  K  U  S  L  E  E  P  A  G  T  S  E  R  L
N  O  D  W  Y  T  D  M  N  Y  A  R  E  N  B
I  O  D  I  X  O  P  I  X  P  E  S  I  H  B
Z  B  L  M  D  E  G  K  B  A  U  T  S  E  U
O  V  E  M  R  E  L  A  D  R  L  R  U  A  B
D  N  O  I  T  A  T  I  D  E  M  E  M  L  M
W  F  N  N  W  H  N  Y  R  H  E  T  R  T  D
F  G  C  G  E  G  R  U  F  T  R  C  R  H  T
T  T  E  A  S  T  C  U  M  A  U  H  L  H  S
S  E  R  E  N  I  T  Y  W  M  C  G  G  A  M
R  L  D  U  D  D  E  O  L  O  I  I  U  D  U
E  A  O  E  A  O  L  S  J  R  N  N  A  P  S
E  C  P  F  P  S  O  E  T  A  A  Q  S  L  I
T  A  E  R  T  E  R  G  S  A  M  E  P  U  C
```

AROMATHERAPY
BUBBLE BATH
CANDLES
COUNTRY WALK
CUDDLE
CUP (of) TEA
DAY OFF
DOZING
EARLY NIGHT
FACIAL
GOOD BOOK
HEALTH SPA
JACUZZI
MANICURE
MASSAGE
MEDITATION
MUSIC
PAMPERING
PEDICURE
READING
RELAX
REST
RETREAT
SAUNA
SERENITY
SIESTA
SLEEP
SLOW DOWN
STRETCH
SWIMMING
YOGA

INITIAL REACTION

Identify the well-known proverb from the first letters in each of its words.
Example: L.B.Y.L. Answer: Look Before You Leap

L. I. B. _____

★ Sudoku

Fill in the blank boxes so that every row, column, and 3x3 box contains all of the numbers 1 to 9.

			9	8	4			7
	8				1		5	
	9		5			6		
2		3		9			4	1
7			3		2			6
5	1			4		8		3
		2			7		6	
	5		6			1		
9			1	3	8			

MIXAGRAMS

Each line contains a five-letter word and a four-letter word that have been mixed together (the order of the letters in each word has not been changed). Unmix the two words on each line and write them in the spaces provided. When you're done, find a two-part answer to the clue by reading down the letter columns in the answers. Example: D A R I U N V E T = DRIVE + AUNT

CLUE: Sound right

C A S I R T A E T = _ _ _ _ _ + _ _ _ _

A C U G R I B L E = _ _ _ _ _ + _ _ _ _

H O O P U N S O R = _ _ _ _ _ + _ _ _ _

R I L I G E N I D = _ _ _ _ _ + _ _ _ _

★ Sign Here by Sally R. Stein

ACROSS

1 Fairy-tale-writing brothers' surname
6 Touch down, as a plane
10 Historian's interest
14 Therefore
15 Jai __
16 Wish sincerely
17 Ancient Peruvians
18 Moistens
19 Tiny bit of liquid
20 Big Declaration of Independence signature
23 Part of a sock
24 UFO pilots
25 Dangerous
27 Beautician's creation
31 Pay a call on
33 Square-mile fraction
34 Most important
36 Batted balls that don't count
40 Declaration of Independence signer/author
43 Mexican mister
44 GI offense
45 Exxon's former name
46 Changes course suddenly
48 Philanthropist Carnegie
50 Seem to be
53 Conk out
54 Compete
55 Declaration of Independence signer
62 Boat paddles
64 "For Pete's __!"
65 Mechanical man
66 Monogram part: Abbr.
67 Looked at
68 Lloyd Webber musical

69 Toy in a carriage
70 H. __ Perot
71 Discourage

DOWN

1 Quartet after F
2 Nevada city
3 Fraction of a foot
4 Thom of shoe fame
5 Fitted together nicely
6 Suburban grassy spots
7 Actor Baldwin
8 Western alliance
9 Item thrown by Olympic athletes
10 Prof.'s degree
11 Main artery
12 Parody
13 Wigwam relative
21 Parts of molecules
22 Steak cutter
26 Kept for later
27 Fedoras and derbies
28 Feel sore
29 Barbell metal
30 Delete
31 Looks at
32 The lowdown
35 Slightly open
37 Cold War adversary
38 Misplace
39 Ski surface
41 Neighborhoods
42 Swing wildly
47 Pencil end
49 Got close to
50 Keep away from
51 "Grand" instrument
52 Jeopardy
53 Heroic acts
56 Sandwich spread, for short
57 Luau music makers
58 Bird of peace
59 Slightly
60 Dust speck
61 Leading performer
63 Mo. city

★ Fences

Connect the dots with vertical or horizontal lines, so that a single loop is formed with no crossings or branches. Each number indicates how many lines surround it; squares with no number may be surrounded by any number of lines.

```
3 2 0 2   1 0 1

1                 1
  2     3 1 2
  3 1 2       0
1             3

2 1 2   1 2 1 2
```

ADDITION SWITCH

Switch the positions of two of the digits in the incorrect sum at right, to get a correct sum.

Example: 955+264 = 411. Switch the second 1 in 411 with the 9 in 955 to get: 155+264 = 419

$$
\begin{array}{r}
349 \\
+283 \\
\hline
641
\end{array}
$$

★★ Line Drawing

Draw three straight lines 2" long or more, each from one edge of the square to another edge, without touching or crossing any of the geometric figures.

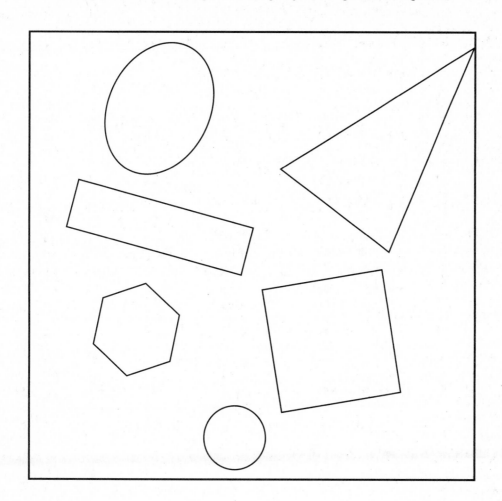

THREE OF A KIND

Find the three hidden words in the sentence that, read in order, go together in some way. Example: I sold Norma new screwdrivers (answer: "old man river").

Yellow hats are considered stylish in West Virginia.

★ Sporting Chance

Find these Summer Olympics venues that are hidden in the diagram, either across, down, or diagonally. Individual words of all multiple-word answers are hidden separately. Ignore words contained within parentheses.

```
C S A T N A M R E G S
A I T K L O S B L D H
N U L O D N O D N O L
A O A G C F R A N C E
A L N R Q K L C I T I
A I T O O R H T U O S
K I A K E L Y O N L G
S A L H Y A U I L E D
M I T A Y E L O R M N
U E R H R R N M E J A
N U O A E T A D A S L
I D H B P N S P Y A N
C T O G Y O S U S S I
H G N O K M X U A H F
P C G A D A N A C L I
A M S T E R D A M K K
R S O A A S E R N F M
I P C I N R W I O E D
U A I O O T S E L M G
W I X K L L W B D R E
J N E Q E A O E E E P
A M M H C U T E R P N
P M S Z R J C I U P C
A O U N A E H N N H E
N R E I B E I J I N G
S E L E G N A N T F R
O Y K O T L A V E P S
M O S C O W E X D A S
I T A L Y C Z B A J U
```

AMSTERDAM	LOS ANGELES
ANTWERP	MELBOURNE
ATHENS	MEXICO CITY
ATLANTA	MONTREAL
AUSTRALIA	MOSCOW
BARCELONA	MUNICH
BEIJING	NETHERLANDS
BELGIUM	PARIS
BERLIN	ROME
CANADA	SEOUL
CHINA	SOUTH KOREA
FINLAND	SPAIN
FRANCE	(St.) LOUIS
GERMANY	STOCKHOLM
GREECE	SWEDEN
HELSINKI	SYDNEY
HONG KONG	TOKYO
ITALY	UNITED KINGDOM
JAPAN	USA
LONDON	USSR

WHO'S WHAT WHERE?

The correct term for a resident of Beirut, Lebanon, is:

A) Beirutian   B) Beiruti

C) Beirano   D) Beirutite

★ Woodwork by Gail Grabowski

ACROSS

1 Plane-tracking device
6 Explosion sound
10 Vicinity
14 Wear away
15 __ mater
16 Short-term worker
17 Standoffish
18 Rip
19 Doily material
20 "__ favor, señor"
21 Stock-exchange worker
24 Dress smartly
26 Emphatic agreement
27 Take long steps
29 Trim, as expenses
31 Desertlike
32 Door handle
34 "Same here!"
39 Look (at)
40 Half-off store events
42 Go yachting
43 Manicurist's board material
45 Dust particle
46 Competent
47 Mine deposits
49 Largest mammals
51 Nome's state
55 Treaty topic
56 Poker player's pack
59 Baseball great Gehrig
62 Female horse
63 Sound quality
64 Reaches across
66 "Now it's clear!"
67 Has breakfast
68 Knight's weapon
69 Examination
70 Numbered roads: Abbr.
71 Church official

DOWN

1 Gather, as crops
2 Folk singer Guthrie
3 Reward at a raffle
4 "Without further __ ..."
5 Was a football official, casually
6 Bandleader's stick
7 Butter substitute
8 Sharif of film
9 Joan of Arc, for one
10 Book of maps
11 All set
12 Game-show host
13 Imitative types
22 Onion relatives
23 Wind-instrument insert
25 Bus passenger
27 Wise person
28 Airport conveyance
29 Short-sleeve shirts
30 Aid in a crime
33 Identify
35 Sir __ Newton
36 Mesa
37 Kitchen flooring piece
38 Bullring cheers
41 Assembled, as a skirt
44 __ Ono
48 Roof support
50 Big bother
51 Word on a ticket
52 Rental agreement
53 Ranchland units
54 Clay-pigeon sport
55 Use a steam iron
57 Windbreaker, for one
58 Poker payment
60 Fairy-tale beginning
61 Computer operator
65 Friend

★ Number-Out

Shade squares so that no number appears in any row or column more than once. Shaded squares may not touch each other horizontally or vertically, and all unshaded squares must form a single continuous area.

2	4	1	5	1
2	1	4	5	5
2	2	5	1	3
4	5	2	2	2
5	3	1	3	4

OPPOSITE ATTRACTION

Unscramble the letters in the phrase RARE FAN to form two common words that are opposites of each other. Example: The letters in SLED INFO can be rearranged to spell FIND and LOSE.

_____   _____

★ Sequence Maze

Enter the maze, pass through all the color squares exactly once, then exit, all without retracing your path. You must alternate between passing through red and blue squares.

THREE AT A RHYME

Rearrange these letters to form three one-syllable words that rhyme.
Example: A A A B C E K S W X X = AXE, BACKS, WAX

D E K N O O O S W

_____   _____   _____

★ Celebrities of the Month by Sally R. Stein

ACROSS

1 Addition totals
5 Run-down neighborhood
9 *Wheel of Fortune* host
14 Source of shade
15 Walking stick
16 Display, as charm
17 "Winning __ everything!"
18 Probability quote
19 Put to rest
20 Anjelica Huston's hubby in *The Addams Family*
22 Appears to be
23 Propelled a kayak
24 Greeting for the villain
25 Army officer
28 Outfield material
29 Spinach or broccoli, for short
32 Burden
33 Tick by
36 Abel's mom
37 Stare at
38 Andrews of *The Sound of Music*
39 On the house
40 Inventor Whitney
41 Folklore tale
42 Country hotels
43 Scooby-__ (cartoon dog)
44 Expert pilot
45 Greek island
46 Brief blast of wind
48 Dealer's deck
51 Graceful birds
53 *Gypsy* composer
57 Conversation starter
58 Suggest strongly
59 Part of USA
60 Comedian Hardy's nickname

61 Isn't truthful
62 Champagne bucket
63 Schemes
64 Days of __ (ancient times)
65 Most scoutmasters

DOWN

1 Agitate
2 __ Minor (Little Dipper)
3 Diner handout
4 Release
5 Clean thoroughly
6 Soup server
7 Opened, as a tie
8 Phoenix suburb

9 Oceanfront
10 Car's wheel bars
11 Captain Nemo's creator
12 Abel's dad
13 Door openers
21 Mayo holder
24 Cheated, slangily
25 Bellowed, as a bovine
26 __-Saxon
27 California winemaker
28 *Wheel of Fortune* turn
30 Big happening
31 51 Across relatives
33 DVD player button

34 Winter Olympics sled
35 British brew
39 Medic's treatment
41 Rodeo ropes
45 S&L offerings
47 Not illuminated
48 Knickknack
49 Author Horatio
50 Oscar winner Witherspoon
51 Patronize a mall
52 Rural water source
53 Theme of this puzzle
54 Neighborhood youth org.
55 Require
56 Makes a mistake

★ One-Way Streets

The diagram represents a pattern of streets. A and B are parking spaces, and the black squares are stores. Find the route that starts at A, passes through all stores exactly once, and ends at B. Arrows indicate one-way traffic for that block only. No block or intersection may be entered more than once.

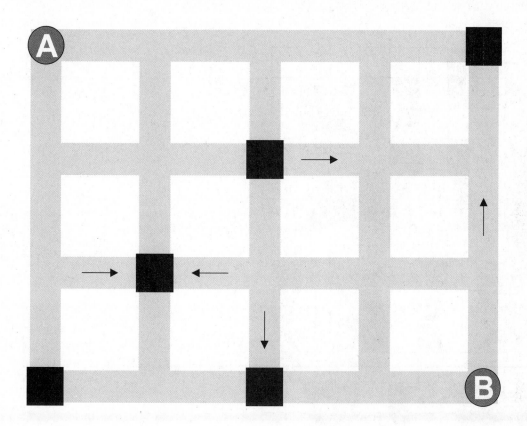

SOUND THINKING

The only common uncapitalized word whose only consonant sounds are Y, F, and R, in that order, has four syllables and eight letters. What is it?

_____

★★ Split Decisions

In this clueless crossword puzzle, each answer consists of two words whose spellings are the same, except for the consecutive letters given. All answers are common words; no phrases or hyphenated or capitalized words are used. Some of the clues may have more than one solution, but there is only one word pair that will correctly link up with all the other word pairs.

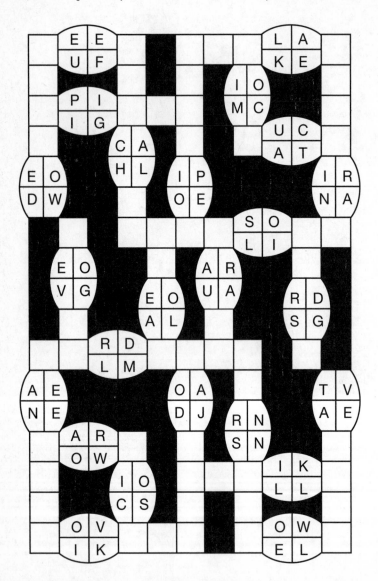

TRANSDELETION

Delete one letter from the word CROUPIERS and rearrange the rest, to get a word meaning "high-quality."

_____

★ Star Search

Find the stars that are hidden in some of the blank squares. The numbered squares indicate how many stars are hidden in the squares adjacent to them (including diagonally). There is never more than one star in any square.

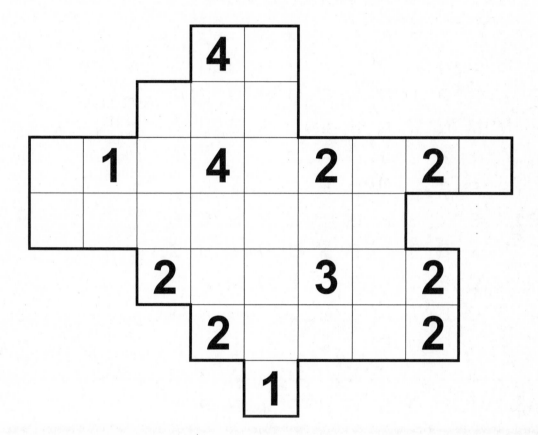

TELEPHONE TRIOS

	ABC	DEF
1	**2**	**3**
GHI	JKL	MNO
4	**5**	**6**
PRS	TUV	WXY
7	**8**	**9**
*	**0**	**#**

Using the numbers and letters on a standard telephone, what three seven-letter words or phrases from the same category can be formed from these telephone numbers?

233-2253 _ _ _ _ _ _ _

264-2253 _ _ _ _ _ _ _

267-3425 _ _ _ _ _ _ _

★ Sincerely Yours

Find these "innocent" words that are hidden in the diagram, either across, down, or diagonally. There's one additional eight-letter answer in the category, not listed below, that's also hidden in the diagram. What's that word?

```
E  B  P  R  U  P  G  A  F  G  S  S  S  G  T
Z  L  L  W  L  H  U  A  N  I  R  U  N  R  A
U  R  P  A  P  O  I  R  N  G  O  E  U  E  R
P  U  T  M  M  N  L  L  E  L  E  S  E  E  T
T  O  N  C  I  E  E  J  U  R  T  L  S  G  L
S  L  E  R  S  S  L  D  G  F  E  E  I  D  E
E  U  C  U  S  Y  E  E  U  I  L  V  H  C  S
N  D  O  P  X  R  S  L  S  T  B  U  I  U  S
O  E  N  U  C  E  S  L  R  S  I  Q  M  A  P
H  R  N  R  C  S  T  A  I  N  L  E  S  S  N
V  C  I  Y  N  O  D  E  I  L  L  U  S  N  U
L  A  R  U  T  A  N  N  A  T  U  R  A  B  K
C  H  A  S  T  E  O  N  T  H  G  I  R  P  U
H  A  R  M  L  E  S  S  I  N  L  E  S  T  P
```

ANGELIC
ARTLESS
BLAMELESS
CHASTE
CREDULOUS
GREEN
GUILELESS
GULLIBLE
HONEST
INNOCENT
INNOCUOUS
NAIVE
NATURAL
PURE
SIMPLE
SINLESS
STAINLESS
TRUSTFUL
UNSULLIED
UPRIGHT

IN OTHER WORDS

There is only one common uncapitalized word that contains the consecutive letters MBB. What is it?

_____

★ Pairs of Fives by Gail Grabowski

ACROSS

1 Sheltered inlet
5 Numerical fact, for short
9 Desirable quality
14 Egg-shaped
15 Mystical glow
16 Window ledges
17 Steakhouse handout
18 Broad smile
19 Part of a vise
20 They say "I do"
23 '50s Ford
24 Place to park
25 Ghost's shout
28 Play-__ (kiddie clay)
29 Did a salon treatment
33 Erie or Superior
34 Hockey great Gretzky
35 Submarine detector
36 Old-fashioned transportation
40 Actor Sal
41 Decline to participate
42 Smooth out
43 Swapped
45 Talk too much
48 __ Misérables
49 General Grant's opposite
50 Die down
52 Haphazard method
57 Muffin toppings
59 "That makes sense"
60 Diarist __ Frank
61 Train station
62 Quote, as a reference source
63 Religious group
64 Frisbees, for example
65 Talk back to
66 French holy women: Abbr.

DOWN

1 Arranged, as hair
2 Cook too long
3 Disappear quickly
4 Get away from
5 Long story
6 Make a left, perhaps
7 Bone-dry
8 Hair knot
9 Wide tie
10 Grain-storage building
11 Excitingly fast-paced
12 Shade tree
13 Recipe amt.
21 Texas city
22 Fishing pole
26 "Fine by me!"
27 Above, in verse
30 Hurricane center
31 Single-helix molecule
32 High-IQ group
33 Company emblem
34 Small songbird
35 Ice-cream parlor offering
36 Bees' home
37 Ragtime dances
38 Pa
39 "So long!"
40 Actor Gibson
43 Hot drink
44 Mementos from the past
45 January birthstone
46 Right now
47 Artists' caps
49 Shopping aids
51 Orchestra section
53 Chess corner piece
54 China's continent
55 Badminton barriers
56 Low grades
57 Strange
58 Hawaiian necklace

★ Hyper-Sudoku

Fill in the blank boxes so that every row, column, 3x3 box, *and* each of the four 3x3 gray regions contains all of the numbers 1 to 9.

		1	3		9	2		7
			2	8	5			6
	6	5		1				9
3	1							
	9			2	1		7	
					3			1
9	5		6				1	8
6	8	3	1			5	9	
	7	2				3		

MIXAGRAMS

Each line contains a five-letter word and a four-letter word that have been mixed together (the order of the letters in each word has not been changed). Unmix the two words on each line and write them in the spaces provided. When you're done, find a two-part answer to the clue by reading down the letter columns in the answers.

CLUE: Ivory rival

C U L A B R E G E	=	_ _ _ _ _	+	_ _ _ _
S T I R K U B E D	=	_ _ _ _ _	+	_ _ _ _
F L A O G R O G A	=	_ _ _ _ _	+	_ _ _ _
E B U L U D Y E S	=	_ _ _ _ _	+	_ _ _ _

★★ You're Booked

From the comments below, match each poolside reader with his or her book.

DON — My book's fiction

JEN — My book's author's male

STEVE — I can't bear fiction

VANESSA — NO COMMENT

Climb That Career Ladder — By Rich Pocket — Buy me and I'll become a millionaire

Darcy the Divine — By Milly Boone — A woman has taken me on holiday

Dracula's Dilemma — By Mina Harker — NO COMMENT

KNIGHTS OF Passion — An account of the crusades — By Felix Fitzgeorge — My print is so small, you need glasses to read me

BETWEENER

What three-letter word belongs between the word at left and the word at right, so that the first and second word, and the second and third word, each form a common compound word?

BOX __ __ __ PORT

★ 123

Fill in the diagram so that each rectangular piece has one each of the numbers 1, 2, and 3, under these rules: 1) No two adjacent squares, horizontally or vertically, can have the same number. 2) Each completed row and column of the diagram will have an equal number of 1s, 2s, and 3s.

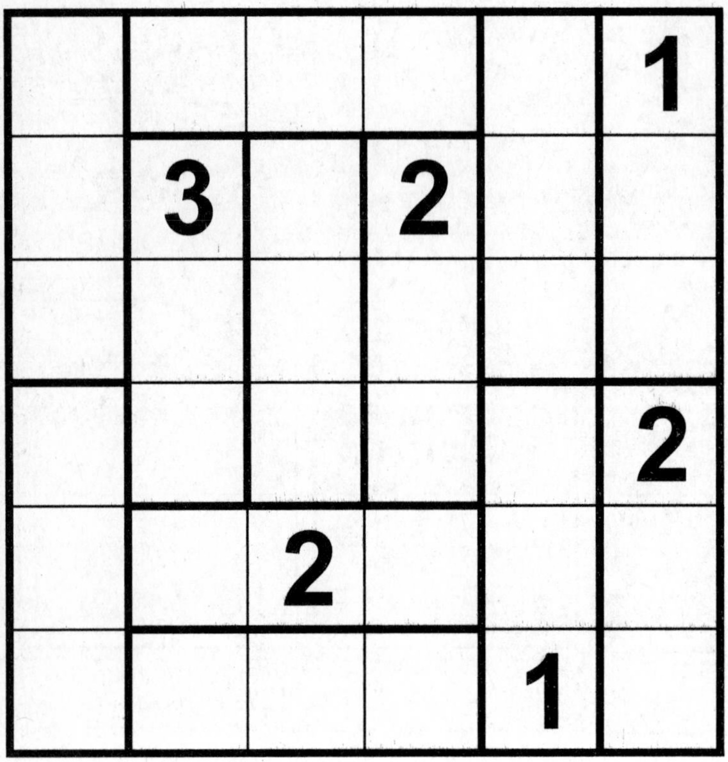

					1
	3		**2**		
					2
		2			
				1	

SUDOKU SUM

Without repeating any digits, complete the sum at right, by filling one digit in each of the five blanks.

```
    4 2 _
+   _ 0 8
    _ _ _
```

★ Soon Enough by Sally R. Stein

ACROSS

1 Hint
5 End of a shirt arm
9 Catches sight of
14 Sword handle
15 Capital of Norway
16 Sioux dwelling
17 Very soon
20 Earns
21 First book of the Bible
22 Make into law
23 Locale in 21 Across
25 Overturn
27 Puts on an act
32 Historical periods
36 Turntable speed: Abbr.
37 Lampoon
38 Very soon
41 Beer brewer's grain
42 Prefix for angle
43 __ and needles
44 Lampoon
45 Mails away
47 Schedule stats.
48 Milky gems
53 Unworried
58 High-pitched
59 Very soon
62 Ease off
63 Cleveland's lake
64 Mountain lion
65 Earns
66 Copenhagen resident
67 Getz of jazz

DOWN

1 Doorbell sound
2 Sheets or pillowcases
3 The U in UHF
4 Moral code
5 Pros and __
6 Take advantage of
7 Where 10 Down is: Abbr.
8 Fail to remember
9 Surprise greatly
10 St. __ (city near Tampa)
11 Numbered musical work
12 Actress Hatcher
13 Catches sight of
18 Julius Caesar phrase
19 Swampland
23 Catch sight of
24 Lowered in rank
26 Mice, to owls
27 Ceiling appliance
28 On the summit of
29 New Zealand bird
30 "__ go bragh!"
31 Hardens
32 Eases off
33 Gather up crops
34 Spherical hairdo
35 Fly alone
37 Slide on ice
39 Hockey official
40 Coffee brewers
45 Cooked slowly
46 Angry
47 Earth-friendly prefix
49 Crooks, to cops
50 Approximately
51 Andes beast
52 Family car
53 Open slightly
54 Marching-band instrument
55 H.S. junior's exam
56 Ending for novel
57 Citrus drinks
58 "My country, 'tis of __ ..."
60 Gun owners' org.
61 Metal in pewter

★ ABC

Enter the letters A, B, and C into the diagram so that each row and column has exactly one A, one B, and one C. The letters outside the diagram indicate the first letter encountered, moving in the direction of the arrow. Keep in mind that after all the letters have been filled in, there will be one blank box in each row and column.

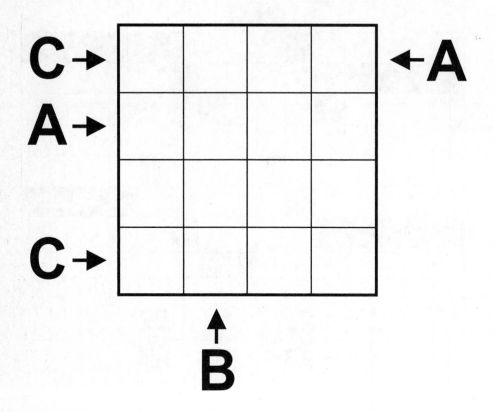

CLUELESS CROSSWORD

Complete the crossword with common uncapitalized seven-letter words, based entirely on the letters already filled in for you.

★ Find the Ships

Determine the position of the 10 ships listed to the right of the diagram. The ships may be oriented either horizontally or vertically. A square with wavy lines indicates water and will not contain a ship. The numbers at the edge of the diagram indicate how many squares in that row or column contain parts of ships. When all 10 ships are correctly placed in the diagram, no two of them will touch each other, not even diagonally.

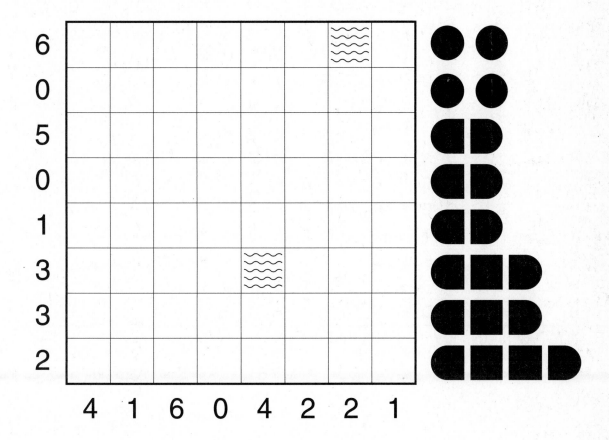

TWO-BY-FOUR

The eight letters in the word OUTDATED can be rearranged to form a pair of common four-letter words in two different ways. Can you find both pairs of words?

— — — —   — — — —

— — — —   — — — —

★ Ports of Call

Try to find these ports of the world that are hidden in the diagram, either across, down, or diagonally, and you'll find that one of them has sailed away. What's the missing port?

```
G  R  E  J  B  S  E  S  O  P  O  S  I  D  N  I  R  B
X  E  T  N  A  N  H  P  G  I  R  U  E  D  O  V  E  R
S  M  N  I  F  A  O  K  M  I  F  E  G  A  Q  V  D  G
E  K  T  E  N  R  B  Z  U  I  T  R  W  E  T  U  E  A
V  S  R  G  T  P  I  R  A  E  U  S  L  T  N  T  D  D
O  N  H  O  T  S  N  H  I  B  A  O  O  K  N  E  L  K
D  A  E  H  Y  L  O  H  M  S  O  R  I  J  N  A  C  E
I  M  A  F  N  Y  B  A  S  P  B  R  I  N  D  I  S  I
Z  R  T  A  D  W  H  E  R  E  K  A  C  P  R  N  Y  S
M  U  T  L  D  O  O  E  R  H  T  D  N  E  G  E  B  E
I  M  E  M  N  E  V  T  L  G  A  N  M  E  D  W  S  L
R  A  L  O  O  I  H  E  E  D  E  I  A  V  A  P  M  P
A  D  L  U  L  W  V  P  F  E  L  N  F  N  N  O  I  A
I  E  A  T  L  O  N  D  O  N  R  S  I  A  S  R  R  N
B  X  V  H  D  N  E  T  S  O  J  F  T  Z  K  T  G  V
```

ADEN	IZMIR
ANTWERP	LIMERICK
BERGEN	LIVERPOOL
BRINDISI	LONDON
BRISBANE	MURMANSK
DOVER	NANTES
DUNKIRK	NAPLES
ESBJERG	NEWPORT
FALMOUTH	OPORTO
FREETOWN	OSTEND
GDANSK	OSTIA
GRIMSBY	PIRAEUS
HAIFA	ROTTERDAM
HAMBURG	SEATTLE
HOLYHEAD	SHANGHAI
	VALLETTA

INITIAL REACTION

Identify the well-known proverb from the first letters in each of its words.

L. F. L. S. _____

★ Out of Shape by Sally R. Stein

ACROSS

1 Income-tax experts: Abbr.
5 Minor arguments
10 Swelled heads
14 Poison-ivy reaction
15 Trial locale
16 Doll's word
17 In addition
18 Come into a room
19 Applaud
20 Talking too much
23 Female deer
24 Vegas cubes
25 Had leftovers, perhaps
28 Cowboy rope
30 Shoemaker's tool
33 Alaska city
34 Family room
35 Saudi __ (Mideast nation)
37 Exerting pressure
40 Minor arguments
41 Young fella
42 Short distance
43 Fractions of a mi.
44 Ziti shapes
46 Watermelon throwaways
47 Sensible
48 Sounds of satisfaction
49 Kidding
56 Stood up
57 Base before home plate
58 Full of grease
59 Nodder's phrase
60 Blake of jazz
61 Package of paper
62 Highest-quality
63 Bottoms of wine barrels
64 Solar-system centers

DOWN

1 Complainer, slangily
2 Drained of color
3 Trade grp.
4 Most carelessly done
5 Vista
6 Ping-__
7 Parking-space filler
8 Signs of the times
9 Singer Barbra
10 Banquet host
11 Big party
12 Actor Sharif
13 Maple product
21 Charged atom
22 Sports-report info
25 Fidgety
26 Pulled from behind
27 Gives off
28 Author Deighton
29 Ulterior motive
30 Ease off
31 Did electrical work
32 Night-table devices
34 Separated
36 Local tax authorities
38 Sum up
39 W. Hemisphere alliance
45 Heston film with a chariot race
46 That woman
47 Frozen rain
48 South American mountains
49 Prepare for a photo
50 Takes off the shelf
51 Taunting remark
52 Not a duplicate: Abbr.
53 In __ of (instead of)
54 Gusto
55 Exercise centers
56 Beef cut

★ Baseball Maze

Enter the maze where indicated, pass through all the baseballs exactly once, then exit. You may not retrace your path.

THREE AT A RHYME

Rearrange these letters to form three one-syllable words that rhyme.

E G H O O O R U W

_____ _____ _____

★ Fences

Connect the dots with vertical or horizontal lines, so that a single loop is formed with no crossings or branches. Each number indicates how many lines surround it; squares with no number may be surrounded by any number of lines.

```
.  .  .  .  .  .  .  .  .
         1  3  3
.  .  .  .  .  .  .  .  .
  2  3              2
.  .  .  .  .  .  .  .  .
  2  0  3     2  0
.  .  .  .  .  .  .  .  .
  2
.  .  .  .  .  .  .  .  .
                     3
.  .  .  .  .  .  .  .  .
      0  1     3  2  3
.  .  .  .  .  .  .  .  .
  1                2  1
.  .  .  .  .  .  .  .  .
   3  3  3
.  .  .  .  .  .  .  .  .
```

ADDITION SWITCH

Switch the positions of two of the digits in the incorrect sum at right, to get a correct sum.

$$789$$
$$+110$$
$$\overline{827}$$

★ About Time

Find these time-related words that are hidden in the diagram, either across, down, or diagonally. There are two additional answers in the category (an eight-letter word and a nine-letter word), not listed below, that are also hidden in the diagram. If the words have opposite meanings, what are they?

```
S O O S T S H P L U D E H C S
D E L A Y E D P A S T I L J M
A B G A N T M E T E L O S B O
L R W L O O D P O N C A S P W
W L L A O M T A O K P E Z R E
A I I U S O A S P R M T S E E
Y E S T E R D A Y I A C Y S K
E U E C S R T P T D H L L E F
M R R N A O E E W E E W R N O
A O F U G W M V D O N E E T R
G D M P A O Y U E G A E M S E
G G A E S W L R A R C R R O V
P A X T N E P O M N O C O O E
H C O P E T C L O C Q F F V K
```

AGE
ALWAYS
CLOCK
DATE
DELAYED
EPOCH
ERA
FOREVER
FORMERLY
MOMENT
OBSOLETE
ONCE
PAST
PRESENT
PUNCTUAL
SCHEDULE
SOMETIMES
SOON
STILL
TEMPORAL
WEEK

WHO'S WHAT WHERE?

The correct term for a resident of Ivory Coast is:

    A) Ivorian   B) Ivorcoaster

    C) Ivorish   D) Coasterian

★ Business Reading by Gail Grabowski

ACROSS

1 Poisonous snake
4 Pronto, in a memo
8 Paper fragment
13 Ballet bend
14 Wholesale quantity
15 Fill with joy
16 Soufflé ingredients
17 Spring flower
18 More adorable
19 Sign on a hotel-room door
22 "Am not!" response
23 Ragtime dance
27 Showed the way
28 Poet Whitman
32 Saloon seats
33 Declares untrue
35 Oaf
36 Sign at a diner
40 Old Italian money
41 Male choir voices
42 BB gun ammo
45 Novelist Ferber
46 Bullring "Bravo!"
49 Curly, Larry and Moe
51 Ready for a nap
53 Sign at a new store
57 Magazine edition
60 Radiant quality
61 ___ of ethics
62 Aspect
63 Fishing-line holder
64 Pub servings
65 Sandwich cheese
66 "Will there be anything ___?"
67 Sun. speech

DOWN

1 2000 presidential candidate
2 Endorsed, as a check
3 Mexican coins
4 Battery fluid
5 Hindu garment
6 Sale condition
7 Sauce made with basil
8 Confidential item
9 Carbonated drink mixers
10 Cat's prey
11 Munched on
12 Part of mph
13 Bicycle part
20 Cloth for drying
21 Young'___ (kids)
24 Hammer or 58 Down
25 Letters after kays
26 L.A. clock setting
29 Whichever
30 Grocery shopper's reference
31 Wigwam relative
33 Two-person talks
34 Drop in the mail
36 Cut calories
37 Folk singer Guthrie
38 Pro and ___
39 Ticked off
40 '60s records
43 Marsh birds
44 Coffee alternative
46 Black-and-orange bird
47 Charger of interest
48 Rims
50 Catch in a trap
52 Ancient Peruvians
54 Fencing contest
55 Raw metals
56 Lacking color
57 "No ___, ands, or buts!"
58 Wood-cutting device
59 Bio. or chem.

★ Sudoku

Fill in the blank boxes so that every row, column, and 3x3 box contains all of the numbers 1 to 9.

7	6			3				4
	4							9
		8	4	2			6	
	3	5	8	1	2			
9	1				3		8	
	8	7	9	3	1			
	1	4	7	8				
2					6			
5			1			3	7	

MIXAGRAMS

Each line contains a five-letter word and a four-letter word that have been mixed together (the order of the letters in each word has not been changed). Unmix the two words on each line and write them in the spaces provided. When you're done, find a two-part answer to the clue by reading down the letter columns in the answers.

CLUE: Planing, sanding, etc.

W A S H D O W E N = _ _ _ _ _ + _ _ _ _

S C O L R O D E O = _ _ _ _ _ + _ _ _ _

C O R U L L E O R = _ _ _ _ _ + _ _ _ _

D I K O N D O B E = _ _ _ _ _ + _ _ _ _

★ 123

Fill in the diagram so that each rectangular piece has one each of the numbers 1, 2, and 3, under these rules: 1) No two adjacent squares, horizontally or vertically, can have the same number. 2) Each completed row and column of the diagram will have an equal number of 1s, 2s, and 3s.

SUDOKU SUM

Without repeating any digits, complete the sum at right, by filling one digit in each of the five blanks.

```
    _  4  _
+   2  _  9
_____
    _  _  6
```

★ Rail Journey by Gail Grabowski

ACROSS

1 Carbonated drinks
6 Hold in one's hand
11 Replace a button
14 Treat badly
15 Singer Page or LaBelle
16 Yes, in Paris
17 Assigned office area
19 Large coffee brewer
20 Playground item
21 Break, as a balloon
22 Denials
23 Elevated flat land
26 Fills, as a van
28 High-school math course: Abbr.
31 Snakelike swimmers
32 River sediment
33 Crop on cobs
35 Spinning toys
37 Toward the Arctic Circle
40 Sir __ Newton
42 Question that sounds like an owl's call
43 About to cry
44 Wicked one
45 Was in the choir
47 Bathtub residue
48 Designer __ Saint Laurent
50 Heap praise on
52 Barbie's beau
53 Bothered
54 Family diagram
55 Knight's title
56 Collar, as a crook
58 Muscle contractions
63 Stars and Stripes land: Abbr.
64 Voter's "crossover" ballot
67 Inventor Whitney
68 Get away from
69 Beijing's country
70 Family room
71 Singer Della
72 Cuddly bear

DOWN

1 Crows' cries
2 Orchestra woodwind
3 Entice
4 Poses a question
5 Big Bird's street
6 College student's avg.
7 Lab-maze runner
8 "Take __ from me!"
9 Bar seats
10 Locate precisely
11 Audio portion of a film
12 Coins in Madrid
13 Finishes first
18 Bird sound
24 Reduces speed
25 Driveway surface
27 Spiny houseplants
28 Corrosive chemical
29 Finish last
30 Source for easy money
34 Gullible
36 Submarine detector
38 Factual
39 Song of praise
41 Scouring powder
46 Invited visitor
49 Paper fastener
51 Portray
53 Airplane walkway
55 Took to court
57 Jeans color
59 Feel sore
60 Slip and slide
61 Repair, as a tear
62 Remain
65 Proof-of-age items, for short
66 Golf platform

★ One-Way Streets

The diagram represents a pattern of streets. A and B are parking spaces, and the black squares are stores. Find the route that starts at A, passes through all stores exactly once, and ends at B. Arrows indicate one-way traffic for that block only. No block or intersection may be entered more than once.

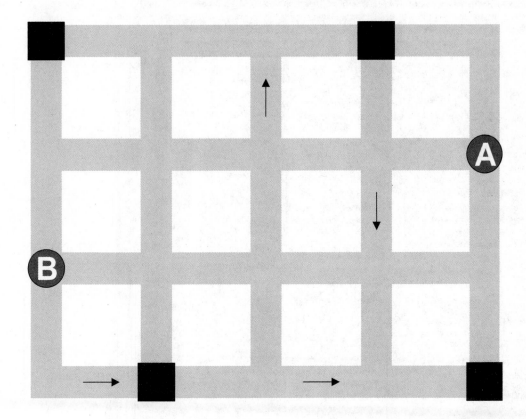

SOUND THINKING

There is only one common uncapitalized word whose only consonant sounds are B, S, and J, in that order. What is it?

_____

★ Maple Leaf Maze

Enter the maze where indicated, pass through all red stars exactly once, then end on the blue star in the center. You may not retrace your path.

SAY IT AGAIN

What three-letter word can be either a type of toy or a verb meaning "exceed"?

— — —

★ Star Search

Find the stars that are hidden in some of the blank squares. The numbered squares indicate how many stars are hidden in the squares adjacent to them (including diagonally). There is never more than one star in any square.

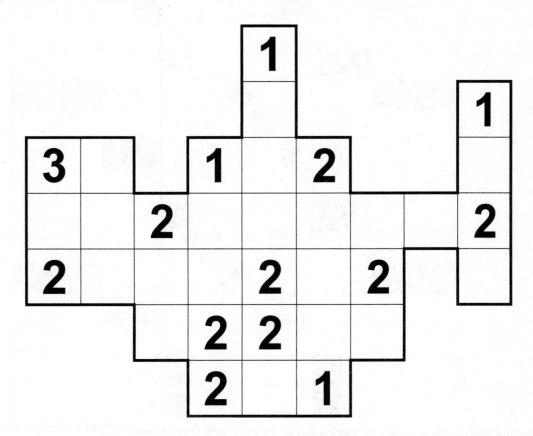

TELEPHONE TRIOS

1	ABC **2**	DEF **3**
GHI **4**	JKL **5**	MNO **6**
PRS **7**	TUV **8**	WXY **9**
*	**0**	#

Using the numbers and letters on a standard telephone, what three seven-letter words or phrases from the same category can be formed from these telephone numbers?

688-5463 _ _ _ _ _ _ _

786-3696 _ _ _ _ _ _ _

786-6279 _ _ _ _ _ _ _

★ In the Trenches by Sally R. Stein

ACROSS

1 Pumpkin eater of rhyme
6 Facts, for short
10 Nevada city
14 Old saying
15 Sound of distress
16 Margarine
17 Solar plexus
20 One __ time (individually)
21 Wither, as plants
22 Doesn't want to comply
23 Hold tightly
25 Benefit
27 "Amen!"
30 Order-taking employee
34 Taking advantage of
35 Wintry
36 Spanish gold
37 Fulfills a golf dream
41 Hawaiian instrument
42 Flying mammals
43 Send payment
44 Business co-owners
47 Business owners
48 __ good example
49 Isn't, nonstandardly
50 Agitate
53 Acting group
55 Toothpaste-tube cover
58 Final, desperate attempt
62 Part of the eye
63 Unimportant
64 Major blood vessel
65 Reporter's post
66 Corporate VIP
67 Attire

DOWN

1 Mama's spouse
2 Spruce up a manuscript
3 Brit's farewell
4 Part of the psyche
5 Hockey official
6 Informal "Understood!"
7 Christmas season
8 Pitcher's "blazing" pitches
9 Toronto's loc.
10 Marc Antony and Julius Caesar
11 Israeli airline
12 Narrow part of a bottle
13 __ and aahs
18 Poke fun at
19 Bassoon kin
23 Chromosome component
24 Fixes illegally
26 Ye __ Tea Shoppe
27 Give a recap
28 Japanese city
29 One pedaling
30 Dirties, as a chimney
31 Hotel accommodations
32 Golfer Els
33 Verse writers
35 Personal integrity
38 Assist in a crime
39 Steam-making appliance
40 Home for a hawk
45 "Naughty, naughty!"
46 Require
47 Small snack
49 Cookout residue
50 Lost traction
51 Rabbit relative
52 Auction condition
54 Land measure
55 Apple center
56 __ and crafts
57 Sch. auxiliaries
59 Little devil
60 Short-lived craze
61 In favor of

★ Airport Whodunit

Solve this mystery by discovering which one of these six suspects, six weapons, and six locations is missing from the diagram. The others are all hidden either across, down, or diagonally. The individual words of all multiple-word answers are hidden separately. Ignore words contained within parentheses.

AIDAN (the) AIRLINE
   REPRESENTATIVE
BRANDON (the) BAGGAGE
   HANDLER
CEDRIC (the) CHECK-IN CLERK
FLAVIA (the) FLIGHT
   ATTENDANT
PETER (the) PILOT
TORQUIL (the) TOUR GUIDE

DUTY FREE BOTTLE
POISONED COFFEE
SCARF
SILK TIE
SLEEP MASK
SUITCASE STRAP

ARRIVALS
CUSTOMS
DEPARTURE LOUNGE
GATE
RESTAURANT
VIP AREA

```
R C D U J Y W T U D E L S U I T C A S Z F
C P H E R P T E E E D O D L G B C L P R S
U B S E P E G U L P I U E H A N D L E R G
S U I T C A S E D A U N N E T V E H T R A
T O L U G K V T N R G S O Q H E I P E I K
O T K G E V I T A T N E S E R P E R R M L
M J A Q N L T N H U T B I F C T T L R I E
S B I M O T S U C R R R O L E I I O U A E
T U S U D R F R F E C A P A P N R Q U O F
G I N C N R P A R T S N N I E K R D R R F
D G T T A E L T T O B D L T C O F F E Y O
E I I C R R I R D E C O G A T E V A G C C
F Z S G B E I B O T T L X D N A I D A N L
```

IN OTHER WORDS

There is only one common uncapitalized word that contains the consecutive letters NKC. What is it?

_____

bRaIn BREaTHeR
SMART FOOD CHOICES:
SIX TIPS FOR NUTRITIOUS MEALS

Pop some soybeans Soy is a high-protein, low-fat vegetable that tastes so good you might expect the nutrition police to come after you. But forget tofu. We're talking edamame, or soybeans. Buy them frozen or fresh, steam for 5 minutes, and sprinkle with some coarse salt. Now pop the beans out of the pod. Make a lot—you can't eat just one!

Make sweet potato fries Instead of using plain potatoes, prepare "fries" using sweet potatoes. Slice a scrubbed, large sweet potato into one-inch strips, then coat with a tablespoon of canola oil and bake in a preheated oven at 450° F for about ten minutes. Shake the pan to turn the fries and continue baking until crispy, about another 15 minutes.

Eat mushrooms for antioxidants If you're as sick of hearing about the health benefits of "brightly colored vegetables" as we are, here's some good news: Researchers at Pennsylvania State University found you can get the same level of disease-fighting antioxidants in portobello and cremini mushrooms as in the ubiquitous carrots and green peppers. We prefer ours grilled, please, with just a dash of balsamic vinegar.

Eat chocolate—the right kind You're probably already aware that dark chocolate is packed with healthy antioxidants. But what you may not know is that it's also among the best sources of magnesium—a mineral that's vital for everything from heart health to preventing diabetes and osteoporosis.

An apple a day to keep fractures away You already know about the benefits of calcium and vitamin D for strong bones. But what about fruits and vegetables? Yup, chalk up another health advantage to these amazing foods—the more fruits and veggies you eat, the higher your bone mineral content, a fancy way of saying you'll have stronger bones and will be less likely to develop osteoporosis or fractures.

What your grocer won't tell you If you shop only on the periphery of the store—where the "real" foods are based—you're more likely to wind up with a healthier cart of groceries. Only venture down the internal aisles for staples such as spices, sugar, flour, canola oil, vinegar, and such. You may save more money in the long run, too, especially if you stick to fruits and veggies that are in season and meats and poultry on sale.

★★ Line Drawing

Draw three straight lines, each from one edge of the square to another edge, so that each line passes through exactly four letters that spell a common word, reading left-to-right and/or top-to-bottom. None of the lines will cross each other.

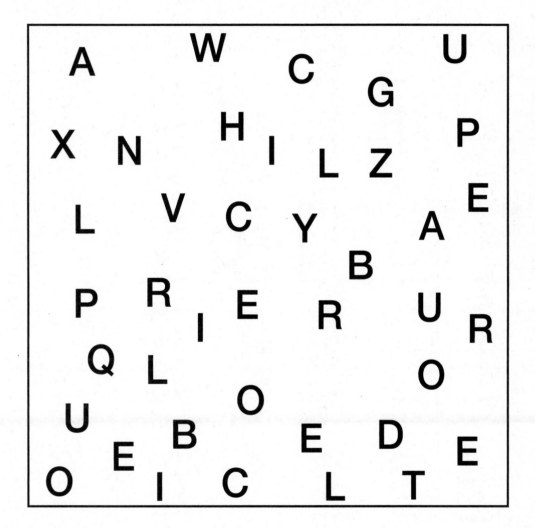

THREE OF A KIND

Find the three hidden words in the sentence that, read in order, go together in some way.

Call Auntie Doris in for supper.

★ ABC

Enter the letters A, B, and C into the diagram so that each row and column has exactly one A, one B, and one C. The letters outside the diagram indicate the first letter encountered, moving in the direction of the arrow. Keep in mind that after all the letters have been filled in, there will be one blank box in each row and column.

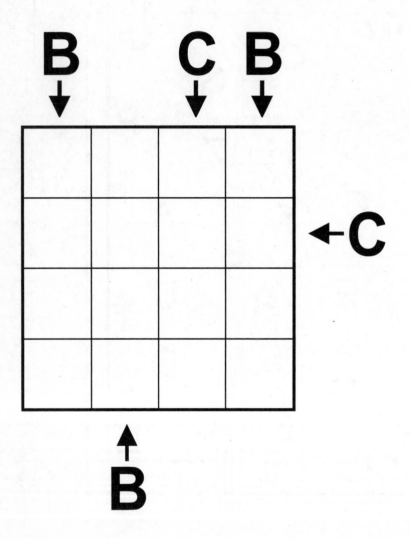

NATIONAL TREASURE

Find the one common uncapitalized six-letter word that can be formed from the letters in ALGERIA.

_ _ _ _ _ _

★ Tabby Toys by Gail Grabowski

ACROSS

1 Make a sound of shock
5 Curved lines
9 Away from port
14 Regarding
15 Toreador's opponent
16 Makes watertight
17 Part of the lower leg
18 Boyfriend
19 Spills the beans
20 Battery-operated computer accessory
23 Get out of bed
24 Dry cleaner's challenge
25 "__ when!" (pourer's request)
28 Pigsty
29 Big shot, initially
32 British sheepdog
34 Newspapers and magazines
36 Get, as a salary
37 Foremost, as a team member
41 School corridor
43 Is in charge of
44 Magic-lamp owner
48 Dazzle
49 Justice Department org.
52 Tiny __ (*A Christmas Carol* boy)
53 Highway
55 Brother of Moses
57 Quadrennial White House party
61 Vietnam's capital
63 Chew like a beaver
64 Poker player's payment
65 Goad
66 Business letter abbr.
67 Glasgow native
68 Unskilled laborers
69 "That __ it!" ("Enough!")

70 Cackling birds

DOWN

1 It's opened for a fill-up
2 On land
3 Add, as to soup
4 Tadpoles' homes
5 Singer Lane
6 Feels remorseful about
7 Student group
8 Doesn't stand straight
9 Sharp-witted
10 Golf platforms
11 Price indicator

12 Kay follower
13 Beast of burden
21 Crowbar, e.g.
22 Cry of delight
26 Atmosphere
27 Japanese currency
30 Passports, for example: Abbr.
31 Center of a peach
33 Camera part
34 Not at all spicy
35 Fireplace residue
37 Pink wading bird
38 Coffee alternative
39 Uncooked
40 Just right

41 Stetson or sombrero
42 __ Baba
45 Sink outlets
46 Letters of debt
47 Hounded
49 Paris' locale
50 Attach securely, as metal plating
51 Coves
54 "Beats me!"
56 Embarrass
58 Lunch time, often
59 Timed contest
60 Leather-punching tools
61 With it, once
62 Mature, as wine

★★ Five by Five

Group the 25 numbers in the grid into five sets of five, with each set having all of the numbers 1 through 5. The numbers in each set must all be connected to each other by a common horizontal or vertical side.

BETWEENER

What four-letter word belongs between the word at left and the word at right, so that the first and second word, and the second and third word, each form a common compound word?

DRIFT __ __ __ __ CHUCK

★ ? ? ?

Find these "questioning" words and phrases that are hidden in the diagram, either across, down, or diagonally.

```
S  V  Y  T  N  I  A  T  R  E  C  N  U  E
T  E  I  C  O  N  U  N  D  R  U  M  B  C
O  P  I  N  I  O  N  P  O  L  L  O  R  D
Q  N  O  I  T  C  E  J  B  O  R  O  C  I
U  L  E  T  A  E  W  L  P  P  S  A  H  F
I  L  L  S  M  F  R  U  Z  S  K  S  A  F
Z  I  D  E  R  W  M  R  E  Z  R  C  L  I
Q  R  D  U  O  P  E  X  O  N  U  M  L  C
N  G  I  Q  F  M  A  I  O  G  E  P  E  U
S  P  R  E  N  M  Y  I  V  L  A  D  N  L
Q  U  L  R  I  T  T  S  B  R  E  T  G  T
U  Z  R  N  K  S  S  O  T  M  E  A  E  Y
E  Z  E  V  E  H  R  E  A  E  S  T  S  O
R  L  U  U  E  P  A  N  T  X  R  Y  N  I
Y  J  Q  U  S  Y  D  O  U  B  T  Y  G  I
```

ASK
CHALLENGE
CONUNDRUM
CROSS-EXAMINE
DEMAND
DIFFICULTY
DOUBT
GRILL
INTERROGATE
INTERVIEW
MYSTERY
OBJECTION
OPINION POLL
PROBE
PROBLEM
PUMP
PUZZLE
QUERY
QUESTION
QUIZ
REQUEST
RIDDLE
SEEK INFORMATION
SURVEY
TEST
UNCERTAINTY

INITIAL REACTION

Identify the well-known proverb from the first letters in each of its words.

A. W. P. N. B. _____

★ Find the Ships

Determine the position of the 10 ships listed to the right of the diagram. The ships may be oriented either horizontally or vertically. A square with wavy lines indicates water and will not contain a ship. The numbers at the edge of the diagram indicate how many squares in that row or column contain parts of ships. When all 10 ships are correctly placed in the diagram, no two of them will touch each other, not even diagonally.

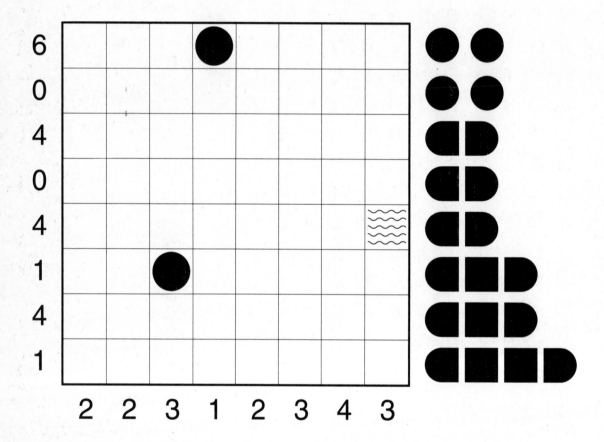

TWO-BY-FOUR

The eight letters in the word PACIFIER can be rearranged to form a pair of common four-letter words in two different ways, if no four-letter word is repeated. Can you find both pairs of words?

_ _ _ _   _ _ _ _

_ _ _ _   _ _ _ _

★★ Sudoku

Fill in the blank boxes so that every row, column, and 3x3 box contains all of the numbers 1 to 9.

	3	4	8					
		9			7			3
	2			4	9			1
5	9				3	2		
3				1				6
		1	4				9	7
9			1	8			5	
1			7			6		
					5	1	7	

MIXAGRAMS

Each line contains a five-letter word and a four-letter word that have been mixed together (the order of the letters in each word has not been changed). Unmix the two words on each line and write them in the spaces provided. When you're done, find a two-part answer to the clue by reading down the letter columns in the answers.

CLUE: Midwest college town

S A V V I E O R S = _ _ _ _ _ + _ _ _ _

B O O M L E G A T = _ _ _ _ _ + _ _ _ _

S T E W A M P O B = _ _ _ _ _ + _ _ _ _

A W A L S K L E W = _ _ _ _ _ + _ _ _ _

★ What's On Today? by Sally R. Stein

ACROSS

1 Farm harvest
5 Once more
10 Capital of Peru
14 Leaf-gathering tool
15 Totaled
16 Yale or Harvard: Abbr.
17 Stare at
18 Pass, as a law
19 Space agcy.
20 In charge, as in a family
23 Pas' spouses
24 Top of an ocean wave
25 Adorable kids
29 Aid in wrongdoing
32 Dramatic musical work
33 Pool sticks
34 "__ the night before Christmas ..."
38 Doing poorly at a casino
41 Pantry pests
42 Gobbles up
43 British coins
44 Snakelike swimmers
45 Most sensible
46 Long stories
50 Nightclub routine
51 Very conservatively
59 Lawyer: Abbr.
60 Ohio city
61 Neighborhood
62 At any __ (nevertheless)
63 A+ or B-
64 Window ledge
65 College club
66 Comic Soupy
67 Spill the beans

DOWN

1 Black bird
2 Anger
3 Tulsa's loc.
4 Jury member
5 Sports stadiums
6 Groups of troublemakers
7 Medical-sch. course
8 Scratcher's target
9 Brief memo
10 Of the moon
11 Silly
12 Fine sprays
13 Nautical "Halt!"
21 "Let me rephrase that ..."
22 What % means: Abbr.
25 Carbonated drink
26 Once __ a time
27 Try out
28 Part of the eye
29 Dad's sisters
30 Flying buzzers
31 Tee preceder
33 Old furnace fuel
34 At that time
35 Corked-bottle contents
36 Circle parts
37 Proofreader's word
39 "That's impressive!"
40 Minor quarrels
44 Point opposite WNW
45 Parts of a play
46 Neck-warming cloth
47 Church platform
48 Must, slangily
49 So far
50 Battery terminal
52 Touches with a baseball
53 Cajun vegetable
54 Kind of vaccine
55 Immense
56 Only four-letter Great Lake
57 Offer at retail
58 Statuesque

★ Fences

Connect the dots with vertical or horizontal lines, so that a single loop is formed with no crossings or branches. Each number indicates how many lines surround it; squares with no number may be surrounded by any number of lines.

```
2 1         2
      2   3 0 3
      2     2
    3       3 2
    2 1       2
      3     3
  3 1 0   0
      2       1 2
```

ADDITION SWITCH

Switch the positions of two of the digits in the incorrect sum at right, to get a correct sum.

```
  5 2 5
+ 3 9 6
-------
  8 3 1
```

★★ Triad Split Decisions

In this clueless crossword puzzle, each answer consists of two words whose spellings are the same, except for the consecutive letters given. All answers are common words; no phrases or hyphenated or capitalized words are used. Some of the clues may have more than one solution, but there is only one word pair that will correctly link up with all the other word pairs.

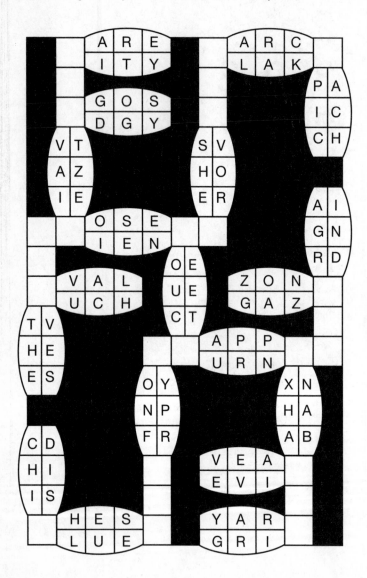

TRANSDELETION

Delete one letter from the word SNOWIEST and rearrange the rest, to get a courtroom term.

_____

★ **123**

Fill in the diagram so that each rectangular piece has one each of the numbers 1, 2, and 3, under these rules: 1) No two adjacent squares, horizontally or vertically, can have the same number. 2) Each completed row and column of the diagram will have an equal number of 1s, 2s, and 3s.

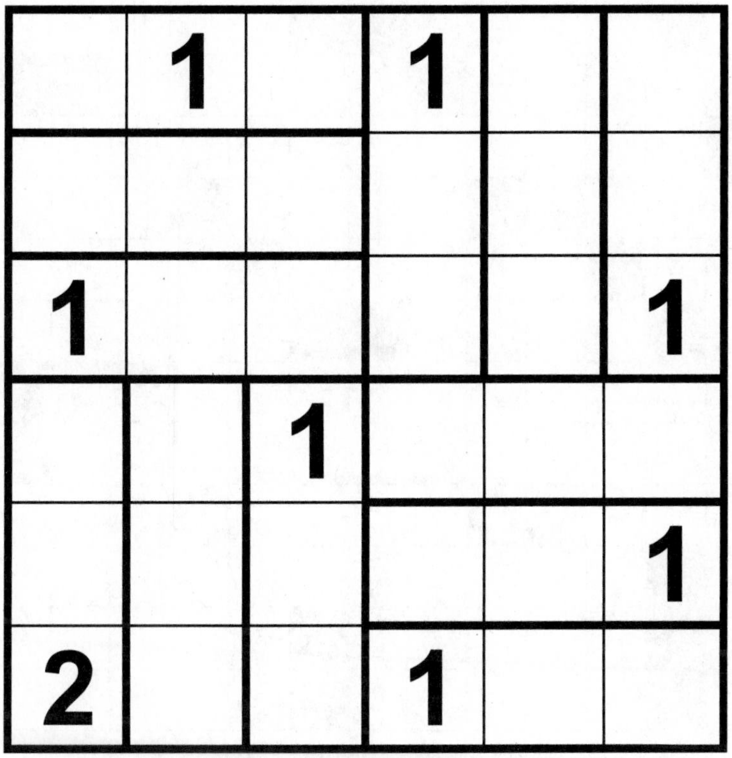

	1		1		
1					1
		1			
					1
2			1		

SUDOKU SUM

Without repeating any digits, complete the sum at right, by filling one digit in each of the five blanks.

```
  5 7 _
+ _ 1 4
-------
  _ _ _
```

★ Crispy by Gail Grabowski

ACROSS

1 At the present time
6 Illegal payment
11 Place a wager
14 Musical drama
15 Tablecloth material
16 Noteworthy time
17 One who breaks into a vault
19 Feel poorly
20 __-mo replay
21 "Get me out of __!"
22 Pound fraction
24 Small sofa
26 Cat in the Hat creator
28 Best man's salute
32 Tartan pattern
35 Violent anger
36 General Grant's foe
37 Be deserving of
38 Golf hazards
40 Ewes' mates
41 Fix, as a fight
42 Any minute now
43 Financial review
44 Awkward situation, slangily
48 Hospital employee
49 Library patron
52 Singer Page or LaBelle
54 Future flower
55 Golf-ball platform
57 Inventor Whitney
58 Tiny gemstone
62 Long period of time
63 Flynn of films
64 "Fame" singer Cara
65 Pod vegetable
66 Drill instructor, slangily
67 Like the Vikings

DOWN

1 Prepare, as a salad
2 Milky birthstones
3 *Robinson Crusoe* author
4 "__ you sure?"
5 Went sailing, fancily
6 Proclaimed noisily
7 Chinese side dish
8 Pen filler
9 Stinging insect
10 In transit
11 Vegetarian course
12 Guitarist Clapton
13 Folk story
18 Clarinet insert
23 GI show sponsor
25 Look-alike
26 Ginger cookie
27 Soufflé ingredients
29 Teheran native
30 Highway hauler
31 True-false, for one
32 Criminal, to a cop
33 Wild animal's home
34 Buenos Aires locale
38 Playpen items
39 Thick cord
40 Regretted
42 Takes long steps
43 Magic-lamp owner
45 Boy king of Egypt
46 New Orleans cuisine
47 Sharp, as wits
50 Old-time anesthetic
51 Bridle straps
52 Chick's sound
53 Lotion ingredient
54 Urban pollution
56 Fencing weapon
59 Keogh alternative
60 Part of ETA: Abbr.
61 __-Magnon man

★ Number-Out

Shade squares so that no number appears in any row or column more than once. Shaded squares may not touch each other horizontally or vertically, and all unshaded squares must form a single continuous area.

2	4	1	1	3
4	3	1	4	5
4	1	1	3	5
1	3	4	5	5
1	5	3	2	4

OPPOSITE ATTRACTION

Unscramble the letters in the phrase DOVE DEN to form two words that are opposites of each other.

_____   _____

★★ Tanks A Lot

Enter the maze at top center, pass over all tanks from behind (thereby destroying them), then exit. You may not pass through any square more than once, and may not enter a square in the line of fire of a tank you have not yet destroyed.

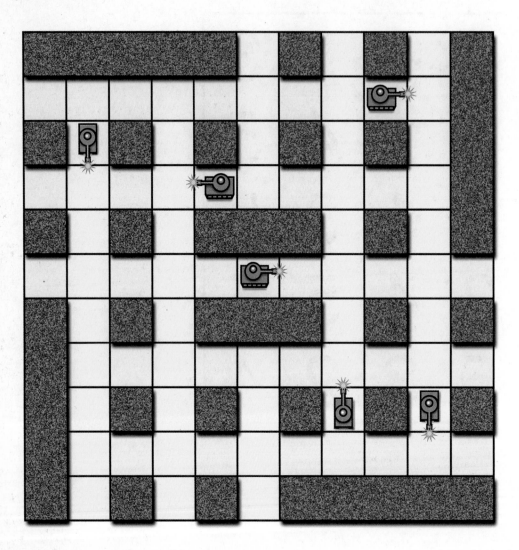

SAY IT AGAIN

What three-letter word can be either the past tense of a verb or a noun meaning "small quantity"?

— — —

★ The Main Thing

Find these "most important" words that are hidden in the diagram, either across, down, or diagonally. There's one additional nine-letter answer in the category, not listed below, that's also hidden in the diagram. What's that word?

```
N E C E S S A R T Q C H I E F
M A J O Y G N I D A E L W I E
C E N T R A L K F I R S N S P
X L A T N E M A D N U F S O R
P R I N C I P A L P A E C L I
N L L V I T A U R L N H A T M
F E A J P E N E F T T I R N A
I R C T K R M U I S C C D A R
R O I E I E E A O U E E I N Y
S J T P S V L M R M R N N I V
T A I K C S E C I M A T A M I
K M R E E R A R I E K R L O T
E E C Z O Y P R E D R A A D A
V U M F J G P Y Y B M I R P S
```

CARDINAL
CENTRAL
CHIEF
CRITICAL
CRUCIAL
DOMINANT
FIRST
FOREMOST
FUNDAMENTAL
KEY
LEADING
MAJOR
NECESSARY
PARAMOUNT
PREMIER
PRIMARY
PRIME
PRINCIPAL
SUPREME
VITAL

WHO'S WHAT WHERE?

The correct term for a resident of Rio de Janeiro, Brazil, is:

A) Riodejanero   B) Janeirian

C) Riosito   D) Carioca

★ At the Barber by Sally R. Stein

ACROSS

1 Notions
6 Singer Horne
10 Vampire writer Rice
14 "I cannot __ lie"
15 Wide-eyed
16 Place to swim at a motel
17 Grocery money-saving strategy
20 Corned-beef concoction
21 Three-piece suit part
22 Orange __ tea
23 Monkey relatives
25 __ Major (Big Dipper)
27 Makes a deep-sea dive
30 Anger
31 Not as much
35 Enjoyed lunch
36 __ sanctum
38 Genetic material
39 On a diet, perhaps
42 Mao __-tung
43 Venice waterway
44 Walks back and forth
45 Eastern European
47 Distress signal
48 Military guard
49 Actor Sharif
51 Mexican abode
52 Sneeze sound
55 French friends
57 Young deer
61 Yuletide decoration ritual
64 Find a new home
65 Summit
66 Pager sounds
67 Moved quickly
68 Butterfly catchers
69 Unruly kids

DOWN

1 Scratch target
2 Designer Oscar __ Renta
3 Yale students
4 Kindergarten lesson
5 Tree fluid
6 Bowling alleys
7 "Over easy" order
8 Up at night, as owls
9 In the past
10 Post-verdict legal tactic
11 Sheltered spot
12 Something taboo
13 Alternatively
18 Currier's partner
19 Increases
24 Sudden fright
26 Projectionist's spool
27 Religious groups
28 Bring about
29 Speak
30 Ancient South Americans
32 Royal order
33 Villainous look
34 Smart-mouthed
36 Lack of knowledge
37 Lariats
40 Cape Canaveral org.
41 Chased
46 Made a loud sound
48 Wide belt
50 Dad's partner
51 Gives as an example
52 S&L cash sources
53 Corn or soybeans
54 Bee's home
56 Grp. in charge
58 Neck of the woods
59 Cried
60 Loch __ monster
62 Author Fleming
63 Recede

★★ One-Way Streets

The diagram represents a pattern of streets. A and B are parking spaces, and the black squares are stores. Find a route that starts at A, passes through all stores exactly once, and ends at B. Arrows indicate one-way traffic for that block only. No block or intersection may be entered more than once.

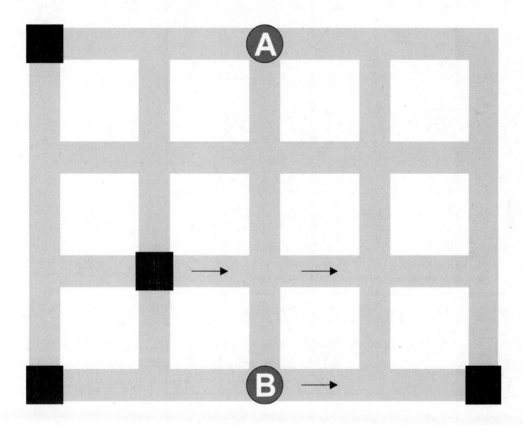

SOUND THINKING

The longest common uncapitalized word whose only consonant sounds are D, T, and Z, in that order, has three syllables and eight letters. What is it?

_____

★ Hyper-Sudoku

Fill in the blank boxes so that every row, column, 3x3 box, *and* each of the four
3x3 gray regions contains all of the numbers 1 to 9.

4	5				7		6	8
	9							1
			4	5				
3	2	6			9	8		
	1			3		5	9	
		9	1		2	6		3
		3	2		5	7		
	6					9	3	4
			3				2	

CENTURY MARKS

Inserting plus signs and minus signs, as many as necessary, in between the nine digits below,
create a series of additions and subtractions whose final answer is 100. Any digits without a
sign between them are to be grouped together as a single number.

$$1 \quad 1 \quad 8 \quad 3 \quad 6 \quad 1 \quad 1 \quad 4 \quad 9 \quad = \quad 100$$

★ Star Search

Find the stars that are hidden in some of the blank squares. The numbered squares indicate how many stars are hidden in the squares adjacent to them (including diagonally). There is never more than one star in any square.

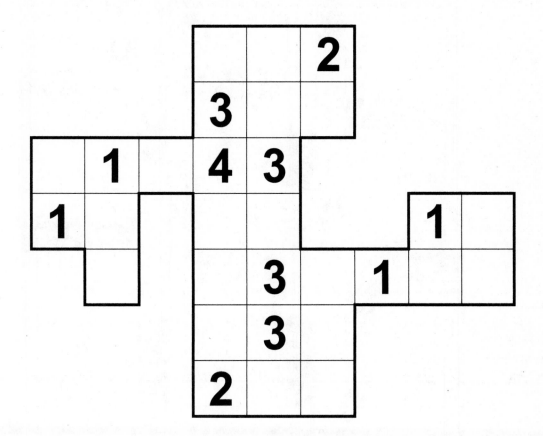

TELEPHONE TRIOS

1	ABC 2	DEF 3
GHI 4	JKL 5	MNO 6
PRS 7	TUV 8	WXY 9
*	o	#

Using the numbers and letters on a standard telephone, what three seven-letter words or phrases from the same category can be formed from these telephone numbers?

274-6487 _ _ _ _ _ _ _

636-8466 _ _ _ _ _ _ _

784-4378 _ _ _ _ _ _ _

★ Flying Starts by Gail Grabowski

ACROSS

1 Wide belt
5 Checkers or chess
9 Mar. 17 honoree
14 __ mater
15 Enjoying a cruise
16 Capital of Egypt
17 Mortgage, for example
18 Leading actor
19 Playful aquatic mammal
20 Decorative item on a couch
23 Soup container
24 Literary spoof
25 Unexciting
27 "Ditto!"
31 Creative thought
34 Endures
38 Doily material
39 Fourth planet
40 Dole out
41 Health resort
42 Piece of bacon
43 Recipe direction
44 Part of a sock
45 Nudges
46 Boy Scouts, for example
47 Available at a reduced price
49 "I'm amazed!"
51 Brings together
56 Research site
58 Have trouble sleeping
62 Angry
64 Airplane part
65 Author Wiesel
66 More pleasant
67 Skin-lotion additive
68 Little rodents
69 Occupied, as a seat
70 Tadpole's home
71 Practice for a bout

DOWN

1 Seasons, as French fries
2 Luau greeting
3 Intelligent
4 Capital of Vietnam
5 Sounded shocked
6 Italian wine region
7 Dinner, for example
8 English nobleman
9 Angry look
10 Tit for __
11 Like a moonless night
12 Vicinity
13 Ripped apart
21 Place for a watch
22 Woodwind instrument
26 "We __ please" (store sign)
28 Showbiz twin Mary-Kate or Ashley
29 Repairs, as papers
30 Florida city
32 One of the Great Lakes
33 Poisonous snakes
34 Scottish girl
35 Choir voice
36 Shoe with a strap
37 Sculpted figure
42 Go shopping
44 Sounds from Santa
48 Leaped suddenly (at)
50 Back of a ship
52 List entries
53 Dutch flower
54 Author Jong
55 Villain's look
56 Clothes-dryer fuzz
57 Opera solo
59 Trade
60 Farm tower
61 Of unknown authorship: Abbr.

★ ABC

Enter the letters A, B, and C into the diagram so that each row and column has exactly one A, one B, and one C. The letters outside the diagram indicate the first letter encountered, moving in the direction of the arrow. Keep in mind that after all the letters have been filled in, there will be one blank box in each row and column.

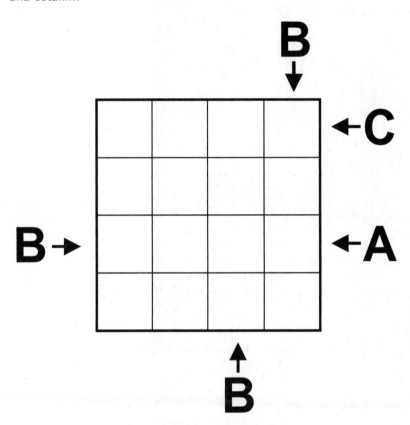

CLUELESS CROSSWORD

Complete the crossword with common uncapitalized seven-letter words, based entirely on the letters already filled in for you.

★★ Dicey

Group the dice into sets of two or more whose sums equal nine. The dice in each set must be connected to each other by a common horizontal or vertical side.

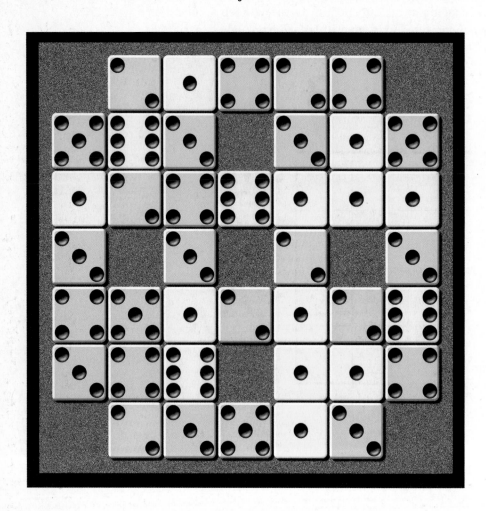

BETWEENER

What four-letter word belongs between the word at left and the word at right, so that the first and second word, and the second and third word, each form a common compound word?

COTTON __ __ __ __ SPIN

★★ Sudoku

Fill in the blank boxes so that every row, column, and 3x3 box contains all of the numbers 1 to 9.

3			9					
		1			8		5	
	8			6	5	1		
1						2	7	
		3		4		9		
	4	9						5
		5	8	2			1	
	2		6			3		
					3			8

MIXAGRAMS

Each line contains a five-letter word and a four-letter word that have been mixed together (the order of the letters in each word has not been changed). Unmix the two words on each line and write them in the spaces provided. When you're done, find a two-part answer to the clue by reading down the letter columns in the answers.

CLUE: Easy mark

G O S P O D O K S = _ _ _ _ _ + _ _ _ _

B O V U R S A L T = _ _ _ _ _ + _ _ _ _

A M S E S L E T T = _ _ _ _ _ + _ _ _ _

T A R C H O R N S = _ _ _ _ _ + _ _ _ _

★ Family Viewing by Sally R. Stein

ACROSS

1 Highest-quality
5 Unwanted lawn plant
9 Dislike intensely
14 Station wagon, for one
15 Wheel bar
16 Jeweled headpiece
17 Factual
18 Stand up
19 Marsh bird
20 Oversentimental journalist
22 Like Jabba the Hutt
23 Prosecutors: Abbr.
24 Dog's coat
25 *CSI* or *The Sopranos*
29 Race winner of fable
34 Angelic toppers
35 Evergreen tree
36 Excursion
37 Israeli airline
38 Was concerned
39 Sharpen
40 Broadway award
41 Pub servings
42 Fractions of a British pound
43 Sculpture and collage
45 Kentucky Derby mounts
46 Hill-building insect
47 Guy's date
48 __ and raves
51 Cub Scout official
57 Honolulu greeting
58 Nonwritten exam
59 Keep out of sight
60 Group of experts
61 Lo-cal, on food labels
62 Dry as a desert
63 Breathe loudly while sleeping
64 Experiment
65 Makes moist

DOWN

1 Fliers in caves
2 Money in Spain and Italy
3 Injure, as one's 4 Down
4 Sock contents
5 Poland's capital
6 Ways off highways
7 Otherwise
8 Moose relative
9 Went to a diner, perhaps
10 Frat pledge's sponsor
11 Race loser of fable
12 Metal-filled rocks
13 Evaluate
21 Wedding vows
24 Astaire of filmdom
25 Greek letter
26 Bravery in battle
27 Tilt
28 Title for the pope
29 Gets weary
30 Change for a five
31 Works on laundry
32 From that time
33 Fencing swords
35 Coconut tree
38 Golfer's vehicle
42 Game on horseback
44 At a discounted price
45 Small town
47 Small flies
48 Knocks on a door
49 Economist Greenspan
50 Something prohibited
51 Muttonhead
52 Northwest Pennsylvania city
53 Defrost
54 Add to the payroll
55 Polish, as an essay
56 Crimson and cherry

★★ Line Drawing

Draw three straight lines, each from one edge of the square to another edge, so that the sum of the numbers in each of the four regions is an odd whole number less than 10.

$$
\begin{array}{l}
2 \qquad \dfrac{1}{2} \qquad \dfrac{1}{4} \qquad 1 \qquad 7 \\[2mm]
\qquad\qquad\qquad\qquad 2 \qquad \dfrac{4}{4} \\[2mm]
\dfrac{3}{4} \qquad 1 \qquad\qquad 1\dfrac{1}{4} \\[2mm]
\qquad\qquad\qquad\qquad\qquad 3 \\[2mm]
\qquad\qquad\qquad \dfrac{1}{2} \\[2mm]
\dfrac{1}{4} \qquad 5 \qquad\qquad\qquad \dfrac{1}{2}
\end{array}
$$

THREE OF A KIND

Find the three hidden words in the sentence that, read in order, go together in some way.

Pago Pago, in general, is a mystery to people from Norway.

★★ Find the Ships

Determine the position of the 10 ships listed to the right of the diagram. The ships may be oriented either horizontally or vertically. A square with wavy lines indicates water and will not contain a ship. The numbers at the edge of the diagram indicate how many squares in that row or column contain parts of ships. When all 10 ships are correctly placed in the diagram, no two of them will touch each other, not even diagonally.

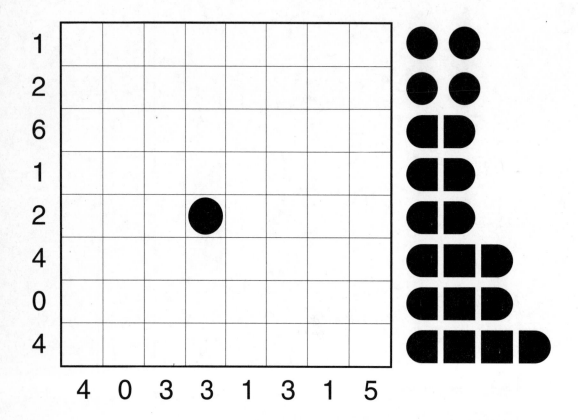

1
2
6
1
2
4
0
4

4 0 3 3 1 3 1 5

TWO-BY-FOUR

The eight letters in the word QUAINTLY can be rearranged to form a pair of common four-letter words in only one way. Can you find the two words?

__ __ __ __   __ __ __ __

★★ Fences

Connect the dots with vertical or horizontal lines, so that a single loop is formed with no crossings or branches. Each number indicates how many lines surround it; squares with no number may be surrounded by any number of lines.

```
1  2        2    3

      2  2  2

   2           2

 1  3     3  1

   3  0     0  2

1         3

 3  3  2

3     2        1  2
```

ADDITION SWITCH

Switch the positions of two of the digits in the incorrect sum at right, to get a correct sum.

```
  3 0 9
+ 2 7 5
-------
  6 8 5
```

★ Cosmetic Counter by Gail Grabowski

ACROSS

1 Visit a store
5 Smart-mouthed
10 Mimicked
14 Exterior of a boat
15 Die down
16 Ripped
17 Region
18 Diet-food label claim
19 Small-size bed
20 Explain away
22 Ocean motions
23 Fork prong
24 Skin opening
25 Allows inside
28 Lost one's footing
32 Small amount
33 Farm storage buildings
34 Bikini part
35 Stir-fry pans
36 Toss
37 ___ as a pancake
38 St. crosser
39 Salad-oil holder
40 Remote-control button
41 Gatherings for graduates
43 Prepares baby food, perhaps
44 ___ moss (gardener's buy)
45 Valentine flower
46 Place for a cookout
48 Pink alcholic drink
53 Designer Cassini
54 Unskilled laborers
55 Whirlpool
56 Luxurious
57 Spine-tingling
58 Shakespearean king
59 Tennis-match units
60 Small songbirds
61 Canoeing locale

DOWN

1 Thick carpet
2 Toss
3 Muffin topping
4 Milk-bottle materials
5 Hairdressers' workplaces
6 Higher than
7 Ump's call
8 Galaxy unit
9 "Are we there ___?"
10 Clothing
11 Pastel shade
12 Great Lake bordering Pennsylvania
13 Family rooms
21 Location

22 Preschoolers
24 Farm implement
25 Engaged in battle
26 Had control of the wheel
27 Absent student's exam
28 Forest ranger's worries
29 Tremendously
30 Wipe away
31 Goes out with
33 Avoid
36 Horse's gait
37 Parting word
39 Italian version of 37 Down

40 Propel a grocery cart
42 Sounds from a horse
43 Sheriffs' groups
45 Disagreeable encounter
46 Bursts, as a balloon
47 Spiny houseplant
48 Keg contents
49 Traditional knowledge
50 Notion
51 Bismarck's state: Abbr.
52 *Jane* ___ (Brontë novel)
54 Church bench

★★ Knot or Not?

When Octavia the Octopus extends her tentacles in the four pictures, in which ones will she get knotted, and in which will she not?

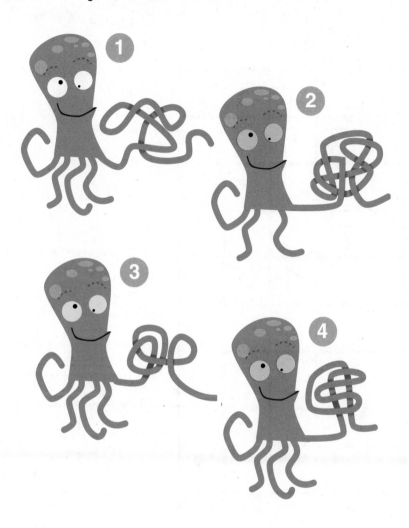

THREE AT A RHYME

Rearrange these letters to form three one-syllable words that rhyme.

A B E E E E K L N

_____ _____ _____

★★ 123

Fill in the diagram so that each rectangular piece has one each of the numbers 1, 2, and 3, under these rules: 1) No two adjacent squares, horizontally or vertically, can have the same number. 2) Each completed row and column of the diagram will have an equal number of 1s, 2s, and 3s.

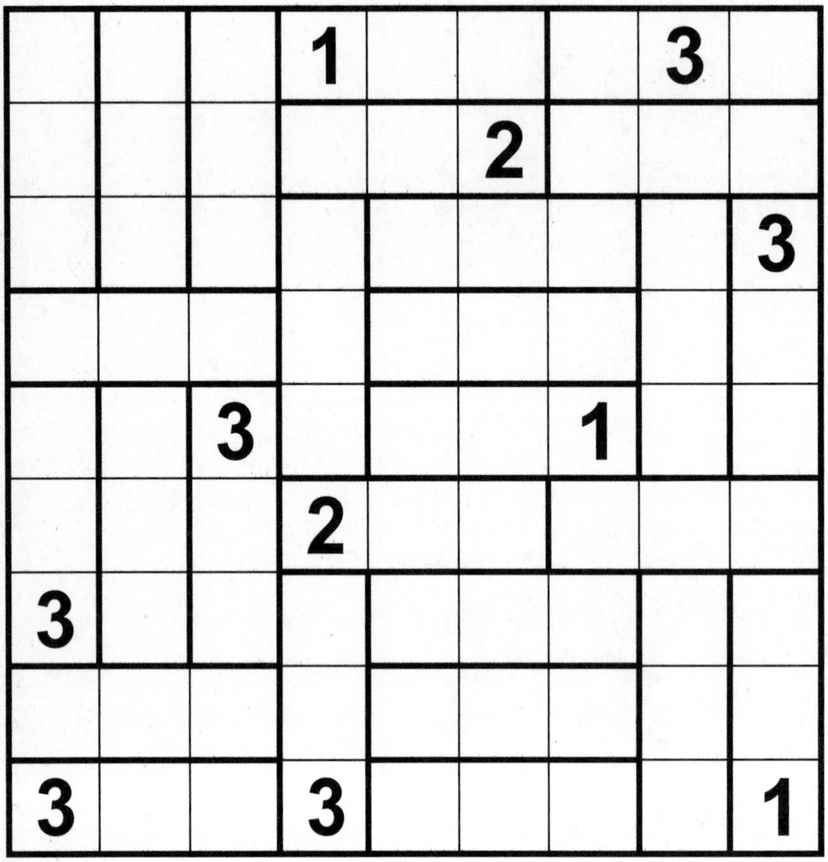

			1				3	
					2			
								3
		3				1		
			2					
3								
3			3					1

SUDOKU SUM

Without repeating any digits, complete the sum at right, by filling one digit in each of the five blanks.

$$2\ \_\ 4$$
$$+\ \_\ 8\ \_$$
$$\overline{\_\ 7\ \_}$$

★ Number-Out

Shade squares so that no number appears in any row or column more than once. Shaded squares may not touch each other horizontally or vertically, and all unshaded squares must form a single continuous area.

4	1	5	1	3
5	5	5	3	4
5	4	2	1	3
3	4	1	4	2
1	2	5	5	5

OPPOSITE ATTRACTION

Unscramble the letters in the phrase FOWLS SAT to form two common words that are opposites of each other.

_____   _____

★ By the Pound by Sally R. Stein

ACROSS

1 Swimsuit tops
5 Tennis pro Kournikova
9 Trench
14 Walked away
15 Make a rip in
16 Montana neighbor
17 Opera solo
18 Tiny branch
19 In the neighborhood
20 As of now
22 Run off to wed
23 Prepare to propose
24 Urban-renewal target
26 NASCAR sponsor
29 As a large group
34 Comic poem
39 Placed in order
40 Regarding
41 Teheran resident
43 Made, as a knot
44 Fifth part of Act I
46 Punch and Judy show skill
48 Entered, as computer data
50 Hot drink
51 Walking pace
53 Scoundrel
58 Robot-novel genre
62 Grumbling under one's breath
65 Nostalgic song
66 Become indistinct
67 Ship's jail
68 Room dividers
69 Place to stand and wait
70 "Suffice __ say ..."
71 Sugary
72 Fencing sword
73 At that time

DOWN

1 Crow's color
2 Broadcast again
3 Blazing
4 "Blank" look
5 Business-envelope abbr.
6 Small salamander
7 Manicurist's concerns
8 Sock pattern
9 Difficult choice
10 Admired one
11 Mexican food
12 British fellow
13 Golfer's objective
21 Otherwise
25 Not ready to harvest
27 Entertaining facts
28 __ capita
30 Poker payment
31 Satirical segment
32 Fortune-teller
33 Whirlpool
34 Flat, circular object
35 Long ago
36 Western author Zane
37 Heredity unit
38 Track circuit
42 Cashew or filbert
45 Most tense
47 Remove, as rind
49 Agile
52 Flower associated with Holland
54 Circle the Earth
55 Circumference
56 Band together
57 Incite
58 Piglets' mamas
59 Talon
60 Not doing anything
61 Smoothing tool
63 Singer's selection
64 Ancestry diagram

★★ No Three in a Row

Enter the maze at bottom left, pass through all the squares exactly once, then exit, all without retracing your path. You may not pass through three squares of the same color consecutively.

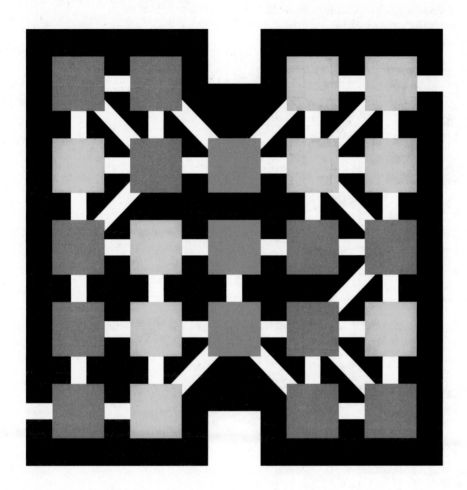

SAY IT AGAIN

What three-letter adjective can mean either "popular" or "peppery"?

— — —

★★ Split Decisions

In this clueless crossword puzzle, each answer consists of two words whose spellings are the same, except for the consecutive letters given. All answers are common words; no phrases or hyphenated or capitalized words are used. Some of the clues may have more than one solution, but there is only one word pair that will correctly link up with all the other word pairs.

TRANSDELETION

Delete one letter from the word PARADING and rearrange the rest, to get a family nickname.

—————————————————

★ Hyper-Sudoku

Fill in the blank boxes so that every row, column, 3x3 box, *and* each of the four 3x3 gray regions contains all of the numbers 1 to 9.

8				1	2	5		3
			8	4				
	1	2	5			4		
3	4							
			2	6			7	
1	2			9		8	5	
	6	8					3	
4	5	9	1		7	6		
	3			5				

MIXAGRAMS

Each line contains a five-letter word and a four-letter word that have been mixed together (the order of the letters in each word has not been changed). Unmix the two words on each line and write them in the spaces provided. When you're done, find a two-part answer to the clue by reading down the letter columns in the answers.

CLUE: Alaskan entrée

T O L A C K E E N = _ _ _ _ _ + _ _ _ _

H S I P I R E N E = _ _ _ _ _ + _ _ _ _

B I V I N A G E L = _ _ _ _ _ + _ _ _ _

R U M B O G U L Y = _ _ _ _ _ + _ _ _ _

★ What's Cooking by Gail Grabowski

ACROSS

1 Oscar or Emmy
6 Hotel posting
10 Pronto, in a memo
14 Hayfield machine
15 Spanish cheers
16 Old Italian money
17 Madonna film role
18 "How clumsy of me!"
19 Urban pollution
20 Vent one's anger
23 French Mrs.
24 RBIs or ERA
25 Glasses and goggles
27 Word-processor spacing feature
30 Fly high
31 __ Town (Thornton Wilder play)
32 Homeowners' documents
36 Part of a shoe size
39 Paid athletes
41 Less moist
43 Ripped
44 Did a carpenter's dusty job
46 Online correspondence
48 Finished first
49 Drug-fighting cop
51 Holy ones
53 Cottonwood relatives
56 That lady's
57 Cry of discovery
58 Approaching the solution
63 Captivated
65 Set of socks
66 Chill-inducing
67 Family-history diagram
68 Vogue rival
69 Latin dance
70 Knitter's need
71 Bird food
72 Secret meeting

DOWN

1 Brother of Cain
2 Surfer's ride
3 Got off the bus
4 Throw again
5 Chose, as for the military
6 Pigeon perch
7 Much (of)
8 Native American abode
9 High-school compositions
10 Capone and Pacino
11 "Don't get so upset!"
12 Kitchen scent
13 Clip-on communicator
21 Destined
22 Calico's cry
26 Stand in line
27 Spinning toys
28 Mystical glow
29 Grocery-bag material
33 Before, in poems
34 Lower, as headlights
35 Baltic or Bering
37 Horse's gait
38 Farmyard egg layers
40 Aquatic mammal
42 Gone up
45 Haul
47 Most massive
50 Thin pancakes
52 "It's true, really!"
53 Birthday celebration
54 Scarlett of fiction
55 No longer fresh
56 Added employees
59 Scrabble piece
60 Military force
61 Barbecue favorites
62 Steak or veal
64 Coffee-break time, often

★ Flights of Fancy

Find these "dreamy" words that are hidden in the diagram, either across, down, or diagonally.

```
M  A  M  B  I  T  I  O  S  T  Y  E  A  R  N
A  A  G  I  R  N  P  D  F  V  R  H  D  O  Y
E  O  B  N  T  O  G  A  R  P  A  A  I  N  A
R  G  L  M  I  I  N  R  P  E  Z  T  N  L  W
D  N  I  G  H  T  M  A  R  E  A  C  W  C  N
W  I  S  U  A  A  A  D  B  R  E  Q  D  E  E
S  S  I  S  M  N  N  O  I  S  U  L  E  D  G
I  S  Y  I  B  I  R  P  L  L  I  C  S  N  F
W  O  J  W  I  G  S  E  A  F  L  W  I  B  I
W  T  K  G  T  A  B  E  V  O  J  N  R  A  T
F  I  O  A  I  M  D  L  U  E  R  S  E  E  A
X  A  S  V  O  I  W  D  I  U  R  S  O  Y  O
L  Q  H  H  N  G  S  Y  T  S  S  I  L  B  L
U  N  R  E  A  L  E  P  O  H  O  W  E  A  F
```

AMBITION
ASPIRATION
BLISS
CLOUDS
DELUSION
DESIRE
DREAM
FANTASY
FLOATING
GOAL
HOPE
IDEAL
IMAGINATION
NIGHTMARE
REVERIE
SLEEP
TOSSING
TRANCE
TURNING
UNREAL
WISH
YAWN
YEARN

IN OTHER WORDS

There is only one common uncapitalized word that contains the consecutive letters OFP. What is it?

_____

bRain BReatHer
GO AWAY!

Travel may be broadening and restorative but it also has its pitfalls, so a sense of humor about it is an indispensable asset to keep with you the next time you leave home. These humorous, and sometimes wry, observations should help to put you in the right frame of mind:

The worst thing about being a tourist is having other tourists recognize you as a tourist.

—RUSSELL BAKER

In America there are two classes of travel—first class, and with children.

—ROBERT BENCHLEY

If God wanted us to fly, He would have given us tickets.

—MEL BROOKS

No place is boring if you've had a good night's sleep and have a pocket full of unexposed film.

—ROBERT ADAMS

Thanks to the Interstate Highway System, it is now possible to travel from coast to coast without seeing anything.

—CHARLES KURALT

When you travel, remember that a foreign country is not designed to make you comfortable. It is designed to make its own people comfortable.

—CLIFTON FADIMAN

The country has charms only for those not obliged to stay there.

—ÉDOUARD MANET

We hit the sunny beaches where we occupy ourselves keeping the sun off our skin, the salt water off our bodies and the sand out of our belongings.

—ERMA BOMBECK

★★ One-Way Streets

The diagram represents a pattern of streets. P's are parking spaces, and the black squares are stores. Find the route that starts at a parking space, passes through all stores exactly once, and ends at the other parking space. Arrows indicate one-way traffic for that block only. No block or intersection may be entered more than once.

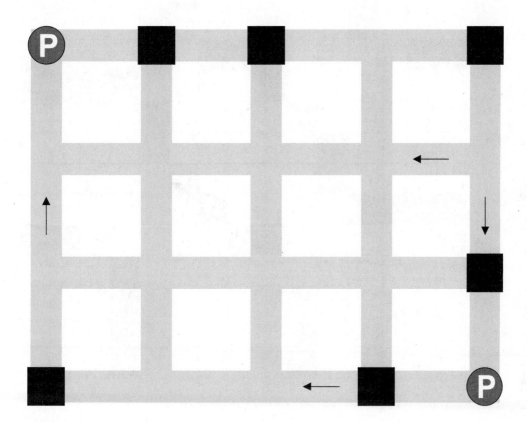

SOUND THINKING

The consonant sounds in the word FISSURE are F, SH, and R. What common uncapitalized eight-letter word is pronounced with the same consonant sounds in the same order?

★ Skiing Is Believing by Sally R. Stein

ACROSS

1 Baseball player's hat
4 Packs of playing cards
9 Leaves of a book
14 *The Sopranos* network
15 Arm of the sea
16 Customary
17 100%
18 Fill with fright
19 Self-assurance
20 Golf gadget
21 Moonshine, slangily
23 Nullifes
25 Escapes in a hurry
26 Rough, as sandpaper
28 The one close by
30 Put up __ (complain)
31 Teddy or grizzly
32 Cellar: Abbr.
36 Farm storage building
37 Hold responsible
38 Suffix for accept
39 Business-envelope abbr.
40 Rowing needs
41 Group of orange trees
42 Quick boxing punches
43 Evolution theorist
44 Jobs for an attorney
47 Muscle
48 Gave new life to
51 That woman
54 Facing the pitcher
55 Rental agreement
56 Wedding vow
57 Irish author Oscar
58 Irate feeling
59 Chinese beverage
60 Cattle-drive beast
61 Christmas carols
62 Conclusion

DOWN

1 Informal conversation
2 Competent
3 Summer Olympics event
4 Don't take seriously
5 Create, as a cryptogram
6 "Santa __ Is Coming to Town"
7 *Show Boat* composer Jerome
8 Proofreader's instruction
9 Ones being taught
10 In unison
11 Museum tour leader
12 Lessens, as a load
13 Whole bunch
22 In flames
24 Actor Welles
26 Home, in Mexico
27 "Think nothing __!"
28 Rips up
29 Bad actors
31 Spill the beans
32 Wilkes-__, PA
33 Friend of the Seven Dwarfs
34 1106, in old Rome
35 Adolescent
37 Toot one's own horn
41 Male geese
42 Clown in a king's court
43 Truck engine
44 Do something satisfactorily
45 Walk slowly
46 Garden tool
47 Performer's platform
48 Parts of a vise
49 Economist Greenspan
50 Nevada city
52 Biblical paradise
53 Hit the __ (leave)

★★ Missing Links

Find the two hoops that are linked together, but linked to no other hoops on the page.

THREE AT A RHYME

Rearrange these letters to form three one-syllable words that rhyme.

D G H I I M M M W Y

_____ _____ _____

★★ Star Search

Find the stars that are hidden in some of the blank squares. The numbered squares indicate how many stars are hidden in the squares adjacent to them (including diagonally). There is never more than one star in any square.

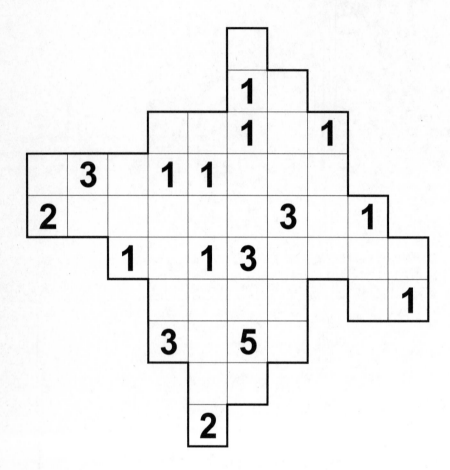

TELEPHONE TRIOS

Using the numbers and letters on a standard telephone, what three seven-letter words or phrases from the same category can be formed from these telephone numbers?

392-6463   _ _ _ _ _ _ _

467-7328   _ _ _ _ _ _ _

627-3783   _ _ _ _ _ _ _

★★ Triad Split Decisions

In this clueless crossword puzzle, each answer consists of two words whose spellings are the same, except for the consecutive letters given. All answers are common words; no phrases or hyphenated or capitalized words are used. Some of the clues may have more than one solution, but there is only one word pair that will correctly link up with all the other word pairs.

TRANSDELETION

Delete one letter from the word CONSULT and rearrange the rest, to get a type of tree.

_____

★★ Speeding by Fred Piscop

ACROSS

1 Joke response, informally
5 Abrasive stuff
9 Up to one's ears
14 Oratorio highlight
15 Move, in Realtor lingo
16 River formation
17 African insect
19 Many a John Wayne film
20 Freight unit
21 Noshed on
22 Saw-toothed
24 Ultimate consumers
27 __ culpa
28 Stanley Cup org.
29 Infinite time
34 On the briny
36 *Cinderella Man* role
37 The __ Scott Decision
38 "Not guilty," for one
39 Bowler's place
40 Catches rays
41 Letters near "O"
42 Having little 4 Down
43 Confined, with "up"
44 Eroded
46 Majorca Mrs.
47 Directional suffix
48 Speculate
53 Ballpark snacks
57 Suffix with scram
58 Bottom line
59 Deck out
60 Wide punctuation
63 Melodic transition
64 Tied up
65 Negative prefix
66 __-fatty acids
67 Yucatán native
68 Family tree abbr.

DOWN

1 Coffeehouse buy
2 Fiery felony
3 Diabolical one
4 Jack Sprat no-no
5 Hansel's sister
6 Direct, as for info
7 "__ be darned!"
8 Santa's sackful
9 Hero worshiper
10 Result of normal use
11 Utah ski resort
12 Editor's "leave it"
13 Big-eared hopper

18 Figure-skater Cohen
23 Nail-file material
25 Error result, perhaps
26 Leak stopper
30 New driver, usually
31 Teheran's land
32 Hiker's setup
33 Gridiron stats: Abbr.
34 Purina competitor
35 Palmist, e.g.
36 Botched
38 Sound of a sock
39 Go __ (agree)

43 Type of tourney
45 Pilotless planes
46 J. Lo title role
49 Hogwash
50 Not very sensible
51 Lemon peels
52 Moral standard
53 Verb with "thou"
54 Baltic Sea feeder
55 *Animal House* attire
56 Goblet part
61 Allegheny Mts. state
62 Family man

★★ ABC

Enter the letters A, B, and C into the diagram so that each row and column has exactly one A, one B, and one C. The letters outside the diagram indicate the first letter encountered, moving in the direction of the arrow. Keep in mind that after all the letters have been filled in, there will be two blank boxes in each row and column.

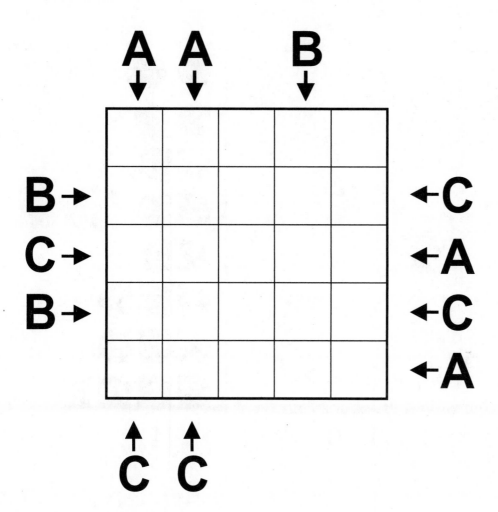

NATIONAL TREASURE

Find the two common six-letter words (not including past-tense verbs) that can be formed from the letters in ICELAND.

_ _ _ _ _ _   _ _ _ _ _ _

★★ Find the Ships

Determine the position of the 10 ships listed to the right of the diagram. The ships may be oriented either horizontally or vertically. A square with wavy lines indicates water and will not contain a ship. The numbers at the edge of the diagram indicate how many squares in that row or column contain parts of ships. When all 10 ships are correctly placed in the diagram, no two of them will touch each other, not even diagonally.

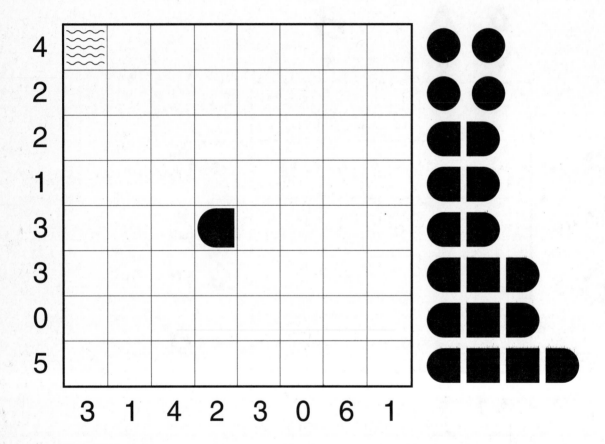

TWO-BY-FOUR

The eight letters in the word RIGATONI can be rearranged to form a pair of common four-letter words in three different ways, if no four-letter word is repeated. Can you find them all?

___ ___ ___ ___   ___ ___ ___ ___   ___ ___ ___ ___   ___ ___ ___ ___

___ ___ ___ ___   ___ ___ ___ ___

★★ On the Circuit by Kevin Donovan

ACROSS

1 Away from work
4 Augment
9 To no __ (useless)
14 Frazier foe
15 *Little House on the Prairie* girl
16 *Rigoletto* composer
17 Junior, to Senior
18 Exclusive group
20 Lyricist Gershwin
21 Auto brand
22 Discussed, with "out"
23 Coho and sockeye
25 Small taste
26 Called up
27 Mexican moolah
28 Actor Kilmer
31 Atlanta university
33 One way to reduce risk
35 Praise highly
36 Home away from home
37 Farm measure
38 Of a city
40 Female voices
41 Ancient
42 Pub potables
43 Secondly
44 Creative pursuits
45 On the loose
48 Go to extremes with
51 Medicinal plant
52 Strong desire
53 Altar presentation
55 Inc., in the UK
56 Flax fabric
57 Part of the whole
58 Chowed down
59 Informal talk
60 More reasonable
61 Okra unit

DOWN

1 Desert haven
2 Plant life
3 Open ender
4 Court-ordered payment
5 Vietnamese port
6 NBA shots
7 Yuletide purchase
8 Boat mover
9 Pilot
10 Work by Whitman
11 Shoe part
12 Doing nothing
13 Bent the truth
19 Stone shaper
24 Tuesday, in Tours
25 Cut at an angle
27 Pocketed breads
28 Winner's "tour"
29 Curly coiffure
30 Caustic solutions
31 *Sesame Street* character
32 Handle roughly
33 Foolish ones
34 Spicy dip
36 __ Head Island, SC
39 Checking IDs
40 Accusatory one
43 Immediately
44 Cosmetics queen Elizabeth
45 Otherworldly visitor
46 Reach
47 Brought to a conclusion
48 Night hunters
49 Face covering
50 Author Ferber
51 Opera offering
54 Some drs.

★★ Two Pairs

Among the 16 pictures below, find the two pairs of pictures that are identical to each other.

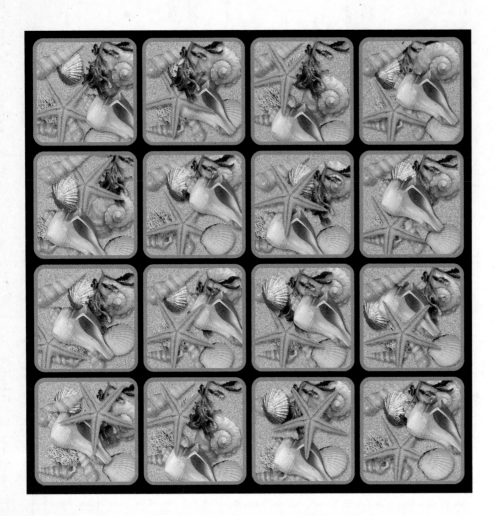

BETWEENER

What four-letter word belongs between the word at left and the word at right, so that the first and second word, and the second and third word, each form a common compound word?

ARROW __ __ __ __ QUARTERS

★★ Sudoku

Fill in the blank boxes so that every row, column, and 3x3 box contains all of the numbers 1 to 9.

8			3	1				4
	1	4	9				2	
						5		
				6			7	2
2				4				5
3	4			7				
	3							
	8				7	1	4	
6				3	2			7

MIXAGRAMS

Each line contains a five-letter word and a four-letter word that have been mixed together (the order of the letters in each word has not been changed). Unmix the two words on each line and write them in the spaces provided. When you're done, find a two-part answer to the clue by reading down the letter columns in the answers.

CLUE: Parking place of a sort

A R A B O F T U T = _ _ _ _ _ + _ _ _ _

A V I K S I N O R = _ _ _ _ _ + _ _ _ _

S K E C L O I N G = _ _ _ _ _ + _ _ _ _

K N E E D I L N Y = _ _ _ _ _ + _ _ _ _

★★ Fences

Connect the dots with vertical or horizontal lines, so that a single loop is formed with no crossings or branches. Each number indicates how many lines surround it; squares with no number may be surrounded by any number of lines.

ADDITION SWITCH

Switch the positions of two of the digits in the incorrect sum at right, to get a correct sum.

$$\begin{array}{r} 3\,8\,2 \\ +\,3\,5\,9 \\ \hline 6\,4\,2 \end{array}$$

★★ Crossing Words by Fred Piscop

ACROSS

1 World book
6 Comedian Kaplan
10 Born's partner
14 Arlo's father
15 On the briny
16 String tie
17 Access one's e-mail
18 *Serpico* author
19 Drop out
20 Newspaper-movie cry
23 Even if, briefly
24 "How silly of me!"
25 Binges
28 Make a pick
31 Fertilizer ingredient
36 Western Indian
37 Cross the plate
39 Pat's letter-turner
40 Ignore wrongdoing
43 Bitter-__ (die-hard)
44 Completely wreck
45 "You __ here"
46 Miniature
48 Dispenser candy
49 Chief exec.
50 Raised rails
52 Poetic preposition
54 Heed sound advice
62 Typesetter's selection
63 No longer valid
64 Push hard
65 Long ago
66 Therefore
67 Fax precursor
68 Paper buy
69 __-do-well
70 Bull sound

DOWN

1 Hole-making tools
2 Horn sound
3 Olympic rings, e.g.
4 Takes on
5 Moog, familiarly
6 Go or go fish
7 PDQ
8 35 Down had one
9 Back off
10 Patio meals, for short
11 Casanova
12 Ivy Leaguers
13 Braille bit
21 Bootlegger's product
22 Beach-pail partner
25 Minty drink
26 Make amends
27 Crystal-lined rock
29 Yeats or Keats
30 Scout unit
32 Surfacing stuff
33 Sadat of Egypt
34 Part of a drum set
35 Grant's successor
37 Main or Wall
38 Suffix with major
41 London's __ Gardens
42 Cruel frat brother
47 Football-team complement
49 Gaudy bird's mate
51 Bunk annoyance
53 Takes five
54 Partnerless
55 Ancient Peruvian
56 Goblet feature
57 Buster's pooch
58 Smell
59 Without company
60 All done
61 Call at a bakery
62 Gift-label word

★★ Number-Out

Shade squares so that no number appears in any row or column more than once. Shaded squares may not touch each other horizontally or vertically, and all unshaded squares must form a single continuous area.

3	6	2	5	4	2
1	4	2	4	5	1
5	3	2	6	2	4
4	5	6	3	5	5
2	4	3	6	6	6
1	5	1	2	3	6

OPPOSITE ATTRACTION

Unscramble the letters in the phrase MILL BAGS to form two common words that are opposites of each other.

_____   _____

★★ Hyper-Sudoku

Fill in the blank boxes so that every row, column, 3x3 box, *and* each of the four
3x3 gray regions contains all of the numbers 1 to 9.

3	9							
7				8		9	3	5
		3	7					
5		4		1			2	
2	1				6			
	4		6				9	
1	3	7				4		
	2		5				8	

CENTURY MARKS

Inserting plus signs and minus signs, as many as necessary, in between the nine digits below,
create a series of additions and subtractions whose final answer is 100. Any digits without a
sign between them are to be grouped together as a single number.

| 1 2 2 5 2 6 4 2 5 | = | 100 |

★★ Article Three by Frances Burton

ACROSS

1 Fake
5 Wild guess
9 Passover feast
14 Venetian explorer
15 Roman formal wear
16 Brown shade
17 Help to do wrong
18 Copycat
19 Between ports
20 WWII feminist icon
23 Pomeranian pest
24 Perfect place
25 Patsy
28 Multi-acre homes
30 Truck compartment
33 Green-card holder
35 Grade-school org.
36 Erstwhile bird
37 Legendary seaman
41 Give the cold shoulder to
42 Mentalist Geller
43 Get down pat
44 "You betcha!"
45 At odds
48 Bishop's domain
49 Crafts' mate
50 "Ta-ta!"
52 Mr. Wilson's bane
59 Chew the scenery
60 Literary foot
61 Pie-cooling spot
62 Yellowstone beast
63 List shortener
64 Time periods
65 In thing
66 Actress Russo
67 Variety

DOWN

1 Practice punches
2 Mulligan stew maker
3 Pub pints
4 Repetitive pattern
5 Says
6 Attire for Astaire
7 Pulitzer author James
8 Hair clip
9 Fends (off)
10 Devoured
11 Sprinkle, as with flour
12 Olympics sword
13 Bring up
21 Actress Verdugo
22 Brainstorms
25 Smart-mouthed
26 Skirt style
27 Prepare to hem
29 Plant parasite
30 Fountain orders
31 Idolize
32 Carried along
34 Fade away
36 Fade away
38 Twosomes
39 More reliable
40 Fish-tank growth
45 Sidekick
46 Deliverer of yore
47 Light on one's feet
49 Playwright Chekhov
51 Beginning
52 What red ink signifies
53 Moslem ruler
54 Snoot
55 Something disliked
56 Light and lively
57 Burst of thunder
58 Additional

★ Lily List

Find these varieties of lilies that are hidden in the diagram, either across, down, or diagonally. Words hidden separately are indicated by slashes.

```
E D Y D I A M Y R I A D P R R D A T S X
A U R T E S N U S Y R E I F A E M W T E
L N G E U T W N Q S K S P S T S A I E E
L A G N A A O E U U A R E E S E R N P U
E J G O I M E N E C E C Z N G R Y K M Q
N E S A L R C B R T R E O N N T L L U L
O Z D A P R E A K E H I N A I F L E R I
R A S L E A M M T C T E F C L L I S T T
T L N S A E N L N C A D A I R O S T M T
I B T G N R O T E O H L V R E W C K J L
C W C T E V E F H G M E B F T E L T A E
J O O L E U R M Q U N E R A S R L I N E
E L Y L N E V A E H S A L M O Y Y N N V
W L E N P M I D N I G H T S T A R K A E
E E I K C A N D E L A B R A U H A E Y N
L Y N Z G T N E M T N A H C N E M R L L
S I V E L V E T G O W N A X U Q A B L T
P Y R A M D U O R P Y N I T S E D E O T
D I S C O V E R Y B A M D U O R P L P I
F L A M E R E D W T U A E B K C A L B L
```

AFRICAN / QUEEN
AGAPANTHUS
AMARYLLIS
BLACK BEAUTY
CANDELABRA
CITRONELLA
DAIRYMAID
DESERT FLOWER
DESTINY
DISCOVERY
DREAMCATCHER
EMERALD / ANGEL
ENCHANTMENT
FIERY SUNSET
FLAME RED
HEAVENLY / TRUMPETS
LEMON MERINGUE
LITTLE EVE
MIDNIGHT STAR
PINK PERFECTION
POLLYANNA
PROUD MARY
SACRAMENTO
SALMON / JEWELS
SECRET LOVE
STERLING STAR
SUNCREST
SWEETHEART
TINKERBELL
TWINKLES
VELVET GOWN
YELLOW BLAZE

INITIAL REACTION

Identify the well-known proverb from the first letters in each of its words.

T. E. B. C. T. W. _____

★★ Sets of Three

Group all the symbols into sets of three, with each set having either all the same shape and three different colors, or all the same color and three different shapes. The symbols in each set must all be connected to each other by a common horizontal or vertical side.

SAY IT AGAIN

What four-letter word can mean either "variety" or "considerate"?

— — — —

★★ Builders' Quartet by Janet R. Bender

ACROSS

1 Sleeve fillers
5 Uses 61 Across
9 Port of Jordan
14 Loud ringing
15 Lotion ingredient
16 *Network* director Sidney
17 Ancient South American
18 World's longest river
19 Conical tent
20 Steady courage
23 "Earth" word form
24 Fixed procedure
25 Make an entrance
28 Have a cold
29 Opposite of post-
30 Roofing material
31 Try to avoid bad luck
36 OPEC's biggest customer
37 Awkward person
38 Corn unit
39 Lyric poems
40 Addams family cousin
41 Dairy-case buy
45 Born: Fr.
46 Really long time
47 Cabinet dept. since 1965
48 Printing mistakes
50 Lasting impression
52 Opponent
55 Former *Dateline NBC* host
58 Long-legged wader
60 Thug
61 Chopping tools
62 Kukla's dragon friend
63 Veep after Quayle
64 Blood fluids
65 Mariners' milieu
66 List of events, casually
67 Waiter's burden

DOWN

1 Copying
2 Actress Zellweger
3 Prefix for economics
4 Eastern European
5 *Star Wars* hero
6 *Middlemarch* author
7 Novelist Tom or Thomas
8 Visualizes
9 Adjusted, as a suit
10 Peculiar
11 Full measure
12 Apiary denizen
13 Had a meal
21 Composer Satie
22 Polynesian tuber
26 Decorative containers
27 Clear the blackboard
28 Pretense
29 Staple of Chinese cookery
31 *Dave* star
32 Observant one
33 Shoe part
34 German refusal
35 Female WWII soldier
39 Venerable British ref. set
41 Foreshadow
42 Speckled steed
43 Like pens at a bank
44 Toss
49 Awesome hotel lobbies
50 Scare off
51 Household task
52 Repairperson
53 Puccini performance
54 Opinion piece
56 Omelet needs
57 Hang in there
58 Great Lakes' __ Canals
59 RN specialty

★★ One-Way Streets

The diagram represents a pattern of streets. P's are parking spaces, and the black squares are stores. Find the route that starts at a parking space, passes through all stores exactly once, and ends at the other parking space. Arrows indicate one-way traffic for that block only. No block or intersection may be entered more than once.

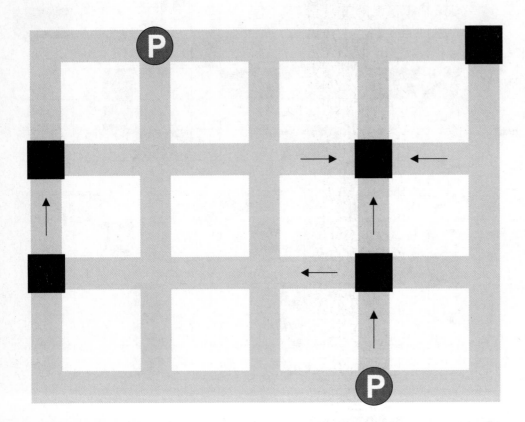

SOUND THINKING

The longest common uncapitalized word whose only consonant sounds are G (as in "go"), L, and R, in that order, is seven letters long. What is it?

_____

★★ 123

Fill in the diagram so that each rectangular piece has one each of the numbers 1, 2, and 3, under these rules: 1) No two adjacent squares, horizontally or vertically, can have the same number. 2) Each completed row and column of the diagram will have an equal number of 1s, 2s, and 3s.

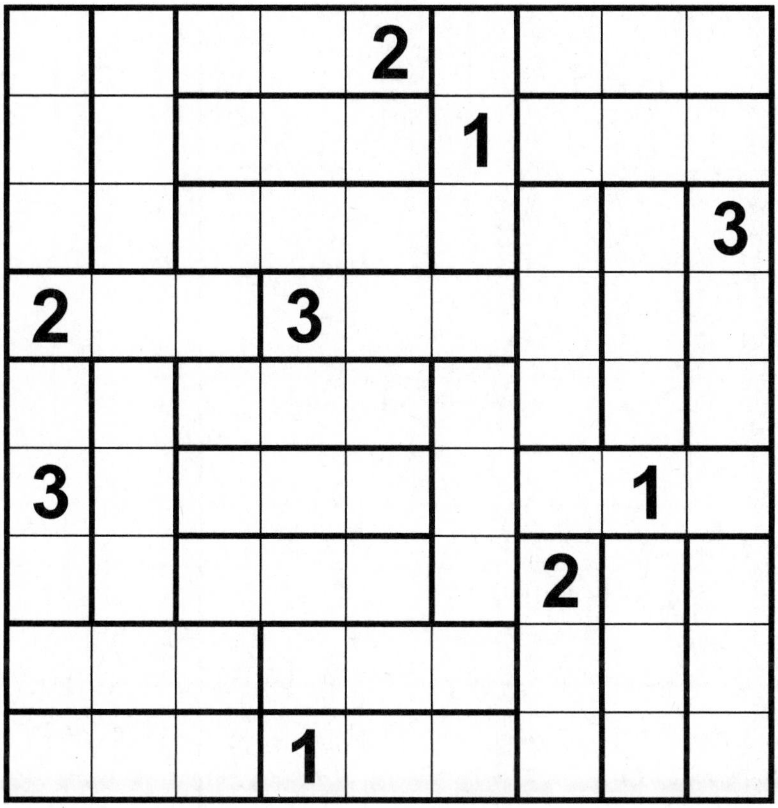

				2				
					1			
								3
2			3					
3							1	
						2		
			1					

SUDOKU SUM

Without repeating any digits, complete the sum at right, by filling one digit in each of the five blanks.

```
    _  8  1
 +  5  _  _
 _____
    _  2  _
```

★★★ Line Drawing

Draw three straight lines, each from one edge of the square to another edge, so that the words in each of the six regions have something in common.

SKI

CHOOSE

THESE

EWE

YEAS

EASE

THY

PLEA

WEIGHS

SIZE

SAYS

GAZED

LAPSE

WISE

ASH

GRASS

FEZ

PLANT

THREE OF A KIND

Find the three hidden words in the sentence that, read in order, go together in some way.

That piranha steak on a makeshift platter—it was terrible!

★★ How Clever by Shirley Soloway

ACROSS

1 Gives off
6 Urban vehicles
10 Assist in malfeasance
14 Yogi of baseball
15 One of the Four Corners states
16 Perry's creator
17 High-level personnel loss
19 Irritate
20 "Return to __" (Elvis tune)
21 Batman and Robin, e.g.
22 Not "fer"
23 Winged god
25 Abhors
27 Start of the day
30 Corrida cry
32 Half hitch or granny
33 Apartment in a complex
34 Fine cotton
36 Writer Jong
39 The Alps, for instance: Abbr.
40 Tweezers target
42 *Uno, __, tres*
43 Michelangelo sculpture
45 Tear apart
46 Till section
47 Playbill listing
49 "Far out, dude!"
50 Big __ (NCAA division)
51 Like some luggage
54 Greek letter
56 Director Reitman
57 Small taste
59 "... __ as a day in June"
63 End of Caesar's boast
64 It's invested by those in the know
66 Classes

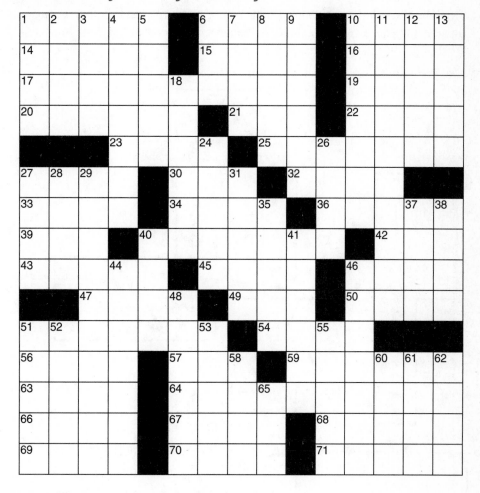

67 Sioux City's state
68 Slip-up
69 Legal tender
70 *Coal Miner's Daughter* subject
71 Chimney output

DOWN

1 Recedes
2 Nothing more than
3 Qom's country
4 Poseidon's spear
5 More rational
6 Mongrel
7 Not much
8 Skater Oksana
9 Patsy
10 Aquarium apparatus
11 Clever solution
12 *Dallas* matriarch
13 Most driver's-ed students
18 Tending to sag
24 More crafty
26 From the top
27 Trash destination
28 One who's against
29 Facetious remarks
31 Live bit of coal
35 Actress Lucie
37 Arguments against
38 Helper: Abbr.
40 "That's a snap!"
41 Least expected
44 Silver flaw
46 Pekoe place
48 It's down in the mouth
51 Municipal
52 Saint Theresa's home
53 Spock portrayer
55 Pyramids, essentially
58 One of 16 chess pieces
60 Part of AD
61 Smell bad
62 Brontë governess
65 Was a candidate

★★ Star Search

Find the stars that are hidden in some of the blank squares. The numbered squares indicate how many stars are hidden in the squares adjacent to them (including diagonally). There is never more than one star in any square.

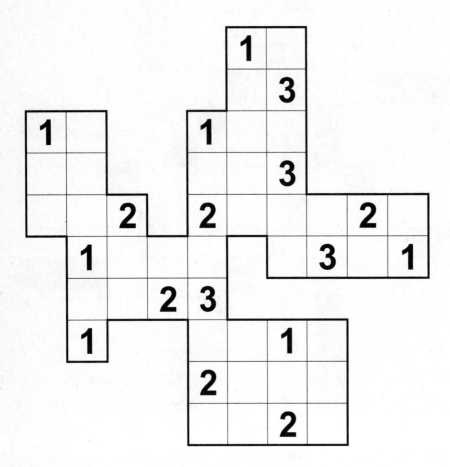

TELEPHONE TRIOS

Using the numbers and letters on a standard telephone, what three seven-letter words or phrases from the same category can be formed from these telephone numbers?

293-7663 _ _ _ _ _ _ _

783-5527 _ _ _ _ _ _ _

782-5463 _ _ _ _ _ _ _

★★ Sequence Maze

Enter the maze where indicated, pass through all the color squares exactly once, then exit, all without retracing your path. You must pass through the color squares in this sequence: red, blue, yellow, red, blue, etc.

THREE AT A RHYME

Rearrange these letters to form three one-syllable words that rhyme.

E I K K K L P R R R U

_____   _____   _____

★★ Women's Day by Randall J. Hartman

ACROSS

1 Othello, for one
5 Trunk fastener
9 __-3 fatty acids
14 Singer Guthrie
15 X and Y on a graph
16 Removes, as rind
17 Judge
18 Modeling material
19 Brief ringing sound
20 Meryl Streep Oscar film
23 Take legal action
24 Possesses
25 Denver hrs.
28 Loaf extremities
31 Title of respect
36 Charley horse
38 Old-time telephone feature
40 Hang around
41 Bay State resort
44 Gladiator's domain
45 Wife of Zeus
46 Plum look-alike
47 Alaska-purchase arranger
49 Delivery to a deejay
51 Mus. version
52 Cry from Homer Simpson
54 Mesozoic or Cenozoic
56 Ira Levin novel
63 Dinnertime for some
64 Former Big Apple stadium
65 Show favoritism
67 *Die Fledermaus* role
68 Furniture wood
69 Gymnast Korbut
70 Part of WWW
71 Life of Riley
72 Black: Fr.

DOWN

1 Alfred E. Neuman's magazine
2 Bauxite and galena
3 Bread spread
4 Wins going away
5 Mexican house
6 Hot-rod rod
7 Black and Bering
8 Univ. major
9 Black, to white
10 French Sudan, today
11 Idle of comedy
12 *Star Trek* creator Roddenberry
13 Pose a poser
21 Tint
22 Scene stealer
25 Tots' parents
26 Heart-pounding event
27 Lobbed
29 Cable alternative
30 Kept for a rainy day
32 "__ who?"
33 Song refrain
34 Blunder
35 Actress Winona
37 Sicilian volcano
39 Former capital of Italy?
42 Got tough
43 Junior, often
48 __ Perignon
50 Sphere
53 Rash action
55 First name in *Who's Who in the Bible*
56 Try again
57 Finished
58 Get purchased
59 Perlman of *Cheers*
60 Affirmative votes
61 Arizona necktie
62 Toon bear
63 Got the picture
66 Veteran mariner

★★ Hyper-Sudoku

Fill in the blank boxes so that every row, column, 3x3 box, *and* each of the four 3x3 gray regions contains all of the numbers 1 to 9.

	6							4
5		7			4			2
	4		3	8				1
				3				7
6			2	9				
	3	9	4					6
3		6						8
1		5				3		
						1		

MIXAGRAMS

Each line contains a five-letter word and a four-letter word that have been mixed together (the order of the letters in each word has not been changed). Unmix the two words on each line and write them in the spaces provided. When you're done, find a two-part answer to the clue by reading down the letter columns in the answers.

CLUE: Ad come-on

C H U R G A F E T = _ _ _ _ _ + _ _ _ _

S H E P A R I E R = _ _ _ _ _ + _ _ _ _

S U T U R F E R T = _ _ _ _ _ + _ _ _ _

A C C I T H E E D = _ _ _ _ _ + _ _ _ _

★★ ABC

Enter the letters A, B, and C into the diagram so that each row and column has exactly one A, one B, and one C. The letters outside the diagram indicate the first letter encountered, moving in the direction of the arrow. Keep in mind that after all the letters have been filled in, there will be two blank boxes in each row and column.

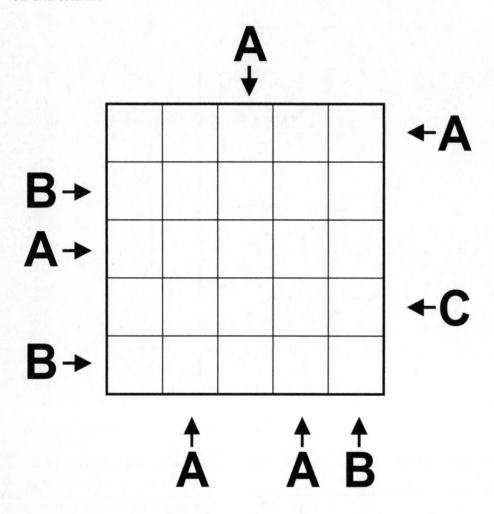

NATIONAL TREASURE

Find the three common uncapitalized six-letter words starting with A that can be formed from the letters in BARBADOS.

— — — — — —   — — — — — —   — — — — — —

★★ Toy Story by Shirley Soloway

ACROSS

1 Curved lines
5 Specifies
10 "It can't be!"
14 Comic actor Lahr
15 Tolkien hero
16 Australian birds
17 Completed
18 Very helpful one
20 Wife of Jason
22 From Rome: Abbr.
23 __-mo replay
24 Erupts in anger
28 Royal address
29 Overseas
33 Civil War side: Abbr.
36 Valuable possession
39 Soup pod
40 Don't patronize
44 Neighborhood
45 Place for a manicure
46 Immigrant's course: Abbr.
47 Talking bird
50 Coal dust
52 Extend cooperation to
58 French friend
61 Latin love
62 Actress Lotte
63 Dismissive exclamation
67 Egyptian biters
68 Facts
69 Former Red head
70 Sharp
71 Votes against
72 Moved sideways
73 RBI, for one

DOWN

1 Fission device
2 Make merry
3 Statement of belief
4 Scatters
5 Gridiron org.
6 *Exodus* hero
7 Starz fare
8 Goes over galleys
9 Piano piece
10 UK lexicon
11 Wellness grps.
12 Void's partner
13 Fjord locale
19 Drop of liquid
21 From Laos, say
25 Hedging words
26 Houses in trees
27 Ship's front
30 *Grapes of Wrath* figure
31 Word after fine or graphic
32 Writer Roald
33 British fellow
34 Mystery author Paretsky
35 State with confidence
37 Epoch
38 Midwest oil city
41 O.K. Corral lawman
42 Fan setting
43 Rounded hill
48 Nivea competitor
49 Mexican food
51 Makes adjustments to
53 Like a pair of oxen
54 Raise, with "up"
55 Map section
56 Assertive personality
57 Lacks
58 Rural resister's word
59 Poet Van Duyn
60 Questionable
64 Spanish article
65 Suit accessory
66 Conclusion

★★ Wheels and Cogs

When Bob needs a boost at the office, he has either coffee or tea. When he turns the handle as indicated, which will he get?

BETWEENER

What four-letter word belongs between the word at left and the word at right, so that the first and second word, and the second and third word, each form a common compound word?

BAG __ __ __ __ LINE

★★ Find the Ships

Determine the position of the 10 ships listed to the right of the diagram. The ships may be oriented either horizontally or vertically. A square with wavy lines indicates water and will not contain a ship. The numbers at the edge of the diagram indicate how many squares in that row or column contain parts of ships. When all 10 ships are correctly placed in the diagram, no two of them will touch each other, not even diagonally.

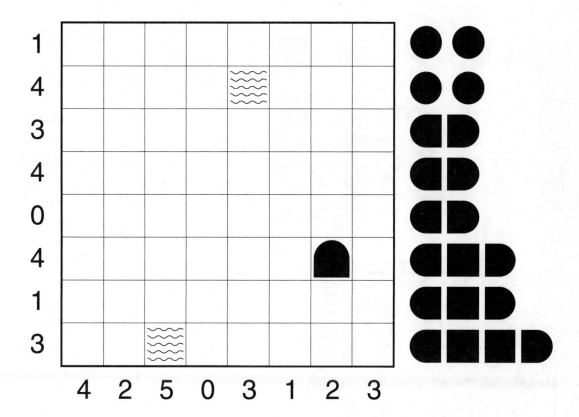

TWO-BY-FOUR

The eight letters in the word RUEFULLY can be rearranged to form a pair of common four-letter words in only one way. Can you find the two words?

— — — —   — — — —

★★ Triad Split Decisions

In this clueless crossword puzzle, each answer consists of two words whose spellings are the same, except for the consecutive letters given. All answers are common words; no phrases or hyphenated or capitalized words are used. Some of the clues may have more than one solution, but there is only one word pair that will correctly link up with all the other word pairs.

TRANSDELETION

Delete one letter from the word TENACIOUS and rearrange the rest, to get another word spelled with three consecutive vowels.

_____

★★ Three in a Row by Fred Piscop

ACROSS

1 Hand over
5 Soda jerk's concoctions
10 Stage accessory
14 Rink leap
15 On one's toes
16 Volcanic outflow
17 Carpet feature
18 Kuwaiti money
19 Diner appliance
20 Loiterer at a ballpark
23 Little one
24 Ram's ma'am
25 Mushy food
28 Bench wood
31 Pull into, as a station
36 Is in the hole
38 Flat-topped formation
40 Clean off
41 Boor's words, perhaps
44 Buy and sell
45 Nintendo rival
46 Singer Sedaka
47 Motion detector, e.g.
49 Scrapped, at NASA
51 Modern evidence
52 Museum-funding org.
54 Edge of a cup
56 Doing as told
63 Old-time poet
64 Giggling sound
65 Split up
67 Surface figure
68 Hostile force
69 Kuwaiti leader
70 Molecule part
71 __ Macabre (Saint-Saëns work)
72 Declare untrue

DOWN

1 Salary max
2 Off-ramp
3 Supermarket section
4 Vote in
5 Traveled quickly
6 Settled down
7 One of your contacts
8 Try to locate
9 Soda-shop supply
10 Stone-in-the-water sound
11 Four-star review
12 "Back to you"
13 Zero-star review

21 Keystone comic
22 __ Eat Cake (Gershwin musical)
25 Annie of Designing Women
26 In the know
27 Praline nut
29 Monster's loch
30 Ruhr Valley city
32 Algerian port
33 Trimmed down
34 Beckon to enter
35 Inventor Nikola
37 Norms: Abbr.
39 Jason's craft
42 Téa of Deep Impact

43 Keen vision
48 Like many tuxedos
50 Salad topper
53 '60s NASA rocket stage
55 Spoke, with "up"
56 Pucker-inducing
57 Black-and-white snack
58 Cheese in a ball
59 After that
60 Skirt lines
61 Reputation
62 Green land
63 Lea call
66 Take a shot

★★ 123

Fill in the diagram so that each rectangular piece has one each of the numbers 1, 2, and 3, under these rules: 1) No two adjacent squares, horizontally or vertically, can have the same number. 2) Each completed row and column of the diagram will have an equal number of 1s, 2s, and 3s.

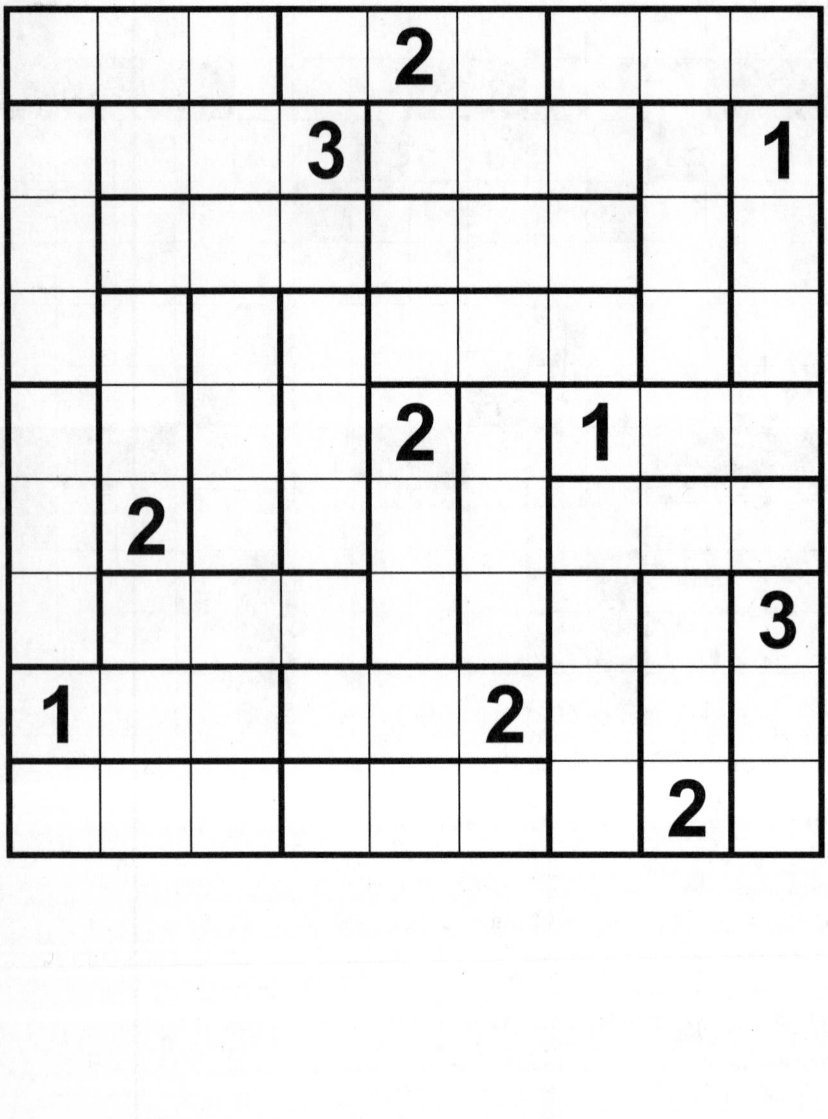

				2				
			3					**1**
				2		**1**		
	2							
								3
1					**2**			
							2	

SUDOKU SUM

Without repeating any digits, complete the sum at right, by filling one digit in each of the five blanks.

$$
\begin{array}{r}
1\ \_\ 8 \\
+\ \_\ 0\ \_ \\
\hline
\_\ 4\ \_
\end{array}
$$

★★ Fences

Connect the dots with vertical or horizontal lines, so that a single loop is formed with no crossings or branches. Each number indicates how many lines surround it; squares with no number may be surrounded by any number of lines.

```
2 1 1       3     3

          2
      2       3 0
  3 0
                3 0
  0 2       1
      3
  3   2     3 3 2
```

ADDITION SWITCH

Switch the positions of two of the digits in the incorrect sum at right, to get a correct sum.

$$\begin{array}{r} 6\ 5\ 3 \\ +\ 2\ 8\ 9 \\ \hline 4\ 3\ 7 \end{array}$$

★★ Face It by Norma Steinberg

ACROSS

1 Variety of cherry
5 Talks big
10 Behold: Latin
14 Abel's father
15 Cowboy competition
16 Three feet
17 Snoop
19 Buffalo's lake
20 Vernacular
21 Word before market or circus
22 Pizzeria appliance
23 "Yeah, sure!"
25 Identification documents
27 Fruity dessert
31 Got up
32 Really liked
33 From Kobe
37 Flintstone pet
38 Send via phone lines
39 Nuptial vows
40 Road-clearing vehicle
43 End a phone call
45 Afrikaner
46 For the most part
47 Singer Brewer
50 Rear part
51 Locale
52 Chunk of ice
54 More unusual
59 Is unable to
60 Insincere agreement
62 Acknowledging expression
63 Lloyd Webber musical
64 Bruce or his daughter Laura
65 Numerical ending
66 Pavarotti, e.g.
67 Poker variety

DOWN

1 Prohibits
2 Role model
3 Astronaut's employer
4 FBI agents
5 Reaction at 40 below
6 Construction-crew member
7 Grownup
8 Actor Hackman
9 Cola, for example
10 Surprisingly informative
11 Officiate at Thanksgiving
12 Colonial news announcer
13 Paradises
18 Light on one's feet
24 Home for roses
26 Alias letters
27 Scoundrels
28 Valhalla bigwig
29 Cher ex
30 Intimidated
31 Floor shine
33 Mandible locale
34 Border
35 Music genre
36 Spot
38 In favor of
41 Opp. of neg.
42 Brochure
43 Solo in *Star Wars*
44 Enthusiasm
46 Isn't honest with
47 Unspoken but understood
48 Expunge
49 Actress Zellweger
50 Invitation to a hitchhiker
53 Exist
55 Netflix inventory
56 Watch carb intake
57 Shade of beige
58 Tear asunder
61 Pitcher part

★★★ Retriever Maze

Enter the maze where indicated, pass through all the stars exactly once, then exit. You may not retrace your path.

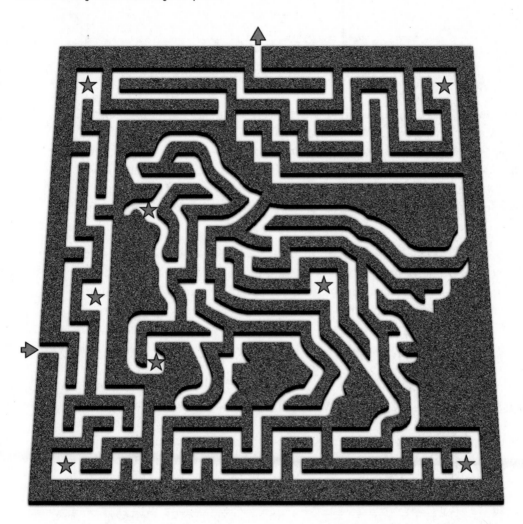

SAY IT AGAIN

What four-letter word can be either a type of flower or a verb meaning "increased"?

— — — —

HOUSEHOLD USES FOR ~~DUCK~~ DUCT TAPE

Duct tape really did start as duck tape. During WW II, the U.S. military turned to Johnson & Johnson for a flexible, durable, waterproof tape. Starting with its own medical tape, J & J developed a tape—army green in color and easy to rip into strips—that was used for everything from sealing ammunition cases to repairing jeep windshields. GI's nicknamed it duck tape because it was waterproof, like a duck's back. After the war, the first use of the now-silver tape was in joining heating and air conditioning ductwork, and so it became known as duct tape.

Reinforce book binding
Duct tape is perfect for repairing a broken book binding. Using a nice-colored tape, run the tape down the length of the spine; cut shorter pieces to run perpendicular to that if you need extra reinforcement.

Make a bandage in a pinch
You've gotten a bad scrape. Here's how to protect it until you get a proper bandage. Fold tissue paper or paper towel to cover the wound and cover this with duct tape. It may not be attractive, but it works in a jam.

Catch pesky flies
You've just checked into a rustic cabin on the lake and you're ready to start your vacation. Everything would be perfect if only the flying insects were not part of the deal. Grab your roll of duct tape, roll off a few foot-long strips, and hang them from the rafters as flypaper. Soon you'll be rid of the bugs and you can roll up the tape to toss it in the trash.

Bumper sticker
Got something you want to say? Cut a length of duct tape and affix it to your bumper. Then use permanent markers or paint markers, in black and/or colors, to pen your message.

Replace a shower curtain grommet
How many times have you yanked the shower curtain aside only to rip through one of the delicate eyelets? Grab the duct tape to make a simple repair. Once the curtain is dry, cut a rectangular piece and fold it from front to back over the torn hole. Slit the tape with a mat knife, razor blade, or scissors, and push the shower curtain ring back in place.

Temporarily hem your pants
You've found a great pair of jeans, but the length isn't right. You expect a little shrinkage anyway, so why bother with hemming right away? Fake the hem with duct tape. The new hem will last through a few washes, too.

★ Lots of Locks

Find these words that all contain the consecutive letters L-O-C-K, that are hidden in the diagram, either across, down, or diagonally. There's one additional 12-letter answer in the category, not listed below, that's also hidden in the diagram. What's that word?

```
B W K B O L D I R G K P U K C O L W K K
E L F C Y U K C O L E C R H A F A C C R
C F O F O G X L V O S N O A I R L O C K
O E R C E L D G L C I Q N L L L L T L Y
L T E P K I W O O K W C E O R B L E Q Q
B L L U L B C O C K K B C C N E I O A B
N O O O K K U O R E C K U U E P T J V D
U C C N E M L S Y E O L S L S K K N E K
S K K T W F W K T P L O O N L C C A I C
S U N L O C K E D E C C E U O O D O J O
L O C K S M I T H R R K H L I L C J L L
W T D M D F X L R U C J T H O B S K N Y
K K L K P O L T R O X A A C F D Q S J H
U C X C A O Z O L J M W K Z F A H C H S
E T O O P B L G C B O C D K C O L D E W
K C O L T N I L F K O I N T E R L O C A
C I L M D L D D O L I E G A K C O L B Z
O V S E N I M G L C H N P A D L O C K P
L Z E H I V R I I M K G G A K C O L B P
X C O L M E H G L O C K E N S P I E Y S
```

AIRLOCK
BLOCKAGE
BLOCKBUSTER
BULLOCK
CLOCKWISE
DEADLOCK
FETLOCK
FLINTLOCK
FLOCKING
FORELOCK
GOLDILOCKS
GRIDLOCK
HEMLOCK
HILLOCK
INTERLOCK
LOCKET
LOCKJAW
LOCK-KEEPER
LOCKSMITH
LOCKUP
MATLOCK
PADLOCK
POLLOCK
ROADBLOCK
ROWLOCK
SHYLOCK
SUNBLOCK
UNLOCKED
WARLOCK
WEDLOCK

WHO'S WHAT WHERE?

The correct term for a resident of Kosovo is:

A) Kosovite   B) Kosovar

C) Kosovino   D) Kosovian

★★ Hyper-Sudoku

Fill in the blank boxes so that every row, column, 3x3 box, *and* each of the four 3x3 gray regions contains all of the numbers 1 to 9.

			8	9				
			5					
1		9		7		5		
		2	1		8			
4		6				8		2
		7		4			6	
		1	6					9
	8				9			6
	9					2	7	

MIXAGRAMS

Each line contains a five-letter word and a four-letter word that have been mixed together (the order of the letters in each word has not been changed). Unmix the two words on each line and write them in the spaces provided. When you're done, find a two-part answer to the clue by reading down the letter columns in the answers.

CLUE: Vegas neighbor

D U A L M I K P E = _ _ _ _ _ + _ _ _ _

E G A L R E N L Y = _ _ _ _ _ + _ _ _ _

O K A L A Y A S S = _ _ _ _ _ + _ _ _ _

R U P E D E N A L = _ _ _ _ _ + _ _ _ _

★★★ Exit Lines by Robert H. Wolfe

ACROSS

1 Any of 16 Benedicts
5 Big stirs
9 Light wood
14 Russian river
15 Airport shuttles
16 Peppard's TV group
17 9-to-12er
19 Satisfy, as a thirst
20 Nonwinners
21 First word of "Cheek to Cheek"
22 Tennis gear
23 Out of date
24 Kids' game
27 Coastal city, often
30 Objective
33 Healing plants
35 Thin fog
36 Bullets, e.g.
37 Parlor seat
38 Dyes
39 Sheepish comments
40 One grand
41 Kin of contra-
42 Woolen fabric
43 Jug handle
44 Have as a target
46 Primary
47 Role player
49 AT&T part
51 Five iron
53 Matter zilch
58 Lagoon former
59 Have as a work holiday
60 Birch craft
61 Midmonth time
62 Regarding
63 Outer boundaries
64 Attention getter
65 Make a pitch

DOWN

1 Insect stage
2 Kind of tradition
3 Links scores
4 First name of *Lestat*'s composer
5 Fly
6 "__ the torpedoes!"
7 Small bills
8 Former geopolitical letters
9 Least moral
10 Big book
11 Cause damage, perhaps
12 Japanese drink
13 Last word
18 Braided hair
21 Male deers
23 Attention-getting note
24 Have a sample of
25 "Hi, Ho!"
26 Sell very cheaply
28 Key of Mendelssohn's Symphony #3
29 Type of bean
31 Mental representation
32 Walk slowly
34 __ de Cologne
36 *Simpsons* grandpa
38 Western lake
42 Pool member
44 Steps over fences
45 Bear witness
48 *Smallville* girl
50 Lite
51 Kitchen spice
52 Not much
53 Rogues
54 Small strings
55 Should that be the case
56 Barracks furnishings
57 Son of Seth
59 Dinner charge-slip line

★★ One-Way Streets

The diagram represents a pattern of streets. P's are parking spaces, and the black squares are stores. Find the route that starts at a parking space, passes through all stores exactly once, and ends at the other parking space. Arrows indicate one-way traffic for that block only. No block or intersection may be entered more than once.

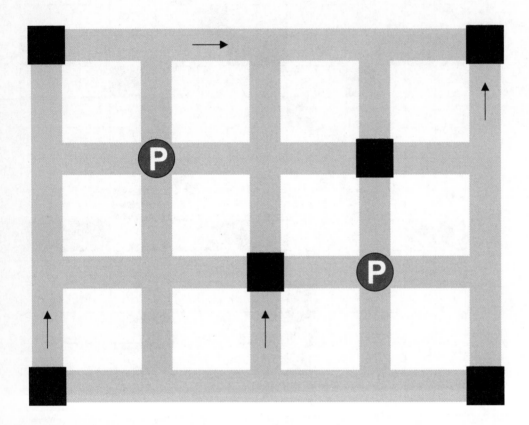

SOUND THINKING

The consonant sounds in the word HARK are H, R, and K. What common uncapitalized three-syllable word is pronounced with the same consonant sounds in the same order?

_____

★★ Star Search

Find the stars that are hidden in some of the blank squares. The numbered squares indicate how many stars are hidden in the squares adjacent to them (including diagonally). There is never more than one star in any square.

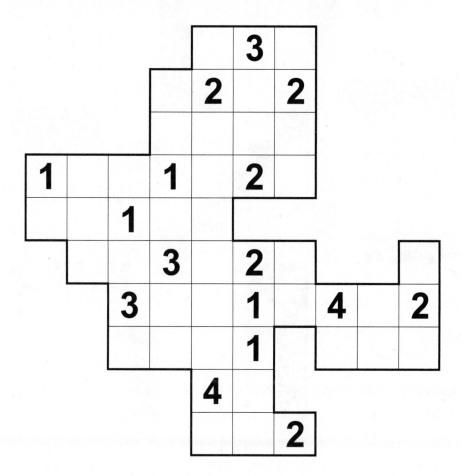

TELEPHONE TRIOS

Using the numbers and letters on a standard telephone, what three seven-letter words or phrases from the same category can be formed from these telephone numbers?

363-6773   _ _ _ _ _ _ _

776-6767   _ _ _ _ _ _ _

787-7678   _ _ _ _ _ _ _

★★★ Best Regards by Daniel R. Stark

ACROSS

1 Nincompoop
5 Band at a wedding
9 Withdraws, with "out"
13 Diva's rendition
14 Hollywood favorite
15 More than mean
17 Bottom edges
18 Furnace duct
19 Shinbone
20 "Get with it!"
22 Places for pies
23 Nota __
24 Peels, as potatoes
25 Quite white
29 Ploy
32 Sandpaper grade
34 Pulp Fiction name
35 Olympic event
39 Canvas users
41 Trouser lengths
43 Lake fish
44 Shoe width
46 Phonograph needle
47 Game-show question
50 Malcolm in the Middle brother
51 Swimming stroke
54 Hubby of Lucy
56 Surfer wannabe
57 Opinion
62 Rare violin
63 Well-qualified
64 Lasting mark
65 Change for a shilling
66 Malamute's load
67 Darth's daughter
68 Sounds of appreciation
69 Brontë heroine
70 Paris hub

DOWN

1 Willy Wonka creator
2 Black-and-white snack
3 Prom rental
4 Chore
5 Biathlon weapon
6 Wasting time
7 __ riche
8 Winner's feeling
9 Ink producers
10 Spade, for one
11 Spud, for one
12 River of Paris
16 Scottish miss
21 Lowest depth
25 Strikebreaker
26 Ibsen character
27 Dobbin's dinner
28 Arm accessory
30 Start of this century
31 Makes taboo
33 Greek letters
36 Ashen
37 Flightless birds
38 Latin 101 verb
40 European airline
42 Commercial district
45 Aloud
48 Radio-station format
49 Kitchen gadget
51 Bloke
52 Bard's teen
53 Fictional bell town
55 Nobel, for one
57 Florist's need
58 Harald V's capital
59 Cake decorator
60 Hit precisely
61 Meal holder

★★★ Go With the Flow

Enter the maze where indicated, pass through all the yellow circles exactly once, then exit. You must go with the flow, making no sharp turns, and you may use paths more than once.

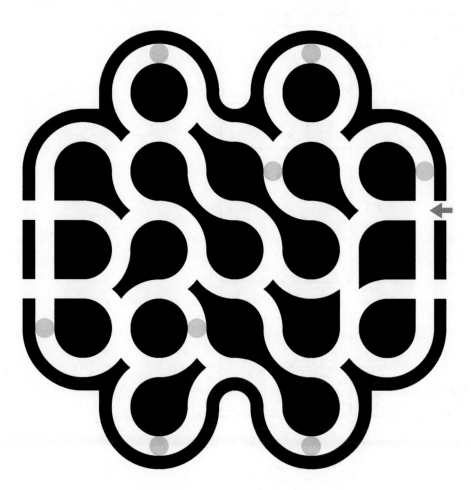

THREE AT A RHYME

Rearrange these letters to form three one-syllable words that rhyme.

A E E E E K K K P T

_____ _____ _____

★★ Sudoku

Fill in the blank boxes so that every row, column, and 3x3 box contains all of the numbers 1 to 9.

4		1		6		7	
	1	8			3		
2					5		
2						9	7
		7		2			
1	8						2
9					1		
	4			3	8		
6		2		9		3	

CENTURY MARKS

Inserting plus signs and minus signs, as many as necessary, in between the nine digits below, create a series of additions and subtractions whose final answer is 100. Any digits without a sign between them are to be grouped together as a single number.

2   3   4   7   7   1   0   3   3   =   100

★★★ Hugs & Kisses by Shirley Soloway

ACROSS

1 Stinging insect
5 Desi Arnaz's birthplace
9 Hall monitor's request
13 Blunt blade
14 Unwritten test
15 In any way
17 Mattress support
19 Renée, in *Chicago*
20 Banderas film of 2001
21 Apple-pie order
23 Pro vote
24 Went through, as an article
25 For each
26 Raucousness
29 Newcastle's river
31 "Wow!"
33 *Jaws* island
35 Hugely annoying
39 Judd Hirsch sitcom
40 Many racetracks
41 One who's against
42 Clear in court
44 Spread, as finger paint
45 TV promo word
46 Perry's creator
48 Any ship
49 In shape
51 Sounds of surprise
53 Court fig.
55 Electrical accessory
57 Straddling
61 Italian island
62 Hunters' helpers
64 Teen series set in California
65 Model Macpherson
66 Layer of paint
67 Greek mountain
68 Some verses
69 Irish singer

DOWN

1 Fly traps
2 Each
3 Alluring
4 A bit of a bother
5 *Marat/Sade* character
6 *QB VII* author
7 Keep out
8 Aquarium growth
9 Self-contradictory statement
10 Place for positrons
11 Some reeds
12 Playground feature
16 Not-nice look
18 Religious devotion
22 Former African capital
24 Money-back offers
26 E-mail info
27 Cinerama descendant
28 Watergate hearings evidence
30 Sort of star
32 River Kwai locale
34 Fork part
36 Padre or Astro
37 Six-sided state
38 Kingly address
40 Word form for "straight"
43 Unusual things
44 Donnybrook
47 Mascara target
49 Sure thing
50 Neighbor of 37 Down
52 Monteverdi opera
54 Cessation of hostilities
56 They're paid to play
57 Wheel connector
58 A part of
59 6/6/44
60 Part of "to be" in Spain
63 Like the Curiosity Shop

★★ Split Decisions

In this clueless crossword puzzle, each answer consists of two words whose spellings are the same, except for the consecutive letters given. All answers are common words; no phrases or hyphenated or capitalized words are used. Some of the clues may have more than one solution, but there is only one word pair that will correctly link up with all the other word pairs.

TRANSDELETION

Delete one letter from the word DUNGAREE and rearrange the rest, to get a word that means "angry."

_____

★★ Number-Out

Shade squares so that no number appears in any row or column more than once. Shaded squares may not touch each other horizontally or vertically, and all unshaded squares must form a single continuous area.

1	1	2	6	4	3
4	1	5	3	3	3
3	1	6	5	4	2
4	4	4	1	2	6
5	2	1	6	6	4
2	3	3	4	1	1

OPPOSITE ATTRACTION

Unscramble the letters in the phrase BIND GENE to form two common words that are opposites of each other.

_____ _____

★★★ All at Sea by Alison Donald

ACROSS

1 Computer lists
6 Actor Omar
10 Curves made by fly balls
14 Water sterilizer
15 Darjeeling et al.
16 Strong wind
17 Wool product
20 Arabian Nights name
21 Hone
22 Salaried group
23 Foil alternative
25 Heedless
27 Boy's outfit
31 S&L client
35 Battery terminals
36 __ tetra (aquarium fish)
38 Wash. neighbor
39 ABA members
40 Ave. crossers
41 Glowing coal
43 "Be prepared" org.
44 Cosmonaut Gagarin
46 Long looks
47 Part of CBS
49 Dolphin kin
51 Flag down
53 Roman orator
54 Flawless
57 Italian wine region
59 Gloomy guy
62 Memorable kids' TV host
66 Rock guitarist Clapton
67 Related
68 Metal bar
69 Computer expert
70 Designate
71 Refusals from 44 Across

DOWN

1 Soft shoe, briefly
2 Book before Nehemiah
3 Christmas carol
4 Cumbersome
5 Voter on treaties: Abbr.
6 Draws with acid
7 Lap dog, for short
8 Crullers and cream puffs
9 Wind dir.
10 Hercule's creator
11 Pro __
12 Sheet-music marking
13 Lowly worker
18 Water pitchers
19 Snaky shape
24 Verses
26 From __ Z
27 Cars from Sweden
28 All keyed up
29 Little bits
30 Up to
32 Hooded snake
33 Fishing basket
34 Of few words
37 Cereal box abbr.
40 Indian Ocean nation
42 Reddish-brown
45 Reuters rival
46 Splotch
48 Colonial roofing material
50 Gas rating
52 __ mode
54 Rapper/actor
55 Be bold
56 Heroic tale
58 Read quickly
60 Prod
61 Chimney buildup
63 Writer Fleming
64 Tonic partner
65 Tie breakers: Abbr.

★★ ABC

Enter the letters A, B, and C into the diagram so that each row and column has exactly one A, one B, and one C. The letters outside the diagram indicate the first letter encountered, moving in the direction of the arrow. Keep in mind that after all the letters have been filled in, there will be two blank boxes in each row and column.

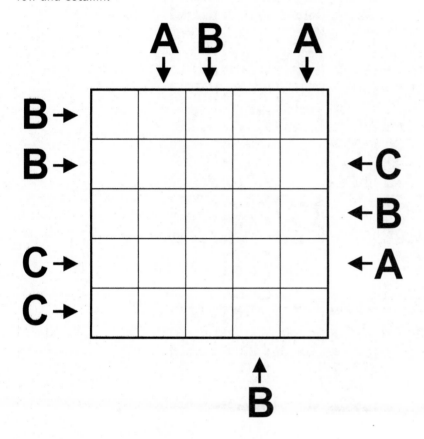

CLUELESS CROSSWORD

Complete the crossword with common uncapitalized seven-letter words, based entirely on the letters already filled in for you

★★ Piece It Together

Fill in the blue design using pieces with the same shape outlined in black.

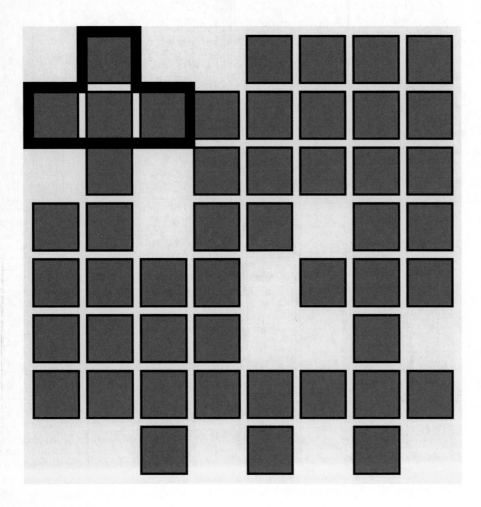

BETWEENER

What five-letter word belongs between the word at left and the word at right, so that the first and second word, and the second and third word, each form a common compound word?

FIRE _ _ _ _ _ READ

★★★ Line Drawing

Draw four straight lines, each from one edge of the square to another edge, so that each circle is tangent to at least two lines. That is, the lines touch—but do not enter—the circles. One line is shown to get you started.

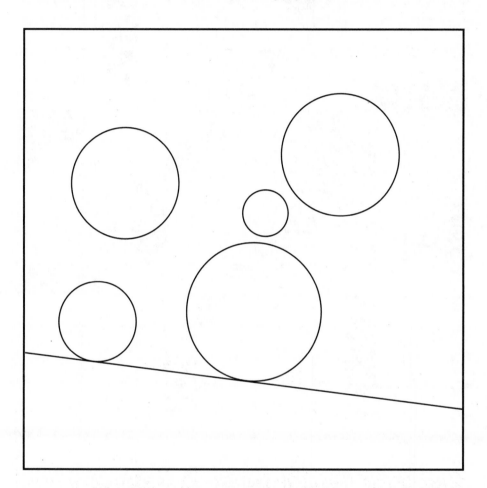

THREE OF A KIND

Find the three hidden words in the sentence that, read in order, go together in some way.

Serve the stew or dessert with eighty–proof vermouth.

★★★ One-Octave Spread by Fred Piscop

ACROSS

1 Mediterranean nation
6 Cobbler flavor
11 Part of an airport lineup
14 Trojan War epic
15 *Gigi* star
16 Ex of Frank and Mickey
17 Data or music holder
19 Quick punch
20 Russian plain
21 Just okay
22 Play for a 30 Across
23 List-ending abbr.
25 Household pests
27 Religious offshoot
30 Gullible one
32 Appear to be
33 "Yuck!"
34 Drops the ball
36 Defeat handily
38 Mouth part
40 Patton portrayer
42 Capital on a fjord
44 Fraudulent scheme
46 Circle dance
47 John, in Scotland
48 Roman poet
50 Cold-storage candidate
51 Very top
52 Holds fast
55 Eliot Ness, for one
57 Old hand
58 Surface figure
60 Inquiring types
64 __ soda (sodium carbonate)
65 Tuneup pro
67 Prefix with log
68 Onions partner
69 Susan Lucci role
70 "Just a __!"
71 Tennis pro Dementieva

72 2000 presidential candidate

DOWN

1 Boom-box plug-ins
2 Oodles
3 Margarita garnish
4 Valve-moving part
5 Show flexibility
6 Take steps
7 Places for notes
8 Monastic head
9 Red-ink figures
10 Not easily read
11 Zydeco, e.g.

12 Salt's "Halt!"
13 Innocent ones
18 Puts an end to
24 Tree of the pine family
26 Prefix for nautical
27 Big __, CA
28 Swelled heads
29 Certain candy fiend
31 Rye-bottle word
35 Cocky walk
37 Campy explosive sound
39 Top pick, slangily
41 Runway surface

43 Singleton
45 Extraordinary event
49 Go off the track
51 Turkey's capital
52 Basilica spots
53 Hang loosely
54 Start a volley
56 Pale with fright
59 "Right on!"
61 Author Bagnold
62 Red-beans partner
63 *The Lion King* villain
66 Notable time

★★ Find the Ships

Determine the position of the 10 ships listed to the right of the diagram. The ships may be oriented either horizontally or vertically. A square with wavy lines indicates water and will not contain a ship. The numbers at the edge of the diagram indicate how many squares in that row or column contain parts of ships. When all 10 ships are correctly placed in the diagram, no two of them will touch each other, not even diagonally.

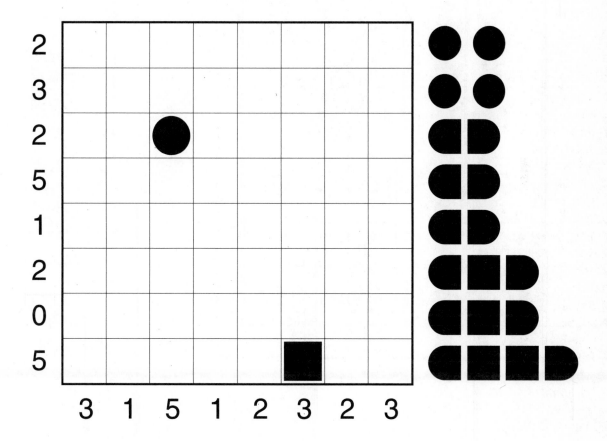

TWO-BY-FOUR

The eight letters in the word TUMBLING can be rearranged to form a pair of common four-letter words in only one way. Can you find the two words?

___ ___ ___ ___   ___ ___ ___ ___

★★★ Hyper-Sudoku

Fill in the blank boxes so that every row, column, 3x3 box, *and* each of the four
3x3 gray regions contains all of the numbers 1 to 9.

		9	7			6	
			3	2	7	5	1
	3		5				9
		6	8		1		
3							
				7			
8	2			5			7
	9			1			5
				9			

MIXAGRAMS

Each line contains a five-letter word and a four-letter word that have been mixed together (the order of the letters in each word has not been changed). Unmix the two words on each line and write them in the spaces provided. When you're done, find a two-part answer to the clue by reading down the letter columns in the answers.

CLUE: African capital

F A S T C O P E T = _ _ _ _ _ + _ _ _ _

A B O M D A S S Y = _ _ _ _ _ + _ _ _ _

P A T W I P E R N = _ _ _ _ _ + _ _ _ _

S T O N E C E R N = _ _ _ _ _ + _ _ _ _

★★★ Pinnacles by Robert H. Wolfe

ACROSS

1 Tibetan priests
6 Singer Reese
11 Use diligently
14 Arkansas' __ Mountains
15 French spa
16 Zsa Zsa's sister
17 High-level meetings
19 Broadcast
20 Comic writer Bombeck
21 Approached rapidly
22 Protective covering
23 Lets in again
25 Engineering school, for short
27 Narrow shoe width
28 Film-script direction
31 Write quickly
34 Kevin of *De-Lovely*
37 Become accustomed (to)
38 Higher than
40 Lab runner
41 Flowerless plants
42 Is gloomy
43 Old counting devices
45 Defunct flier
46 Also
48 *Leave __ to Heaven*
50 Son of Seth
51 Started gradually
56 Curved paths
58 Make an assertion
60 Voice quality
61 Scratch up
62 King-to-be
64 The night before
65 Like the Capitol
66 Hardly humble
67 Gross less expenses
68 Water vessels
69 Christmas song word

DOWN

1 Also-ran
2 Blue shade
3 "__ mia!"
4 Fleet of warships
5 Go downhill for fun
6 Coup __
7 Dale or Maurice
8 Jaunty rhythm, in music
9 Sioux Indian
10 Part of Q and A
11 Busiest times
12 57, in old Rome
13 Tall tale
18 Experiment
22 Panorama
24 Gets by
26 Enlightens
28 Soft cheese
29 Large vases
30 Experiment
31 Door part
32 Woodwind
33 For certain eyes only
35 Roth and SEP
36 Catch
39 Places for ore
44 Title holder
47 Real-estate account
49 Hit the hay
51 Cat, often
52 Deer females
53 Gift giver
54 Bring upon oneself
55 Impoverished
56 Last word
57 Great notice
59 Capital of Togo
62 Alphabetic trio
63 Turntable abbr.

★★★ Fences

Connect the dots with vertical or horizontal lines, so that a single loop is formed with no crossings or branches. Each number indicates how many lines surround it; squares with no number may be surrounded by any number of lines.

```
3 3 3           3

2       1       1

    3   2

                0 3

3 0

    3   2

1       0       2

3           3 2 3
```

ADDITION SWITCH

Switch the positions of two of the digits in the incorrect sum at right, to get a correct sum.

```
  4 8 7
+ 4 0 3
-------
  7 9 1
```

★★★ Dotty

Draw a line from square to square, moving either horizontally or vertically, so that all squares have been visited once. You may pass from one square to another only if it contains a dot of the same color and size. Note that many squares have small dots on top of large dots.

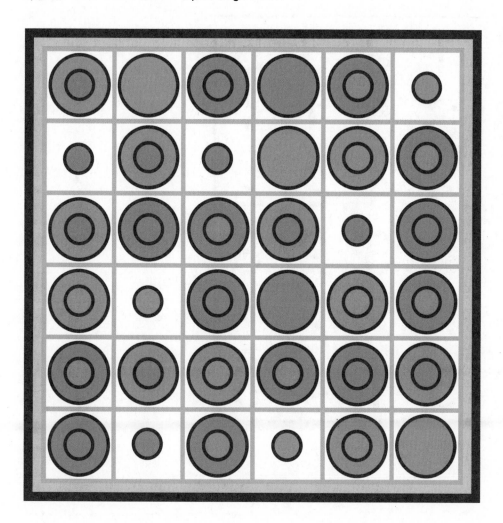

SAY IT AGAIN

What four-letter verb can mean either "drill" or "weary"?

— — — —

★★ Number-Out

Shade squares so that no number appears in any row or column more than once. Shaded squares may not touch each other horizontally or vertically, and all unshaded squares must form a single continuous area.

6	4	1	3	3	5
3	3	3	5	1	1
5	6	3	4	2	2
5	1	4	3	2	3
4	5	2	2	2	1
2	2	5	1	4	6

OPPOSITE ATTRACTION

Unscramble the letters in the phrase MEDAL WIT to form two common words that are opposites of each other.

_____   _____

★★★ Looking for Help by Fred Piscop

ACROSS

1 Zodiacal border
5 Puts up, as tomatoes
9 Bargains
14 Home to most
15 Resting on
16 Amassed, as a tab
17 Chocolate units
18 Turkish currency
19 Fight venue
20 Ruth nickname
23 Smoothing devices
26 *Krazy* __
27 Slangy suffix
28 Head honcho
31 *Speed* star
36 Give for a time
38 Beer topper
40 Zoo heavyweight
41 *Mary Poppins* helper
44 *Otello*, for one
45 Hemingway nickname
46 Stadium topper
47 Tiled art
49 Cub Scout units
51 __ Moines, IA
52 *Seinfeld* uncle
54 Volcanic rock
56 Bloodhound's asset
62 Tire feature
63 Stable babe
64 Left speechless
68 __ acid (protein component)
69 Cut and paste
70 Brilliant star
71 Ancient Greek physician
72 Ewes' guys
73 Provoke

DOWN

1 Pickup part
2 Yank's home
3 Mick Jagger title
4 So last year
5 Cancels
6 Working away
7 *A Doll's House* character
8 Punish, in a way
9 Constitution creators
10 Corn units
11 From square one
12 Moon goddess
13 Set-to
21 City area, informally
22 Sculler's tool
23 "__ Prison Blues" (Johnny Cash song)
24 Syrian city
25 Lake rentals
29 Lunch course
30 Lunch course
32 Olmert of Israel
33 Abe of *Fish*
34 Tooth cover
35 Most achy
37 "Explorer" of kids' TV
39 Wear a long puss
42 Fastened, in a way
43 Service-station supply
48 Corp. VIP
50 "My Gal __"
53 Job seeker's success
55 Like "dis"
56 Men-only
57 Witty writer Bombeck
58 Singer Diamond
59 Well-thought-out
60 Bubbly drink
61 Hurt badly
65 Try to win
66 Stowe heroine
67 "Dear old" one

★★★ 123

Fill in the diagram so that each rectangular piece has one each of the numbers 1, 2, and 3, under these rules: 1) No two adjacent squares, horizontally or vertically, can have the same number. 2) Each completed row and column of the diagram will have an equal number of 1s, 2s, and 3s.

					3			
1								
				1				
		3			1			
1								
						2		
		1						
2								1

SUDOKU SUM

Without repeating any digits, complete the sum at right, by filling one digit in each of the five blanks.

```
    _  _  5
 +  1  8  _
    _  9  _
```

★★★ Find the Ships

Determine the position of the 10 ships listed to the right of the diagram. The ships may be oriented either horizontally or vertically. A square with wavy lines indicates water and will not contain a ship. The numbers at the edge of the diagram indicate how many squares in that row or column contain parts of ships. When all 10 ships are correctly placed in the diagram, no two of them will touch each other, not even diagonally.

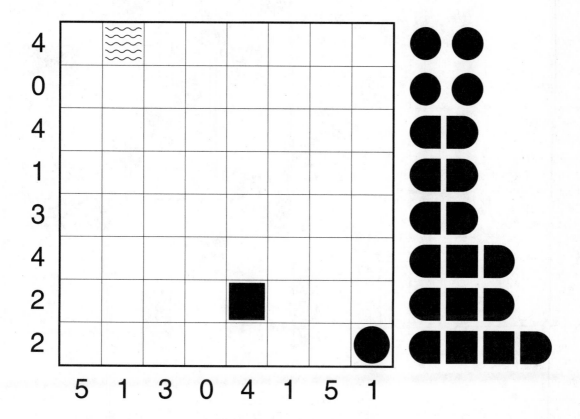

TWO-BY-FOUR

The eight letters in the word UNAFRAID can be rearranged to form a pair of common four-letter words in two different ways. Can you find both pairs of words?

— — — —   — — — —

— — — —   — — — —

★★★ Remark-Able by Robert H. Wolfe

ACROSS

1 Tease derisively
5 Dinghy movers
9 Crude one
14 Military assistant
15 Legal move
16 Those against
17 '20s barroom
19 Emulates Ebert
20 Add spice to
21 NCAA broadcaster
23 Greek letter
24 Degauss a tape
26 Scotch cocktail
28 Erstwhile airline
31 Something invigorating
32 "Wherefore __ thou Romeo?"
33 __ acid (protein building block)
35 Upper atmosphere
38 Pull apart
40 Tired out
42 Vendition
43 Overfills
45 Boundaries
47 Grand __ Opry
48 Keyboard key
50 Like candid shots
52 Stash away
54 Petunia part
55 Actor Wallach
56 Shopping destination
58 They sum it all up
62 Ancient tale teller
64 Modern message taker
66 Triple
67 "__ be fine!"
68 City near Turin
69 Aquatic mammal
70 Land at sea
71 Have to have

DOWN

1 Soviet news agency
2 Clear (off)
3 Brainstorm
4 China service
5 Cordiality, so to speak
6 Miss. neighbor
7 View again
8 Articulates
9 Without exception
10 Single-helix compound
11 Bedlam
12 Connect with
13 English assignment
18 Divided country
22 Paid player
25 Hidden shooter
27 Small pieces
28 Diner sign
29 Painter's calculation
30 Official travel overseas
31 Shoe part
34 Composer Rorem
36 Fashion magazine
37 Swamp stalk
39 Philosopher Descartes
41 Arm of the sea?
44 It's hard to answer
46 Garden tool
49 Govt. watchdog
51 Hemingway title character
52 Defunct defense grp.
53 On one's toes
54 Novel focuses
57 57, long ago
59 Relaxation
60 Religious ceremony
61 Tried to avoid the tag
63 Solo number
65 Corn Belt st.

★★ B__ __ __ __ Time

Find these words that are hidden in the diagram, either across, down, or diagonally. Then figure out the appropriate five-letter word starting with B that completes the title above, and fill it in the blanks.

```
L W O B T R J E H M A C
C P A G E E S I M O R P
F N M C L D L L K N A A
K O O A E A F A L L N Q
L R O P C N F W A T K N
D R Y T A C I R C U I T
H P O A R I S A L A I H
A E O R B N P E H B E U
B S A I R G G C A A L C
I O A R N I D H R N K R
H N A R T T M L S O N I
P U C U U P L A T E A C
```

ANKLE
ARM
BANK
BOWL
BRACELET
CAMP
CHAIN
CIRCUIT
CUP
DANCING
FALL
FOOT
HABIT
HEART
LAW
LEG
MIRROR
NOSE
PACT
PLATE
POINT
PROMISE
RANK
RECORD

IN OTHER WORDS

There is only one common uncapitalized word that contains the consecutive letters PMU. What is it?

_____

★★★ Alternating Tiles

Starting at a yellow tile somewhere at the top and moving either horizontally or vertically, draw a path through the tiles to the bottom. You may not pass through two tiles of the same color consecutively.

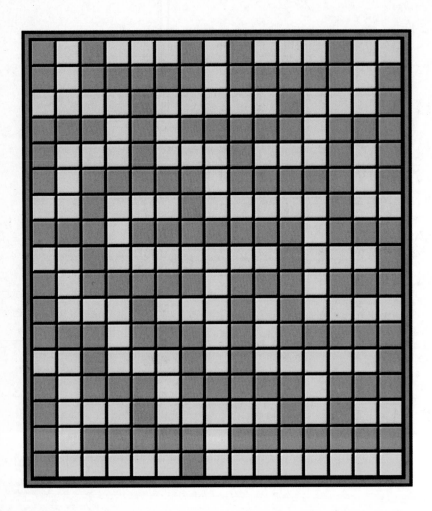

THREE AT A RHYME

Rearrange these letters to form three one-syllable words that rhyme.

A C L L L L O O O R S U

_____   _____   _____

★★★ Star Search

Find the stars that are hidden in some of the blank squares. The numbered squares indicate how many stars are hidden in the squares adjacent to them (including diagonally). There is never more than one star in any square.

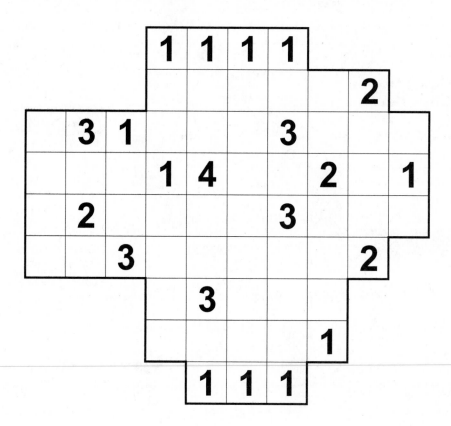

TELEPHONE TRIOS

1	ABC 2	DEF 3
GHI 4	JKL 5	MNO 6
PRS 7	TUV 8	WXY 9
*	O	#

Using the numbers and letters on a standard telephone, what three seven-letter words or phrases from the same category can be formed from these telephone numbers?

227-4246   _ _ _ _ _ _ _

288-7283   _ _ _ _ _ _ _

569-2678   _ _ _ _ _ _ _

★★★ Success-Full by Daniel R. Stark

ACROSS

1 Slightly wet
5 British baby carriage
9 Like some electrical adapters
13 Resorts to
14 Singer Falana
15 Gourmet mushroom
17 Be successful
19 Author Zola
20 Dead heat
21 Axe handle
22 Prepares to be knighted
23 Travels around
24 Motorcycle races
25 Drawing rooms
28 Fresh, as lettuce
29 Blocks
30 Campus figure
31 Not careful
35 Love, in Lima
36 Vacuum tube
37 Its "A" tunes the orchestra
38 Swelter
39 Basilica area
40 Thai or Nepali
41 Realty units
43 Censors
44 Did a slow burn
47 Pigeon talk
48 Jams in tightly
49 Damsel rescuer
50 Tarzan neighbor
53 Bicker
54 Be successful
56 Demeanors
57 What is more
58 "... __ o'clock scholar"
59 Latin 101 verb
60 Gush forth
61 *Star Wars* series teacher

DOWN

1 Fine powder
2 Piedmont province
3 Unimportant
4 Chi follower
5 Answers a judge
6 Puts up shingles
7 Perched
8 Function starter
9 Improves upon
10 Be successful
11 Paint additive
12 Violin relative
16 Inferior
18 Mongol rulers
22 Piece of dinnerware
23 Be successful
24 Wear down
25 Picket-line crosser
26 __ mater
27 "Get a load of that!"
28 Crabby
30 Uttered shrilly
32 Lover of an Irish Rose
33 Shower bar
34 Female lobsters
36 Has the nerve
40 Cool in manner
42 Burger extra
43 Take temporarily
44 Enjoyed the pool
45 Ghostly
46 Narrowly defeats
47 Quit
49 Respond to an SOS
50 It helps fill a lot
51 Dappled
52 Sicilian landmark
54 Undergrad degs.
55 Glimmer of hope

★★★ Sudoku

Fill in the blank boxes so that every row, column, and 3x3 box contains all of the numbers 1 to 9.

			7		4			
	3		5				6	
		5		3	8			
6	7					5		1
		2				4		
9		8					3	2
			6	9		3		
	2				7		8	
			3		2			

MIXAGRAMS

Each line contains a five-letter word and a four-letter word that have been mixed together (the order of the letters in each word has not been changed). Unmix the two words on each line and write them in the spaces provided. When you're done, find a two-part answer to the clue by reading down the letter columns in the answers.

CLUE: Unglamorous crepe

P I J O L A K E F = _ _ _ _ _ + _ _ _ _

S P A S I P E L S = _ _ _ _ _ + _ _ _ _

P A C A N D S A T = _ _ _ _ _ + _ _ _ _

S U K E N U P E N = _ _ _ _ _ + _ _ _ _

★★★ One-Way Streets

The diagram represents a pattern of streets. A and B are parking spaces, and the black squares are stores. Find the route that starts at A, passes through all stores exactly once, and ends at B. Arrows indicate one-way traffic for that block only. No block or intersection may be entered more than once.

SOUND THINKING

The consonant sounds in the name GERONIMO are J, R, N, and M. What common uncapitalized eight-letter word is pronounced with the same consonant sounds in the same order?

_____

★★★ ABC

Enter the letters A, B, and C into the diagram so that each row and column has exactly one A, one B, and one C. The letters outside the diagram indicate the first letter encountered, moving in the direction of the arrow. Keep in mind that after all the letters have been filled in, there will be two blank boxes in each row and column.

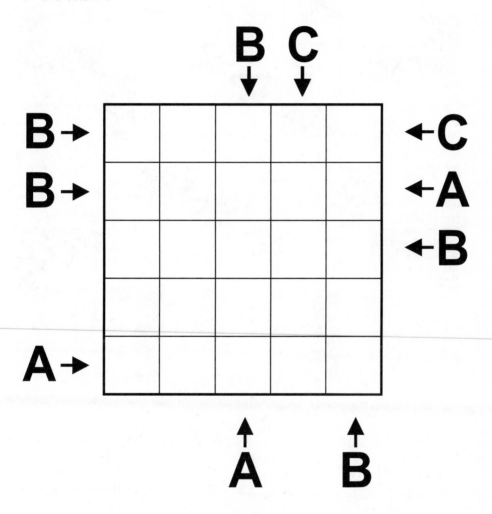

NATIONAL TREASURE

There is only one common uncapitalized eight-letter word that can be formed from the letters in EL SALVADOR. If it's an article of clothing, what is it?

__ __ __ __ __ __ __ __

★★★ Pair-O'-Docs by Fred Piscop

ACROSS

1 Molecule builder
5 Some warrant officers
10 Bonkers
14 Actress Downey
15 Milo of *The Verdict*
16 Canton's home
17 Ho-hum
18 Squirrel's snack
19 Hourly charge
20 Negligible amounts
23 London length
24 Cookie fruit
25 Chinese or Japanese
28 "Solve for x" subj.
29 Linden or Holbrook
32 Cummerbund, e.g.
33 Match up
35 Tankard filler
36 Oil container
40 *A Chorus Line* tune
41 Greek vowels
42 Jane Austen novel
43 Rugrat
44 Many Foreman finishes
45 First-rate
47 MPG part
48 Made dove sounds
50 Place for socks
55 Bog material
56 Post transaction
57 Corrida cries
59 Monopoly payment
60 Furry frolicker
61 Arabian Sea land
62 All wound up
63 Jury members, in theory
64 Flightless bird of yore

DOWN

1 Wall Street figure
2 Snitched
3 Actor Epps
4 Hawaiian fish
5 Talks big
6 Neil Simon slob
7 Did superbly
8 Geeky sort
9 Beach nuisance
10 Coif-covering kerchief
11 Ill-fated whaler
12 Is the right size
13 Ring site
21 Founding Father's nickname
22 Star in Orion
25 Fancy tie
26 Issue a refusal
27 Dot in the sea
28 Circle segments
29 Does damage to
30 Reunion attendees
31 Wallace's '68 running mate
33 Cultural doings
34 Supermodel Carangi
37 Reebok alternatives
38 Slam preventer
39 HBO western drama
45 Apple hollowers
46 Place to graze
47 Two-bit
48 Place for freight
49 More off-the-wall
50 Exploit
51 Called, in a way
52 Art Deco master
53 *Blondie* kid
54 Hit the books
55 Relative of ante-
58 __-Cone (icy confection)

★★★ Ship of Fuels

Which cable fits into each of the three refueling pods?

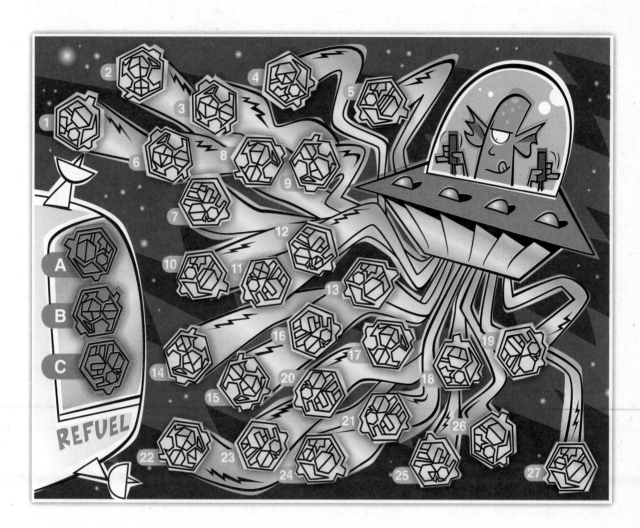

BETWEENER

What four-letter word belongs between the word at left and the word at right, so that the first and second word, and the second and third word, each form a common compound word?

YEAR __ __ __ __ MARK

★★★ Find the Ships

Determine the position of the 10 ships listed to the right of the diagram. The ships may be oriented either horizontally or vertically. A square with wavy lines indicates water and will not contain a ship. The numbers at the edge of the diagram indicate how many squares in that row or column contain parts of ships. When all 10 ships are correctly placed in the diagram, no two of them will touch each other, not even diagonally.

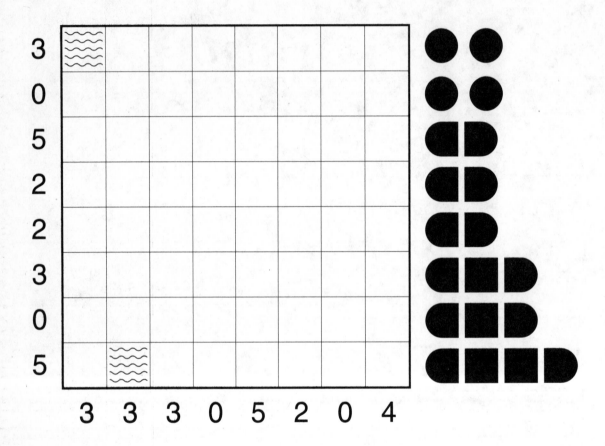

TWO-BY-FOUR

The eight letters in the word VERTICAL can be rearranged to form a pair of common four-letter words in only one way, if no four-letter word is repeated. Can you find the two words?

— — — —   — — — —

★★★ 123

Fill in the diagram so that each rectangular piece has one each of the numbers 1, 2, and 3, under these rules: 1) No two adjacent squares, horizontally or vertically, can have the same number. 2) Each completed row and column of the diagram will have an equal number of 1s, 2s, and 3s.

SUDOKU SUM

Without repeating any digits, complete the sum at right, by filling one digit in each of the five blanks.

```
  _ 5 8
+ 3 0 _
_____
  _ _ _
```

bRain BREaTHer
TAKE A LOOK! TIPS TO COMBAT EYESTRAIN

Your eyes may be the windows to your soul but, when overworked, they become doorways to pain, headaches, and blurred vision. And eyestrain is becoming increasingly common as people spend more time staring into the glare of computer monitors and the tiny screens of PDAs. What to do? Try these remedies below to make life easier on the eyes.

Rest 'em Whenever you're working on a task that requires close concentration, take a break every 20 minutes or so. Look at a faraway object—a picture on the opposite wall or a view out the window—for at least 30 seconds. By allowing your eyes to shift focus, you give them a rest.

Blink 'em Try to blink often—every few seconds or so—when you're paying close attention to your TV or computer screen. Blinking moistens your eyeballs and relaxes your eye muscles.

Close 'em If you have a long task that involves prolonged staring, close your eyes periodically. Even if you just shut your eyelids for a few seconds, you'll get some immediate relief.

Glasses for Your Neck If you wear bifocals, you can get neck strain from working at a computer. That's because bifocals' "reading" lens is at the bottom of the glasses, so you have to tilt your head back to see the computer screen. Ask your eye doctor to prescribe another pair of glasses that will give you clear vision at a distance of 20 inches, so you can read what's on the monitor without awkward head tilting.

Warm relief Another way to relax your eye muscles: Briskly rub your hands together until they grow warm. Then gently place the heels of your palms over your closed eyes and hold them there for a few seconds.

Cool relief If you soak a washcloth or hand towel in cool water, wring it out, and lay it over your eyes for five minutes, it will relieve strain.

Use shades In any bright sun—even in the winter—wear sunglasses to reduce the eyestrain that comes from squinting. Choose yellow, amber, orange, or brown lenses. Light in the blue part of the spectrum is what makes us squint and these lenses block it.

★★★★ Trifecta by Merle Baker

ACROSS

1 Shot in the dark
5 Declines
9 Mideast valley
14 Run smoothly
15 Superabundance
16 Goes out
17 "Waiting for the Robert __"
18 *Bee Season* star
19 Totaled
20 Make palatable
23 Wasn't bashful
24 Short time
25 Carpet feature
26 Arctic sight
28 Mouths, in zoology
31 Cookout leftovers
34 Captain Picard's counselor
35 Golfer's selection
36 Hold accountable
39 Beyond help
40 Leander's love
41 Apple products
42 Sitcom planet
43 Clear partner
44 Ukraine, once
45 Sigma follower
46 Unit of heat
50 Come along
55 Keyed up
56 List heading
57 Fall starter
58 Standard of perfection
59 Maintain
60 Sushi offering
61 Like mosquitoes
62 Delilah portrayer in '49
63 Some: Fr.

DOWN

1 Disgorges
2 Spring bloomer
3 "There __ free lunches"
4 Overfast
5 Breakfast-table item
6 Expurgate
7 Patting object
8 Alteration canceler
9 Elton lyricist
10 Letter-perfect
11 Cattle, old-style
12 Prefix meaning "quintillionth"
13 Dating from
21 Knock it off
22 Bubbling
26 *Famille* member
27 Wolf, in Oaxaca
28 Triple-decker treat
29 Crucifix
30 Rag dolls
31 Lhasa __
32 Musical-phrase connector
33 Hair unit
34 Friends' pronoun
35 Spur-of-the-moment
37 Guitar sound
38 Senate path
43 Somewhat
44 Mouth-watering
45 Fine-tune
46 Needing deciphering
47 Encore performance
48 Cockamamie
49 James and Jones
50 Captain's concern
51 Fictional fiend
52 Unlocks, poetically
53 Egyptian god
54 Gad about

★★★ Fences

Connect the dots with vertical or horizontal lines, so that a single loop is formed with no crossings or branches. Each number indicates how many lines surround it; squares with no number may be surrounded by any number of lines.

```
.   .   . 3 .   .   . 3 3 .   .
       3   0           2
          3 2     3
 3                        3
 1                        2
    3   0 2
 3          1   3
    2 1       2
.   .   .   .   .   .   .   .   .
```

ADDITION SWITCH

Switch the positions of two of the digits in the incorrect sum at right, to get a correct sum.

```
  5 6 9
+ 1 7 7
───────
  9 4 4
```

★★★ Number-Out

Shade squares so that no number appears in any row or column more than once. Shaded squares may not touch each other horizontally or vertically, and all unshaded squares must form a single continuous area.

1	3	6	3	5	4
4	4	5	3	5	2
2	5	4	3	3	6
3	1	5	6	2	3
5	2	2	2	1	3
2	6	1	5	4	3

OPPOSITE ATTRACTION

Unscramble the letters in the phrase SPORT STAT to form two common words that are opposites of each other.

_____   _____

★★★★ French Motto by Donna Levin

ACROSS

1 Letter encl.
5 Designer bag name
10 Shipbuilding wood
14 Support beam
15 Squelched, as a squeak
16 Yemeni capital
17 Faneuil Hall nickname
20 Explosive sound
21 Hoffman film
22 Goes for
25 Soon-to-be grads.
26 Will's ... *Bagger Vance* costar
28 Shakespearean prince
30 See the light
34 Mambo king Puente
35 Apollo preceder
37 Cellular material
38 Democracy, per Plato
41 Sportscaster Berman
42 Squeal on
43 Pain in the neck
44 Parisian pancake
46 __-mo
47 Levee
48 *Stuart Little* monogram
50 C-3PO, e.g.
52 Uncomfortable situation
56 Wound up
60 Sigma Chi, for one
63 Hit the road
64 Aquarium denizen
65 Ripped
66 Skywalker's mentor
67 Greet at the door
68 Some Federal Reserve Notes

DOWN

1 Under the weather

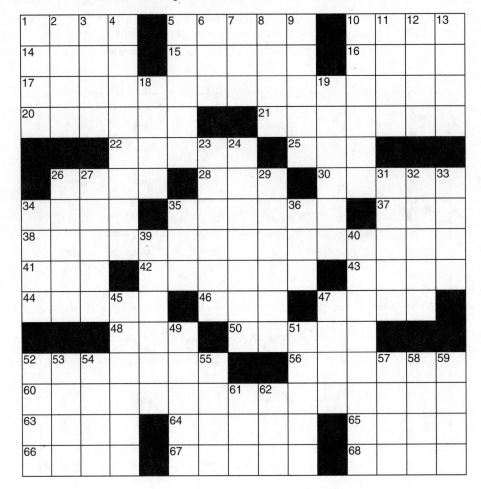

2 Magical beginning
3 Volvo competitor
4 Hospital professional
5 Frost products
6 Carnival location
7 TV alien
8 Shoulder muscle
9 Barcelona bye-bye
10 Fearsome fly
11 Hearing things
12 Against
13 *The Court Jester* star
18 Booty
19 Infamous Italian surname

23 Property crimes
24 Usual
26 Silas Marner, for example
27 Make amends
29 Bar serving
31 Ruse
32 __ main (primarily)
33 Actor Diggs
34 Powder for baby
35 __ long way (last)
36 Bar morsel
39 Whom Ken Jennings questioned
40 Excoriated

45 Former Spanish coin
47 Designer from Normandy
49 Floats, as an aroma
51 Plethora
52 I-80, e.g.
53 Droxie alternative
54 Mind
55 Trap in a corner
57 Symbol of Great Britain
58 To be, to Marie
59 Colors
61 Absorbed, as costs
62 Color or corn starter

★★★ Liberty Bell Maze

Enter the maze where indicated, pass through all the stars exactly once, then exit. You may not retrace your path.

BETWEENER

What five-letter word belongs between the word at left and the word at right, so that the first and second word, and the second and third word, each form a common compound word?

MILE _ _ _ _ _ WALL

★★★ Hyper-Sudoku

Fill in the blank boxes so that every row, column, 3x3 box, *and* each of the four
3x3 gray regions contains all of the numbers 1 to 9.

		6						
	3			6			5	4
5		1	8		2		9	
						3		2
		8			7	5		
4							8	
2			5	8		1		
		5	7				6	

MIXAGRAMS

Each line contains a five-letter word and a four-letter word that have been mixed together (the
order of the letters in each word has not been changed). Unmix the two words on each line and
write them in the spaces provided. When you're done, find a two-part answer to the clue by
reading down the letter columns in the answers.

CLUE: Israeli statesman

A L E G I V A D E = _ _ _ _ _ + _ _ _ _

B O B I R O L I L = _ _ _ _ _ + _ _ _ _

A B U L L S G E O = _ _ _ _ _ + _ _ _ _

A N O B U L N E R = _ _ _ _ _ + _ _ _ _

★★★ "C" Water

Find these seas and bays of the world that are hidden in C-shapes in the diagram. Two answers are shown to get you started.

```
N A G E N S P J X R R O N G K I O B W R
T L K P A Z S I D W U N O B P T U C N T
I J X I R C S T T E A R L B Z A O R F W
M E S K B O N B Z G V N J A S B N Y S K
L R E H Q V F T Q Q I A N L X I P A Y G
P V D R E Y E R Y B E S T A D S T W G H
V A N J H G M I S B Z I F A N Q H E R O
C M N E N Y T O N A N Z I L I E B C K J
U T K B J S C X E H Q I N O R W E R G F
H F O W J E A V G G W J P O I E A N C D
A L I R B V A B U E A T E R B N G N A L
V L X R L F L A G H N P F B B L C G M H
S X E Y W F H M D A U E S D I Z A N D R
Q U L E Y V I N O U O U H O A R A C E B
C E U E S K R Y V M D C N E S O G F A B
O Q R E E W A C A M S R Y T U M B L B P
L X O E S M K L T Y G O N L P A N T A L
V V K L F F E S K N W D E M M T G P I C
D M A D O T N X F Z A Y N Q S Y X T K D
O I Z R D P A Z I E H L C T Y A T E E V
```

ADMIRALTY
AEGEAN
BAFFIN
BALTIC
BENGAL
BERING
BONAVISTA
~~BOTANY~~
BROKEN
CARIBBEAN
DISCOVERY
DRAKE'S
ENCOUNTER
FLORES
FROBISHER
GALVESTON
GREENLAND
HERMITAGE
HUDSON
IONIAN
LAPTEV
MACKENZIE
NAPLES
~~NORWEGIAN~~
PLENTY
TASMAN
YELLOW

INITIAL REACTION

Identify the well-known proverb from the first letters in each of its words.

H. I. W. T. H. I. _____

★★★★ Risk Management by Patrick Jordan

ACROSS

1 Topical treatments
6 Tell it, with "up"
10 Essential part
14 Born in Borneo, say
15 Tra trail
16 Philanthropist Cornell
17 *Golden Boy* girl
18 Like __ of bricks
19 Work wearyingly
20 Start of a Kin Hubbard quip
23 A head of *Time*
24 Emulate werewolves
25 Mrs. George Jetson
28 Biblical jawbone source
30 Done in
33 Commando weapon
34 Court TV concern
36 Conclude
38 Middle of quip
41 Tire pattern
42 Shoemaker's helpers
43 Aware of what's "in"
44 Muppet with a football-shaped head
46 Motion-backing vote
47 Medicine quantity
48 Waiter or bell preceder
50 Spend some time
52 End of quip
58 Rounded lump
59 Folklorist's recital
60 First name of *Catwoman*'s star
61 Terrier of mysteries
62 Bayh of Indiana
63 Spam medium
64 Great Trek participant
65 Accomplished
66 Fastening pin

DOWN

1 Indonesia's "Isle of the Gods"
2 Beginning with
3 Maltese money
4 Earth layer
5 Confused condition
6 Pickup-truck style
7 Appeases the appetite
8 Sluggard's condition
9 Some DVD players
10 Peevish
11 Polo competitor
12 Donald Duck's nephews, for one
13 Evil computer of moviedom
21 Compassionate comment
22 Certain hatchlings
25 Not more than
26 Sky shade
27 Less loutish
29 "Sorry to say ..."
31 Wyoming's statehood predecessor
32 Microwaves, informally
34 Yawn-inducing state
35 Certain film segment
37 Toon skunk
39 Sweet snack
40 Under, in verse
45 Overdid one's part
47 Bundle of energy
49 Ovation shout
51 Voiced amazement
52 On top of that
53 E or G, e.g.
54 Vigorous spirit
55 Tiger's toenail
56 Author Wiesel
57 Find a market for
58 Schmooze

★★ Triad Split Decisions

In this clueless crossword puzzle, each answer consists of two words whose spellings are the same, except for the consecutive letters given. All answers are common words; no phrases or hyphenated or capitalized words are used. Some of the clues may have more than one solution, but there is only one word pair that will correctly link up with all the other word pairs.

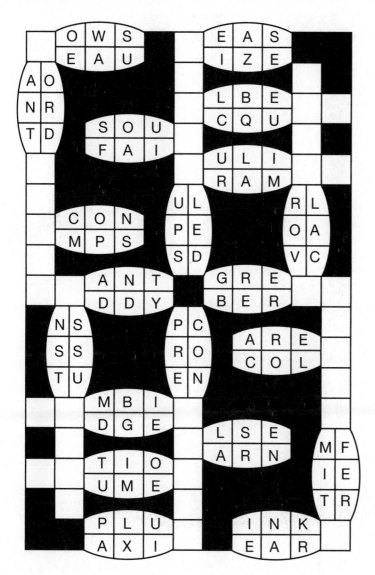

TRANSDELETION

Delete one letter from the word AUGMENT and rearrange the rest, to get a baker's ingredient.

_____

★★★ One-Way Streets

The diagram represents a pattern of streets. A and B are parking spaces, and the black squares are stores. Find the route that starts at A, passes through all stores exactly once, and ends at B. Arrows indicate one-way traffic for that block only. No block or intersection may be entered more than once.

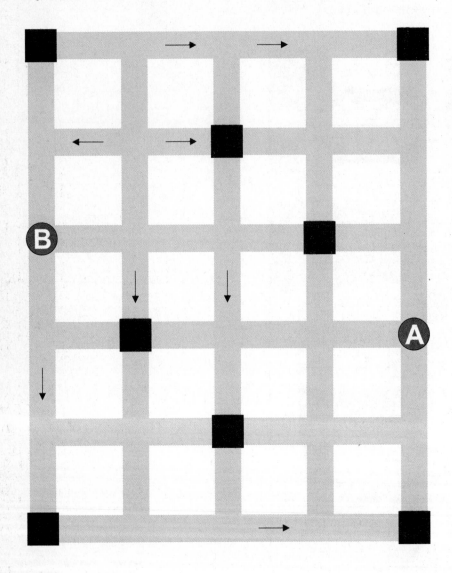

SOUND THINKING

Besides CAT and KITTY, what three-syllable name for a type of mammal is pronounced with the consonant sounds K and T, in that order?

_____

★★★★ Promo Pieces by Doug Peterson

ACROSS

1 "Get lost!"
5 Jazz singer Carmen
10 Palindromic prename
14 Pooch in Oz
15 Make a choice
16 Flatten
17 With expertise
18 Georgia city
19 Classroom challenge
20 Truck-stop sight
23 Olympic skater Cohen
24 Charged atom
25 Stout of whodunits
26 Idyllic setting
28 Formula westerns
31 Doctrines
34 Meal
37 Hamm of soccer
38 "Just what I needed!"
41 Eastern discipline
42 Type of inspection
43 Leather ending
44 Wide neckwear
46 Relaxation
48 Work the soil
49 Homily topic
51 Customary practice
55 Withdrawing one's support
58 Hercules, for one
59 "Honest!"
60 Well-ventilated
61 Desert rarity
62 Vow taker
63 Atlantic fish
64 Dateless
65 Some collars
66 Experiment

DOWN

1 Baseball-card data
2 Mongoose prey
3 Brother of Prometheus
4 Place for dolls
5 Written reminder
6 Orchestra members
7 Right-hand page
8 Squirrel food
9 Site of Vulcan's forge
10 Folded entrée
11 Like many charities
12 Romanov ruler
13 Unit of resistance
21 Smidgen
22 Plenty hot
27 Actresses Moran and Gray
28 Milo of *Barbarella*
29 Knee-slapper
30 Overstuff
31 Chichén __ (Mayan tourist site)
32 Ewes and does
33 Northeast Asian region
35 Letter before omega
36 Drill command
39 Monopoly piece
40 Doesn't dwell on
45 Sri Lanka product
47 Take to court
49 Quick drink
50 Snow shelter
52 Mrs. Kramden
53 Spiritual guides
54 Land of Nefertiti
55 Marsh material
56 *Picnic* playwright
57 Does some tailoring
58 Big hits: Abbr.

★★★ Color Paths

Find the shortest path through the maze from the bottom to the top, by using paths in this color order: red, blue, yellow, red, blue, etc. Change path colors through the white squares. It is okay to retrace your path.

SAY IT AGAIN

What five-letter word can be either a category of living thing or a place where goods are manufactured?

__ __ __ __ __

★★★ Star Search

Find the stars that are hidden in some of the blank squares. The numbered squares indicate how many stars are hidden in the squares adjacent to them (including diagonally). There is never more than one star in any square.

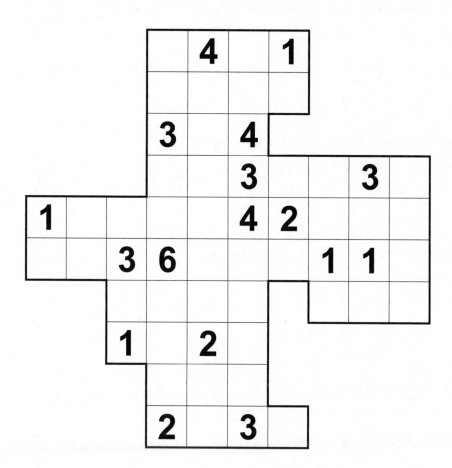

TELEPHONE TRIOS

Using the numbers and letters on a standard telephone, what three seven-letter words or phrases from the same category can be formed from these telephone numbers?

526-7666   _ _ _ _ _ _ _

662-5379   _ _ _ _ _ _ _

825-3633   _ _ _ _ _ _ _

★★★ Sudoku

Fill in the blank boxes so that every row, column, and 3x3 box contains all of the numbers 1 to 9.

		8	2	9	5	3		
		7				6		
9			3		4			6
7								2
2			1		9			8
		9				7		
		1	4	3	8	9		

CENTURY MARKS

Inserting plus signs and minus signs, as many as necessary, in between the nine digits below, create a series of additions and subtractions whose final answer is 100. Any digits without a sign between them are to be grouped together as a single number.

$$4 \quad 1 \quad 1 \quad 7 \quad 4 \quad 8 \quad 2 \quad 9 \quad 1 \quad = \quad 100$$

★★★★ Writers' Might by Doug Peterson

ACROSS

1 King David's father
6 Eugene Levy's '80s show
10 Electronic read
14 "Buenos Aires" musical
15 "Mr. Hockey"
16 Chanel of couture
17 Sax range
18 Leprechaun's land
19 Chooses, with "for"
20 Start of a Tommy Lasorda quote
23 Lose ground
24 PC owner
25 Woolly one
26 www.bucknell.__
27 Citation issuer
29 Passion
31 Engine sound
33 Stage pro
36 Part 2 of quote
38 Part 3 of quote
41 Western neckwear
43 Far from shore
45 Yankee star
48 A person
49 Type of cobra
50 __ carte
51 Maestro Masur
54 Honeybee collection
57 End of quote
60 Stead
61 Man-shaped mug
62 Unclear
64 Hazzard County deputy
65 Party cheese
66 Muscat man
67 Word of warning
68 Tatters
69 Observe covertly

DOWN

1 West Side Story gang member
2 Made equal
3 Cushy position
4 Kitchen fixture
5 Like Mouseketeer hats
6 Former National League park
7 Taint
8 Bits of kindling
9 Trial locale
10 Flat-bottomed floater
11 Made a replica of
12 When Juliet appears on the balcony
13 Fridge raider
21 Bring to mind
22 Muse of verse
23 Dom. __
28 Black-and-white snack
30 Musical McEntire
32 Choir garb
34 Triumphant outburst
35 Comics jungle queen
37 "That's all folks!" sayer
39 Media debut of '82
40 Fence-sitter's phrase
42 Common carry-on
44 Arbor Day mo.
45 Locked up
46 Climate-changing current
47 Go up against
52 Verbalize
53 Mary's upstairs neighbor
55 St. __ fire
56 Glob
58 Lose at blackjack
59 Workout spots
63 Feminine force

★★★ ABC

Enter the letters A, B, and C into the diagram so that each row and column has exactly one A, one B, and one C. The letters outside the diagram indicate the first letter encountered, moving in the direction of the arrow. Keep in mind that after all the letters have been filled in, there will be two blank boxes in each row and column.

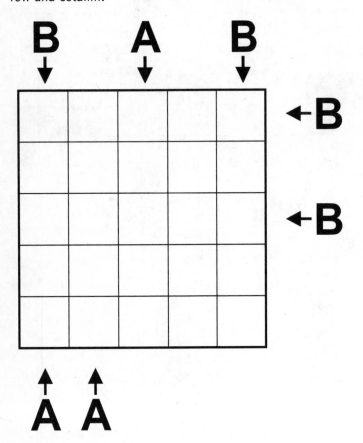

CLUELESS CROSSWORD

Complete the crossword with common uncapitalized seven-letter words, based entirely on the letters already filled in for you.

C		O		T		E
	■		■		■	
B		U		Q		
O	■		■		■	M
	X					
S	■		■		■	
	X			A		T

★★★ Find the Ships

Determine the position of the 10 ships listed to the right of the diagram. The ships may be oriented either horizontally or vertically. A square with wavy lines indicates water and will not contain a ship. The numbers at the edge of the diagram indicate how many squares in that row or column contain parts of ships. When all 10 ships are correctly placed in the diagram, no two of them will touch each other, not even diagonally.

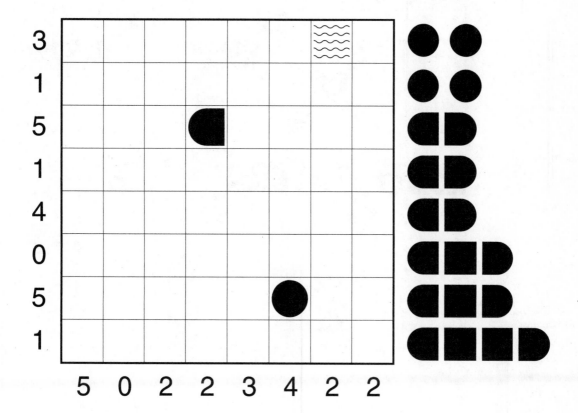

TWO-BY-FOUR

The eight letters in the word WRIGGLED can be rearranged to form a pair of common four-letter words in only one way. Can you find the two words?

— — — — — — — —

★★★★ Money Man by Janet R. Bender

ACROSS

1 Fruit-tree pest
6 Herringlike fish
10 Side of a window
14 Fresh from the chimney, perhaps
15 Carry on
16 *American __* (Fox show)
17 Dam that created Lake Nasser
18 They may be put on
19 Silent-screen star
20 Former Fed chairman
23 Auto trim
25 Blood fluids
26 *Trading Spaces* network
27 Haw preceder
28 Sound of discovery
30 Computer use: Abbr.
32 Russian novelist Ehrenburg
34 With 44 Across, what 20 Across warned against
40 Some strings
42 Railroad unit
43 Arledge of ABC
44 See 34 Across
47 Sci-fi writing award
48 "__ Maria"
49 "Good" cholesterol: Abbr.
51 Stimpy's partner
52 Afterthoughts, briefly
55 Notable periods
58 Ready for marriage
60 What the Fed regulates
63 Give notice
64 On a cruise
65 Laughs, out loud
68 Bruins' sch.
69 Lions' lairs
70 Actress Verdugo
71 __ out a living
72 Word on an octagon
73 "I Am Woman" singer

DOWN

1 Quick-wink link
2 Battery terminal: Abbr.
3 Conversation starter
4 Author Calvino
5 Energetic one
6 Booty
7 *CSI* clues
8 Share an opinion
9 __ *News* (Utah newspaper)
10 Triangular sails
11 Conform
12 Lesson in a tale
13 Chenin __ (wine grape)
21 RC Cola competitor
22 Zenith's opposite
23 Leek relative
24 Spiral
29 Dangerous dolphin
31 Gentle rebuke
33 Actress Jessica
35 Took off
36 Champs Elysées landmark
37 Fed
38 Member of a celestial order
39 Sierra __
41 Cut
45 Peruses again
46 Author Ferber
50 Reformation leader
52 Vex
53 Moved furtively
54 Steps over a wall
56 Item on a depreciation schedule
57 Note taker, for short
59 "__ Street Blues"
61 Greek letters
62 Coarse file
66 Common conjunction
67 Opportunity to speak

★★ Dot to Dot

Draw five squares in the diagram so that the corner of each square is on a dot. The squares may be at any angle. Dots may be used for more than one square, or not be used at all.

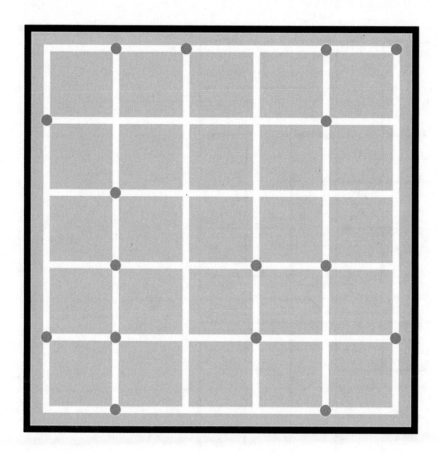

THREE AT A RHYME

Rearrange these letters to form three one-syllable words that rhyme.

A C D D D E E M O O O T W

_____   _____   _____

★★★ 123

Fill in the diagram so that each rectangular piece has one each of the numbers 1, 2, and 3, under these rules: 1) No two adjacent squares, horizontally or vertically, can have the same number. 2) Each completed row and column of the diagram will have an equal number of 1s, 2s, and 3s.

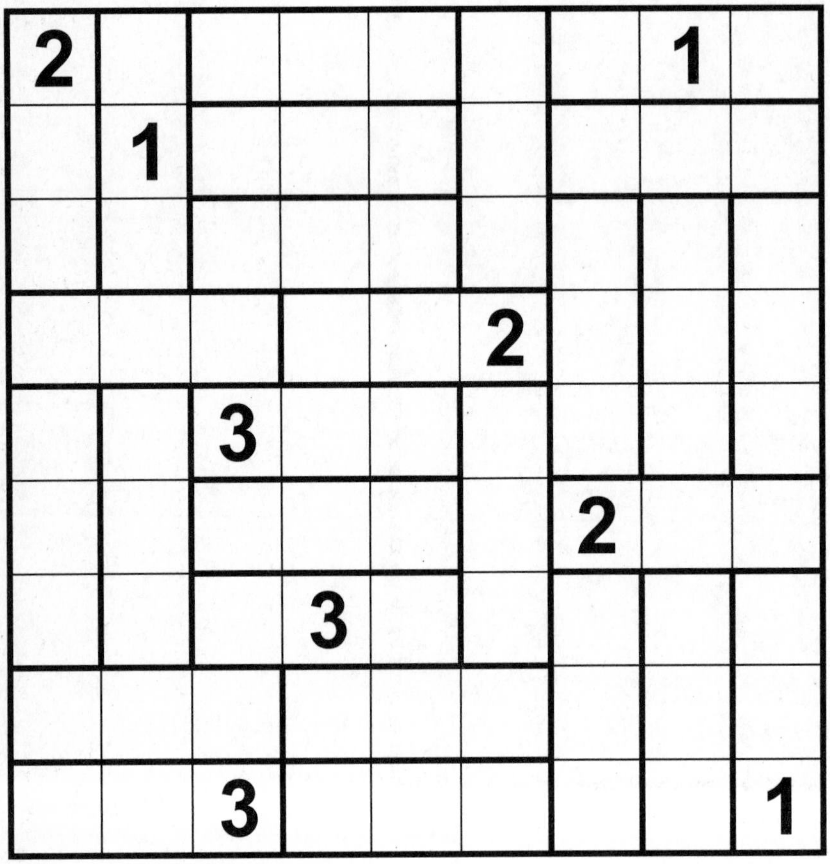

2						1		
	1							
					2			
		3						
						2		
			3					
		3						1

SUDOKU SUM

Without repeating any digits, complete the sum at right, by filling one digit in each of the five blanks.

```
  _ 4 _
+ 2 0 3
-------
  _ _ _
```

★★★ Fences

Connect the dots with vertical or horizontal lines, so that a single loop is formed with no crossings or branches. Each number indicates how many lines surround it; squares with no number may be surrounded by any number of lines.

```
3   3       0 2
   1 3
    0        3
 1           2       2
 3     2              3
      0          3
          1 2
     3 2       2     3
```

ADDITION SWITCH

Switch the positions of two of the digits in the incorrect sum at right, to get a correct sum.

```
  460
+ 135
─────
  650
```

★★★★ Assets Across by Merle Baker

ACROSS

1 Singing brothers' surname
5 Gangling
10 No. crunchers
14 Angled
15 Parting word
16 Dejected
17 "__ girl!"
18 Edible mushroom
19 Rice product
20 Broadway producer's acquisition
23 Biblical judge
24 Dupe
25 Piano keys, essentially
28 Oracle site
30 Beginning on
32 Film-noir classic of '50
33 Boxcars and such
36 "Happy Motoring" sloganeer
39 Big Ten sch.
40 Signs
41 An attractive force
46 Fooled
47 Large volume
48 Add numbers to
52 Navy builder
54 __ Toguri (Tokyo Rose)
55 *Le Monde* article
56 Dental-cleaning target
60 Maui feast
62 Absolute
63 Lo-cal
64 Home for hay
65 Christie et al.
66 Active one
67 *Giant* character
68 Buy alternative
69 Odds partner

1	2	3	4		5	6	7	8	9		10	11	12	13
14					15						16			
17					18						19			
20				21					22					
23				24				25				26	27	
28			29			30	31				32			
		33			34					35				
36	37	38			39					40				
41			42	43			44	45						
46			47				48			49	50	51		
52			53			54				55				
		56			57	58			59					
60	61			62					63					
64				65					66					
67				68					69					

DOWN

1 Degraded
2 Courage and fortitude
3 Involve
4 Alone, at a party
5 Kerosene
6 Decorate
7 Actor Robert De __
8 Don't give up
9 Christmas tradition
10 *CSI* venue
11 Took advantage of
12 Diving bird
13 Holy __

21 Lover of Narcissus
22 Court figures
26 Shake up
27 Neiman Marcus rival
29 High-school social
30 Basilica feature
31 Give the cold shoulder to
34 Rich soil
35 See 45 Down
36 Med. tests
37 Loafer, e.g.
38 Distinguished
42 Virginia willow
43 Having the same rank

44 Coin side
45 With 35 Down, semimonthly event
49 Solar-energy basis
50 Close-knit
51 *Silent Movie* actress
53 Plain-spoken
54 They may come to you
57 Eclectic magazine
58 European erupter
59 Shoppe sign word
60 White House monogram
61 Dubai's grp.

★★★ Hyper-Sudoku

Fill in the blank boxes so that every row, column, 3x3 box, *and* each of the four 3x3 gray regions contains all of the numbers 1 to 9.

	4			1	3			
			8		7	1	3	
		3						
3								
2							4	
1	6			7	9			
						6		
4					5	8	1	
	7			8		9		

MIXAGRAMS

Each line contains a five-letter word and a four-letter word that have been mixed together (the order of the letters in each word has not been changed). Unmix the two words on each line and write them in the spaces provided. When you're done, find a two-part answer to the clue by reading down the letter columns in the answers.

CLUE: Taxi driving?

P I G T H R O W Y = _ _ _ _ _ + _ _ _ _

P H E L E R O A D = _ _ _ _ _ + _ _ _ _

D U P E N C A R E = _ _ _ _ _ + _ _ _ _

F L A B K O O K E = _ _ _ _ _ + _ _ _ _

★★ Split Decisions

In this clueless crossword puzzle, each answer consists of two words whose spellings are the same, except for the consecutive letters given. All answers are common words; no phrases or hyphenated or capitalized words are used. Some of the clues may have more than one solution, but there is only one word pair that will correctly link up with all the other word pairs.

TRANSDELETION

Delete one letter from the word EPITHET and rearrange the rest, to get a word that means "small."

_____

★★★★ Cut It Out by Fred Piscop

ACROSS

1 Goya subject
5 "I dunno" gesture
10 Thick slice
14 Border on
15 Model's asset
16 Heart
17 Something to cut out
19 Logical flaw
20 Literary monogram
21 Attract
22 Publishing person
24 Photo tints
26 *Trinity* author
27 Something to cut out
33 Flower holder
36 Cardinal points
37 Field call
38 Glazier's unit
39 Leader of the
   original Rat Pack
40 Fan mag
41 Successful legislation
42 Capacitance unit
43 Big picture
44 Something to cut out
47 Significant times
48 20 Questions
   category
52 Three-time De Niro
   costar
55 Singer from Nigeria
57 "My turn!"
58 Eccentric one
59 Something to cut out
62 List-ending abbr.
63 *Little House* ...
   daughter
64 Leave in a hurry
65 Declare untrue
66 Continental cash
67 Is good for

DOWN

1 Boom sites
2 Demean
3 Dixie drink
4 Bolted down
5 Other half, so to
   speak
6 Billing unit
7 Ready to retrieve
8 Morale-building grp.
   since 1941
9 Produce
10 Flaky rock
11 Booty
12 Singer Guthrie
13 Tap serving
18 Explorer of 1803-06

23 Morse sounds
25 Twiddling one's
   thumbs
26 Optimistic view
28 They may be crossed
29 *Oliver's Story* author
30 Mideast ruler
31 Writer Jaffe
32 Year-end air
33 Petty clash
34 RPM gauge
35 Chip in
39 No-goodnik
40 Pueblo Indian
42 Hot stuff

43 Like a zebra
45 In a mild manner
46 Patterned cotton
   fabric
49 Metric prefix
50 Shoelace tip
51 Gets whupped
52 Depot posting, for
   short
53 Big bag
54 Horse coloring
55 Provocation
56 Space starter
60 Non-pro sports org.
61 Awry

★★★ Solitaire Poker

Group the 40 cards into eight poker hands of five cards each, so that each hand contains two pairs or better. The cards in each hand must be connected to each other by a common horizontal or vertical side.

BETWEENER

What six-letter word belongs between the word at left and the word at right, so that the first and second word, and the second and third word, each form a common compound word?

FOOT _ _ _ _ _ _ HEAD

★★★ Number-Out

Shade squares so that no number appears in any row or column more than once. Shaded squares may not touch each other horizontally or vertically, and all unshaded squares must form a single continuous area.

2	2	2	5	6	1
5	3	6	4	4	1
4	4	4	2	1	6
4	6	5	1	3	2
6	5	2	1	6	3
3	1	1	1	2	5

OPPOSITE ATTRACTION

Unscramble the letters in the phrase NOBLER WORD to form two common words that are opposites of each other.

_____   _____

★★★ One-Way Streets

The diagram represents a pattern of streets. A and B are parking spaces, and the black squares are stores. Find the route that starts at A, passes through all stores exactly once, and ends at B. Arrows indicate one-way traffic for that block only. No block or intersection may be entered more than once.

SOUND THINKING

The consonant sounds in the scientific term ALKALI are L, K, and L. What two more common un-capitalized six-letter words are pronounced with the same consonant sounds in the same order?

_____   _____

★★★★ Sweet Dreams by Donna Levin

ACROSS

1 Seven-time Wimbledon singles champion
5 Great, to a hip-hopper
9 Start of a Tony Bennett title
14 Leslie Caron title role
15 Honolulu's here
16 Sikorsky spinner
17 Chocolaty dessert
20 Opposite of paleo-
21 Vegan's no-no
22 *Paper Moon* stars
23 Self-satisfied
24 Thug
25 Chocolaty dessert
31 Chronicler of Henry and June
32 Gone by
33 Criminal charge
35 Wonka portrayer in '05
36 Like the 1890s
37 Homer and Marge's middle child
38 Take to court
39 Blueprint detail
41 Minesweeper captain of fiction
42 Chocolaty dessert
46 Light melody
47 Sharpen
48 *Heart of Darkness* locale
51 Informal tops
52 Dickens pen name
55 Chocolaty dessert
58 Transcontinental flight feature
59 Drop-down __
60 Bridge expert Sharif
61 Asparagus unit
62 Margaret Truman's mom
63 It may be held for lunch

DOWN

1 Secluded valley
2 Price increase
3 Gravy Train alternative
4 Certain evergreen
5 Pretender
6 Tries it
7 "There'll be __ time ..."
8 Shabby ship
9 Settle, as details
10 Far from chic
11 Where Vulcan worked
12 Thwart
13 *Uno y dos*
18 Tube awards
19 Bird's eye view?
23 Pass over
24 Outback salutation
25 X-ray units
26 Outdo
27 Private-eye film plot
28 Speedily
29 Hard time, informally
30 Stand for Seurat
34 Beep
36 Guy
37 Singer Lorna
39 Foul-weather apparel
40 Rice dish
41 Knightly activity
43 Actress Witt
44 12-year-olds
45 Type of monkey
48 Rocket interceptors, for short
49 Turkey
50 Go wild
51 Kilmer subject
52 Crimson Tide, familiarly
53 Acceptable
54 Friend of Beetle Bailey
56 Federal book-balancing agcy.
57 Dot follower

★★★ Sudoku

Fill in the blank boxes so that every row, column, and 3x3 box contains all of the numbers 1 to 9.

				2				
	7			4		6		
	4		9		1		7	
		6				7		
7	3						9	5
		2				1		
	9		3		8		5	
		8		6		2		
				5				

MIXAGRAMS

Each line contains a five-letter word and a four-letter word that have been mixed together (the order of the letters in each word has not been changed). Unmix the two words on each line and write them in the spaces provided. When you're done, find a two-part answer to the clue by reading down the letter columns in the answers.

CLUE: Means of escape

```
S H A L O U N E T  =  _ _ _ _ _  +  _ _ _ _
R O B B O I N N Y  =  _ _ _ _ _  +  _ _ _ _
S C O L A L U R E  =  _ _ _ _ _  +  _ _ _ _
A P P L E A V L Y  =  _ _ _ _ _  +  _ _ _ _
```

★★★ Star Search

Find the stars that are hidden in some of the blank squares. The numbered squares indicate how many stars are hidden in the squares adjacent to them (including diagonally). There is never more than one star in any square.

				3		1	
		3					
	2			2		1		
3			2	4				2
						3		2
	1	2		2	2			2
		1				2		
	1	1	1	1	1	1		

TELEPHONE TRIOS

1	ABC 2	DEF 3
GHI 4	JKL 5	MNO 6
PRS 7	TUV 8	WXY 9
*	O	#

Using the numbers and letters on a standard telephone, what three seven-letter words or phrases from the same category can be formed from these telephone numbers?

266-7673   _ _ _ _ _ _ _

266-2628   _ _ _ _ _ _ _

338-3567   _ _ _ _ _ _ _

★★★★ No Resistance by Doug Peterson

ACROSS

1 Campus recruiting grp.
5 Hindu prince
10 Tame, as a bronco
14 Incantation opener
15 Clear soup
16 Reverberate
17 Demonstrates adaptability
20 Take care of
21 "... bug __ rug"
22 Byways
23 Astronaut affirmatives
25 Jagged rock
27 Formally declare
30 Hankerings
32 1860s initials
35 Tibetan title
36 Dude
37 They eschew meat
39 Toes the line
42 Largest Japanese island
43 Blue Jays, on scoreboards
44 Nautical heading
45 Magnate Onassis
46 Chances to swing
48 Piquant
49 Soup pasta
50 Gospel singer Winans
52 Physics lead-in
55 __-locka, FL
57 Violin maker of yore
61 Isn't disruptive
64 Spherical hairdo
65 Casino natural
66 Imitate Daffy Duck
67 Large pipe
68 Publicity
69 Grayish-white

DOWN

1 Tattered duds
2 Orchestral instrument
3 Birch, for one
4 Gilligan and friends
5 Hitter's stat
6 Craftsmanship
7 With 59 Down, New Age composer
8 Stick on
9 LBJ's veep
10 Haze over
11 West Coast sch.
12 Sporting sneakers
13 Transports to the repair shop
18 Serenade, perhaps
19 Chalk-dust collector
24 Israeli commune
26 Parallel-parking gear
27 First in a series
28 Hero's quality
29 Muscat citizen
31 Terra __
32 Type of lily
33 Show disdain
34 Admirable quality
38 Where quetzales are spent
40 Olmert predecessor
41 Quick sellers, supposedly
47 Baby __
49 Director Welles
51 Raven's cry
52 First husband
53 Comfy spot
54 Hatcher of Hollywood
56 Cover, as a road
58 Budget alternative
59 See 7 Down
60 Bill Cosby's first series
62 Culinary meas.
63 Printing widths

★★★ Straight Ahead

Enter the grid where indicated; pass through all of the blue squares, then exit. You must travel horizontally or vertically in a straight line, and turn only to avoid passing through a black square. It is okay to retrace your path.

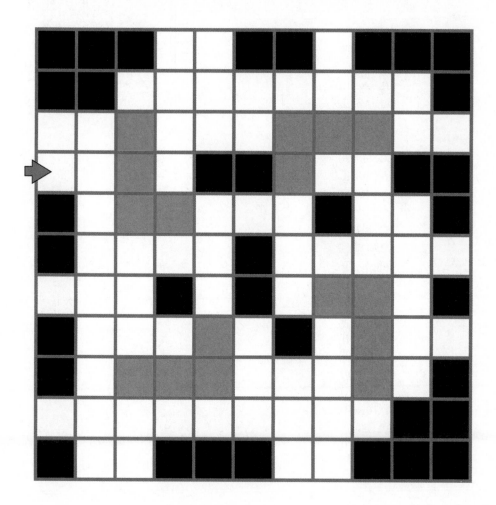

SAY IT AGAIN

What five-letter noun can mean either "category" or "excellence"?

— — — — —

★★★ Musical Spirals

These music terms are arranged in spirals in the diagram, either starting or finishing in the center, either clockwise or counterclockwise. Some of the spirals may overlap. One answer is shown to get you started.

```
C Y N O H A X S O L Y        ACCOMPANY
K O P H X L Y I O F B        ACCORDION
E L Y P C O N G G E L        ALLEMANDE
E D N Q T O T O S O W        ANDANTINO
L A A D L A R A L M O        CANTABILE
L E M B H T N C R I U        CONDUCTOR
D T P M I S E C A N R        CONTRALTO
I M P O X T E L E T S        CRESCENDO
T U R F L S I I B A S        HARMONICS
P M O J G C N Q O T U        HARMONIZE
R W E L A R O U O S N        IMPROMPTU
E E A P R A Y N S T E        INTERLUDE
M G S T O L E D G G D        LACRIMOSO
P O D N E E D U R O T        LARGHETTO
P R C E W N I L O C C        PASTORALE
H E S C K T E R N D U        PIZZICATO
P O L A N D Z E N O T        POLONAISE
S E O N O A A A S H W        POLYPHONY
I A N I T N F X O P O        ROUNDELAY
S I G I B N L A R N Q        SAXOPHONE
R E N X I J T O G N D        SIGNATURE
U T A C C X T E H H R        SIXTEENTH
Z Z O N O A V J S K U        SOLFEGGIO
C V I D R F A V H A R        SOSTENUTO
T B R U S C I Y Z E M
Y N A Y A H N M I N O
C A P P R M O P I Z F
C O M Z C T V T O Z K
M I J O U Q H A C I L
```

WHO'S WHAT WHERE?

The correct term for a resident of Parma, Italy, is:

A) Parmese

B) Parmatine

C) Parmesan

D) Parmian

★★★ ABC

Enter the letters A, B, and C into the diagram so that each row and column has exactly one A, one B, and one C. The letters outside the diagram indicate the first letter encountered, moving in the direction of the arrow. Keep in mind that after all the letters have been filled in, there will be two blank boxes in each row and column.

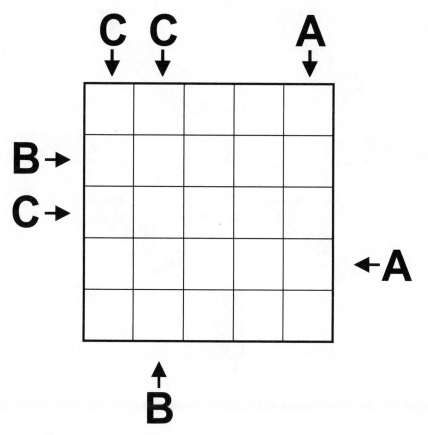

CLUELESS CROSSWORD

Complete the crossword with common uncapitalized seven-letter words, based entirely on the letters already filled in for you.

★★★★★ Themeless Toughie by Daniel R. Stark

ACROSS

1 Flourish
8 Athlete's throw
15 Lie
16 Spaghetti-sauce herb
17 Arrayed
18 Race units
19 __ visit
20 Troy story
22 Lao's neighbor
23 OOO
24 Messy places
25 Bother
26 Italian novelist
27 Distinct
28 Oxford needs
29 Modernize
31 Least restricting
32 R-rating reason
33 Baja food
34 French honey
37 Kind of cash
41 Like some jackets
42 Gets ready for dinner
43 From, in *Namen*
44 Martinique et al.
45 Took a bite of
46 Courteous one
47 __ City (New Haven)
48 Pulitzer candidates
49 *Five Weeks in a Balloon* author
50 Green state
52 Running wild
54 Handled
55 Architectural detail
56 Ways
57 Like a ukulele's neck

DOWN

1 More forward
2 Leaf source
3 Street-corner shape
4 Opens slightly
5 Royal address
6 Countdown word
7 Reflect
8 City near Chicago
9 Expanses
10 Offer for sale
11 Something to poach
12 Garden structure
13 Gets some air
14 Most forward
21 Former Vatican currency
24 Do without
25 Element #86
27 Don't use
28 Beats
30 Folklore giants
31 Was on the ebb
33 Flies
34 Paying customers
35 *High Adventure* author
36 Opposite sides
37 Object of attention
38 Get stuffed
39 Freighter's capacity
40 Signed up
42 Multiplies
45 Tribal symbol
46 Catch on
48 *Our Gang* dog
49 Glen
51 Wine holder
53 Easter starter

bRain BReatHer
SCIENTIFIC ENDEAVOR:
NEVER SAY NEVER

Take the words of these seekers of knowledge to heart and who knows what you might discover!

Basic research is what I am doing when I don't know what I am doing.

—WERNHER VON BRAUN

The greatest obstacle to discovery is not ignorance—it is the illusion of knowledge.

—DANIEL J. BOORSTIN

An inventor is simply a fellow who doesn't take his education too seriously.

—CHARLES F. KETTERING

When you make the finding yourself—even if you're the last person on earth to see the light—you'll never forget it.

—CARL SAGAN

The most exciting phrase to hear in science, the one that heralds new discoveries, is not "Eureka!" (I found it!) but "That's funny …"

—ISAAC ASIMOV

Just because something doesn't do what you planned it to do doesn't mean it's useless.

—THOMAS ALVA EDISON

Talent hits a target no one else can hit; genius hits a target no one else can see.

—ARTHUR SCHOPENHAUER

If we value the pursuit of knowledge, we must be free to follow wherever that search may lead us. The free mind is not a barking dog, to be tethered on a 10-foot chain.

—ADLAI E. STEVENSON

★★★★ Find the Ships

Determine the position of the 10 ships listed to the right of the diagram. The ships may be oriented either horizontally or vertically. A square with wavy lines indicates water and will not contain a ship. The numbers at the edge of the diagram indicate how many squares in that row or column contain parts of ships. When all 10 ships are correctly placed in the diagram, no two of them will touch each other, not even diagonally.

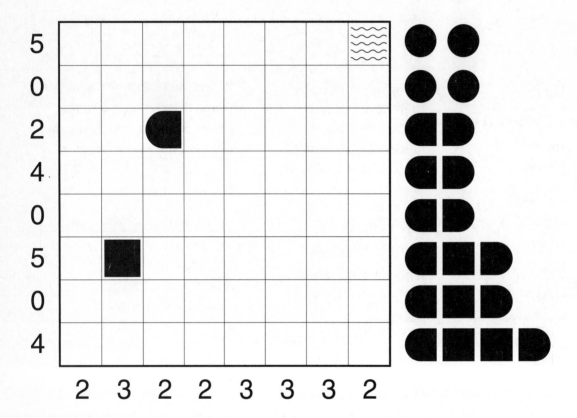

TWO-BY-FOUR

The eight letters in the word YEARNING can be rearranged to form a pair of common four-letter words in only one way. Can you find the two words?

— — — —   — — — —

★★★★ Hyper-Sudoku

Fill in the blank boxes so that every row, column, 3x3 box, *and* each of the four 3x3 gray regions contains all of the numbers 1 to 9.

3						1		7
1					2			5
	7	8					6	
		3						
			4					2
			2		5		8	1
		6						
	5						9	
							5	

BETWEENER

What seven-letter word belongs between the word at left and the word at right, so that the first and second word, and the second and third word, each form a common compound word?

FIRE __ __ __ __ __ __ __ JACK

★★★★★ Themeless Toughie by Merle Baker

ACROSS

1 Frankenstein portrayer in '94
8 Frameworks
15 Loos character
16 Name meaning "aristocrat"
17 He's outta here
18 Stores on the farm
19 2005 World Series participant
20 "Yikes!"
22 *Knight Rider* car
23 Danish-born journalist
24 Aegean island
26 Job-ad letters
27 Ref. set
28 Decorative details
29 Remain with
31 Lack of interest
33 Curses
34 Something on one's agenda
36 Muse of astronomy
39 Leftovers
43 Passover month
44 Like crests
45 MSN competitor
46 USN rank
47 Backfire
49 Fruit in a Durango drink
50 Air force
52 *Alfred* composer
53 Places between hills
54 Frankie's costar
56 Stone Age implement
58 Less sympathetic
59 Reduction of tension
60 Covers, in a way
61 Polar-exploration vehicles

DOWN

1 Made dim
2 Whom the French called "Monsieur Crescendo"
3 Waterproof overshoes
4 Closes on
5 Gravy Train alternative
6 Grand, briefly
7 Longtime Asian ruler
8 Devotes
9 Rapids transit
10 Shaker ___, OH
11 Name of seven Danish kings
12 Backdrops
13 Common solvent
14 Sonnet groupings
21 Local
24 Union, in DC
25 Climb
28 None too easy
30 +1
32 Ethiopian lake
33 Force open
35 Hits, in a way
36 Let go
37 Lambaste
38 At present
40 Homebuilding activity
41 Plastic flute
42 URL elements
44 Travelers
48 Ford flick, often
49 Lost color
51 Be inclined
53 Expression of opinion
55 Curtain holder
57 It may be smoked

★★★ Paper Chase

If a dotted line indicates a cut, and an uninterrupted line indicates a fold, which of the five patterns is produced when you fold and cut each square of paper as indicated?

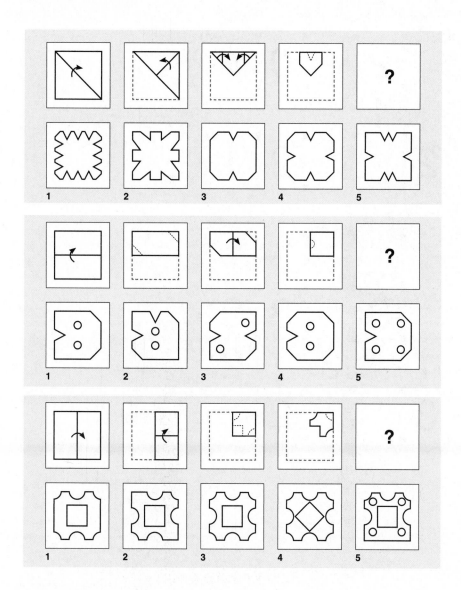

THREE AT A RHYME

Rearrange these letters to form three one-syllable words that rhyme.

B C C D E E H I I L M M M

_____ _____ _____

★★★★ Fences

Connect the dots with vertical or horizontal lines, so that a single loop is formed with no crossings or branches. Each number indicates how many lines surround it; squares with no number may be surrounded by any number of lines.

```
 .   .   .   .   .   .   .   .   .
   3       2     0 1
 .   .   .   .   .   .   .   .   .
   3   2   1
 .   .   .   .   .   .   .   .   .
   3 1   2       2   1
 .   .   .   .   .   .   .   .   .

 .   .   .   .   .   .   .   .   .

 .   .   .   .   .   .   .   .   .
   3 2       3   3 2
 .   .   .   .   .   .   .   .   .
         1     3     2
 .   .   .   .   .   .   .   .   .
   3 1   3       2
 .   .   .   .   .   .   .   .   .
```

ADDITION SWITCH

Switch the positions of two of the digits in the incorrect sum at right, to get a correct sum.

$$\begin{array}{r} 187 \\ +875 \\ \hline 972 \end{array}$$

★★★★★ Themeless Toughie by Daniel R. Stark

ACROSS

1 Warm
8 Bounce back
15 Tosses back and forth
16 Survey
17 Toxicology concern
18 Steals from
19 Organ settings
20 Evoke laughter
22 Dan McGrew's gal
23 Fullest extent
24 Telling it like it is
25 *Mary Poppins* role
26 Compass reading
27 Like some citizenships
28 Candle holder
30 Took apart
33 Was worthy
34 Lighten
35 Major defeat
37 Come out with
40 Changes nothing
45 Some wild families
47 Powell successor
48 Wish undone
49 Rights, so to speak
50 Laughable
52 "No sleep till __": Byron
53 Gibraltar denizen
54 Dry spell
55 Some rentals
56 Beyond repair
58 Limonite, for one
60 Delighting
61 Euro predecessors
62 Half a room, perhaps
63 Sight from Darjeeling

DOWN

1 Feeling chagrin
2 Bar order
3 Shoe parts
4 Well-practiced
5 Hoppers
6 Aloha token
7 Snowballs
8 Summertime offering
9 Has a life
10 Headland
11 Sacred syllables
12 Furious
13 Administer
14 Proved false
21 Strapless slipper
24 NL or NFL team, in headlines
25 Serving pieces
27 *The Wreck of the Mary __* ('59 film)
29 Far from polished
31 Parakeet treats
32 Piece of plumbing
36 Not at present
37 Refreshed
38 Capital on the Mediterranean
39 Language from which comes "lama"
41 Bloke's streetcar
42 Push forward
43 Dawns
44 Most volatile
46 Unvoiced
51 Gentle reminder
52 Tunnel worker
54 Mask part
55 Shake off
57 Polished off
59 Crank up

★★★★ 123

Fill in the diagram so that each rectangular piece has one each of the numbers 1, 2, and 3, under these rules: 1) No two adjacent squares, horizontally or vertically, can have the same number. 2) Each completed row and column of the diagram will have an equal number of 1s, 2s, and 3s.

SUDOKU SUM

Without repeating any digits, complete the sum at right, by filling one digit in each of the five blanks.

```
    5 0 8
+   _ _ _
  _ 3 _
```

★★★ Number-Out

Shade squares so that no number appears in any row or column more than once. Shaded squares may not touch each other horizontally or vertically, and all unshaded squares must form a single continuous area.

2	4	5	1	6	6
1	5	1	3	6	3
6	1	3	5	3	4
4	2	3	4	4	5
4	3	3	2	5	5
4	6	4	4	1	2

OPPOSITE ATTRACTION

Unscramble the letters in the phrase CRUELER CANAL to form two common words that are opposites of each other.

_____   _____

★★★★★ Themeless Toughie by Merle Baker

ACROSS

1 Didn't go through
9 Zen enlightenment
15 Cell accessory
16 Dislodge
17 Audio failures
18 Swindles
19 Evokes fondness
20 Contradict
21 Two Unsers
22 Inspiration for Sally in *Call Me Madam*
23 Not hard by
26 Hide and sneak
27 Hi-__
30 *Where Eagles Dare* author
35 Sicilian, for example
36 Something exploitable
37 Experiences
38 *Howards End* character
39 Belgian-born songwriter
40 *Mayflower* passenger
42 Detective-story pioneer
44 Ballet star
47 Set forth
51 Cold cover
52 Excessive
53 Melodic passage
54 Let up
55 Austere
56 Study of low temperatures

DOWN

1 Ancient British historian
2 Lint source
3 Get moving
4 Plays
5 Hazard to navigation
6 Makes bitter
7 Tolkien creatures
8 *L'Académie __ Sciences*
9 Marilyn Monroe, in *Some Like It Hot*
10 What 4 may stand for
11 Triple
12 Campy punch reactions
13 *The Godfather* composer
14 Wee
20 On point
22 Swipe
23 Comics cry
24 Botany
25 "My __ True" (Elvis Costello song)
26 Stretch across
27 Show *Seinfeld*, say
28 Apollo 11 lunar module
29 Fishhook holder
31 Cartoon Network sister channel
32 Catalyzed
33 Metric measurement syst.
34 Not very graceful
40 Berkshire racecourse
41 Take for a term
42 Chum
43 Eurydice's love
44 Tuner
45 Part of some plots
46 Foreign negation
47 Pirate, for short
48 *Museo* display
49 Numerical suffix
50 Hazard to navigation
52 Arrow trajectory

★★★ Commonwealth Trail

Beginning with GUYANA, then moving up, down, left, or right, one letter at a time, trace a path of these nations in the British Commonwealth.

```
G A N A N Z A N I T E R O O N
U Y A T L E H C A I D E M E L
T U S E L S E Y U N K I A S O
H O T O N D N E K M G N C A T
A S I A G L A N Y O D W A N H
F A N A Z I P E A O T S A N O
R I D W U P A Z B B A D U R U
I T A S A N L I R U N A N A B
C L A I U E E B S E E I A R B
A S M N G W U S H D A N C A A
L O A E U R I I S G L A M I D
O S T A A I T N G N A B I B O
M I K N M T I T A P O A I L S
O P A A S U V A B I R E R A A
N A O M U L A E W R I K T S U
I S L A N D S N Z E A L A N D
```

AUSTRALIA
BANGLADESH
BARBADOS
BELIZE
BOTSWANA
BRUNEI
CAMEROON
CANADA
~~GUYANA~~
INDIA
KENYA
KIRIBATI
LESOTHO
MALTA
MAURITIUS
NAMIBIA
NAURU
NEW ZEALAND
PAKISTAN
PAPUA NEW GUINEA
SAMOA
SEYCHELLES
SINGAPORE
SOLOMON ISLANDS
SOUTH AFRICA
SWAZILAND
TANZANIA
TONGA
TUVALU
UNITED KINGDOM

IN OTHER WORDS

There is only one common uncapitalized word that contains the consecutive letters RDV. What is it?

_____

★★★ Turn Maze

Entering at the bottom and exiting at the top, find the shortest path through the maze, following these turn rules: You must turn right on red squares, turn left on blue squares, and go straight through yellow squares. Your path may retrace itself and cross at intersections, but you may not reverse your direction at any point.

SAY IT AGAIN

What six-letter word can be either the past tense of a verb or a noun meaning "soil"?

___ ___ ___ ___ ___ ___

★★★★★ Themeless Toughie by S.N.

ACROSS

1 Film role for Robert Duvall and Tyrone Power
11 Wholesale
15 Send
16 Help in
17 His best-known song includes "Thee haughty tyrants ne'er shall tame"
18 Office collection
19 Asian language
20 Syndicate
21 In streams
23 Salt Lake County mecca
25 Pinch
27 Burden
28 Fictional soldier
30 Support
32 Didn't support
33 Panhandler?
36 Long in Hollywood
37 Logical remark
41 *Evening Shade* character
42 Edge
43 Word of appreciation
45 Absorbed
46 Decca jazz artist
50 Mini-mission
52 Sovereign's __ (one of the British Crown Jewels)
54 "The Game of the White Dove"
55 Hurt, in a way
57 Pops
59 Garden event each spring
60 Book leather
61 Enable
64 Drive
65 Websterian, perhaps
66 Barely beats, with "by"
67 Tigerish

DOWN

1 Circadian dysrhythmia
2 Doctor's order, at times
3 New growth
4 Model, for short
5 Kingdom east of Sumer
6 Dante sees him in *The Divine Comedy*
7 View from Mumbai
8 Spoil
9 It was above the Greek underworld
10 Isn't self-contained
11 Managed
12 Ditches
13 Get used to things
14 Visited, as 49 Down
22 Doctor's order, at times
24 Speck
26 Popular stuffing
29 Calling up
31 Calendar marking
34 Heading, for short
35 *Ash Wednesday* monogram
37 Turned out
38 Tax
39 Joining
40 Literary pseudonym
44 Nice neighbor
47 Bridge term
48 Three-time NFL MVP
49 Temporary quarters
51 Appointments
53 Viscount St. Albans
56 Defy
58 __ road
62 Close one
63 Shortened preposition

★★★★ ABCD

Enter the letters A, B, C, and D into the diagram so that each row and column
has exactly one A, one B, one C, and one D. The letters outside the diagram
indicate the first letter encountered, moving in the direction of the arrow. Keep
in mind that after all the letters have been filled in, there will be two blank
boxes in each row and column.

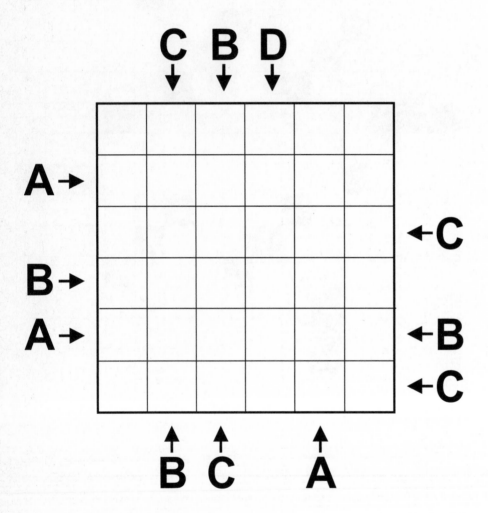

NATIONAL TREASURE

Find the two common six-letter words that can be formed from the letters in KAZAKHSTAN.

— — — — — —   — — — — — —

★★★★ Sudoku

Fill in the blank boxes so that every row, column, and 3x3 box contains all of the numbers 1 to 9.

7								
	5		7		8	1		4
						2		
					7		8	9
3				1				6
2	6		9					
		1						
8		2	1		3		4	
								7

MIXAGRAMS

Each line contains a five-letter word and a four-letter word that have been mixed together (the order of the letters in each word has not been changed). Unmix the two words on each line and write them in the spaces provided. When you're done, find a two-part answer to the clue by reading down the letter columns in the answers.

CLUE: Marlo Thomas role

T A B L O G O Y O = _ _ _ _ _ + _ _ _ _

S H O W A D I L Y = _ _ _ _ _ + _ _ _ _

F A R M O R T E D = _ _ _ _ _ + _ _ _ _

T H O U T A L L A = _ _ _ _ _ + _ _ _ _

★★★★★ Themeless Toughie by Daniel R. Stark

ACROSS

1 Iffy
7 Medieval players
14 Port near Pompeii
15 Thanksgiving guest, often
16 Cherry pickers
17 Agent's cover
18 Asteroids, e.g.
20 Vehicle without wheels
21 Arctic explorer
22 Certain noisemakers
24 Encouraging word
25 Spanish suffix
26 Daffodil digs
27 Annual awards since '49
29 Egg follower
30 Depot stats.
32 Something prized
33 Worked on axles
35 Shows
39 Inc., in Ipswich
40 Witty remarks
41 Natural resource
42 1966 film role for Rudolph Nureyev
45 It's Big on the West Coast
46 "Whew!"
47 Trendy meat
48 Catching one's breath
52 *Pulp Fiction* character
53 Beast, to Bardot
55 Off-key
57 Eventual
59 World's third-largest island
60 Almost grown
61 Stevedore
62 Cast about

63 Decorate, as leather

DOWN

1 Cold
2 Story teller
3 From October 1957 to now
4 Arm bone
5 Cattails
6 German industrial center
7 Was upcoming
8 Out, at the dentist
9 Make a fly
10 Wayfarers' refuges
11 Sport with gates
12 With a whimper
13 Lindbergh's ancestors
15 Narrow squeaks
19 Turn
23 Slow flows
28 When Super Bowl XXXV was played
30 Legally impede
31 Media mogul's moniker
32 Pick up
34 Dark drink
35 Type of column

36 Assault-team member
37 Newbies
38 Toga wearers
40 Unkempt
42 Argues back
43 Folded fare
44 Grumble
45 Was right for
49 Saw
50 Lofty
51 Horse handler
54 German article
56 Like khaki
58 Big mouth

★★★★ One-Way Streets

The diagram represents a pattern of streets. P's are parking spaces, and the black squares are stores. Find the route that starts at a parking space, passes through all stores exactly once, and ends at the other parking space. Arrows indicate one-way traffic for that block only. No block or intersection may be entered more than once.

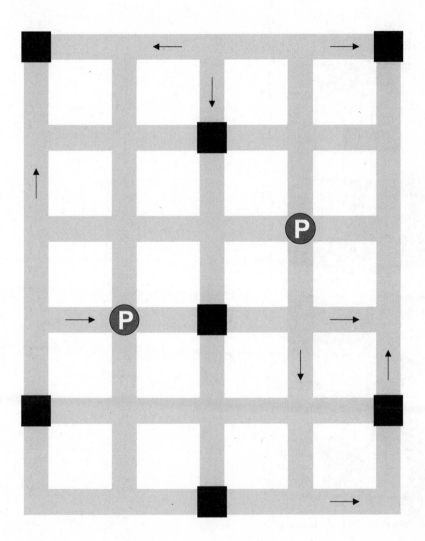

SOUND THINKING

There are three common seven-letter nouns whose only consonant sounds are M, S, T and R, in that order. Two of them are MASTERY and MYSTERY. What's the third?

_____

★★ Split Decisions

In this clueless crossword puzzle, each answer consists of two words whose spellings are the same, except for the consecutive letters given. All answers are common words; no phrases or hyphenated or capitalized words are used. Some of the clues may have more than one solution, but there is only one word pair that will correctly link up with all the other word pairs.

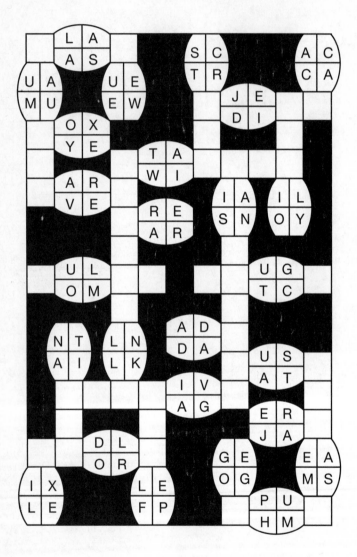

TRANSDELETION

Delete one letter from the word HEURISTIC and rearrange the rest, to get the last name of a famous author.

_____

★★★★★ Themeless Toughie by Doug Peterson

ACROSS

1 Snare sound
8 Tough spot
15 In la-la land
16 Swindled
17 Munster niece
18 Some holds
19 Crude
21 Onetime 44 Across commander
22 Menu warning word
25 Preserve, as beef
26 Not contrived
27 Elated state
28 Name meaning "honeybee"
30 Claim
32 Court, in a way
36 *Cross Creek* Oscar nominee
38 Learns thoroughly
39 Tip sources
41 Holds forth
42 Soul-food flavoring
44 Security org.
45 Estate of old
48 Hosiery shade
49 Dictionary format
50 Summit of Crete
51 Unwanted scales
53 Manager of the 2000 U.S. Olympic baseball team
55 Planetary path
59 Star followers
60 Investment firm employee
61 Colt's spot
62 Triangular sails

DOWN

1 Spirit of the Caribbean
2 Concert finale
3 Equinox mo.
4 Not running
5 Best-selling author of '76
6 Long-horned antelope
7 Whist holding
8 Post men
9 Castling candidate
10 Jackie Robinson's coll.
11 Sounds of confusion
12 Sap
13 Anthony Hope title locale
14 Henry's son
20 Fifth notes
22 Irwin and Robert
23 Job for Twain
24 Frozen digs
26 Regular workers
28 Bugling, for one
29 Brown some
31 Blowout
33 Relatively cool sun
34 On account of
35 Derby holder
37 Polished
40 Navajo art medium
43 __ aisle
45 Refuse
46 Lana Turner's birthplace
47 Sketchbook support
49 B analogue
51 "Fiddlesticks!"
52 It runs down your arm
54 Sacred syllables
56 *Ginger* __ (Newbery Medal winner)
57 ID with dashes
58 Sci-fi staples

★★★★ Looped Path

Draw a continuous, unbroken loop that passes through each of the red, blue, and white squares exactly once. Move from square to square in a straight line or by turning left or right, but never diagonally. You must alternate passing through red and blue squares, with any number of white squares in between. To get you started, part of the path is shown.

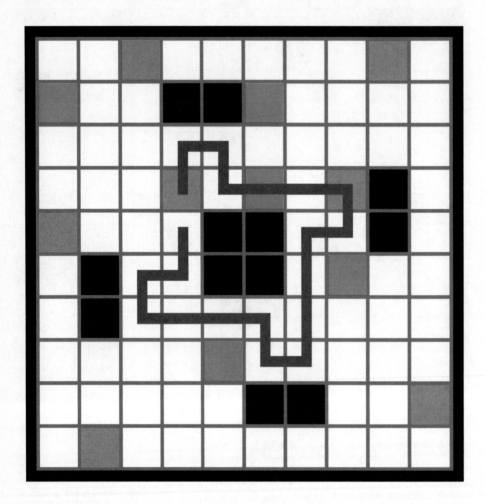

SAY IT AGAIN

What six-letter verb can mean either "oust" or "testify"?

— — — — — —

★★★★ Star Search

Find the stars that are hidden in some of the blank squares. The numbered squares indicate how many stars are hidden in the squares adjacent to them (including diagonally). There is never more than one star in any square.

TELEPHONE TRIOS

	ABC	DEF
1	**2**	**3**
GHI	JKL	MNO
4	**5**	**6**
PRS	TUV	WXY
7	**8**	**9**
*	**0**	**#**

Using the numbers and letters on a standard telephone, what three seven-letter words or phrases from the same category can be formed from these telephone numbers?

262-2537   _ _ _ _ _ _ _

783-3464   _ _ _ _ _ _ _

743-7238   _ _ _ _ _ _ _

★★★★★ Themeless Toughie by Daniel R. Stark

ACROSS

1 Place of action
8 Architectural detail
15 One of the enemy
16 Much of Ohio
17 Strong
18 Doesn't go
19 Barely make do, with "by"
20 Sports Almanac chapter
22 Way with words
23 Some officers
25 Quirk
26 Happen again
27 *Cope Book* aunt
28 Strike out
30 Bunyan's blacksmith
31 Pledged
33 __ suite
35 Moves slowly
37 Back-row cry
38 Give away
39 Hollywood Walk of Fame name since 4/20/06
40 Emerson genre
41 Experience déjà vu
43 Source of flavor
47 Names on pedigrees
49 Presidential nickname
50 More demure
51 Oreg., once
52 *90210* role
54 Superfund administrator
55 Showed well
57 Panoply
59 Throw off
60 Not open
61 Surprise hit
62 Lived

DOWN

1 Swipe
2 Impatient motorist
3 Admire
4 Downed
5 Window treatments
6 Additional
7 Writes over
8 Film repair
9 Son of Aphrodite
10 __-Pan (Clavell novel)
11 Word of Potsdam politesse

12 Geographical indicator
13 Leaflet
14 Small falcon
21 Green shade
24 Last year's
26 Second showing
28 Hackman, in *The French Connection*
29 Butcher buy
32 Gets threadbare
34 The Gem State
35 Very primitive
36 Countermand

37 Nectar source
38 Lineups
39 Instinctive feeling
42 Storage area
44 Shadow's place
45 Do roadwork
46 Laughed rudely
48 "Rubber Duckie" singer
50 *Residencias*
52 Phi __ (honor-society member)
53 Seedy stablishment
56 Surpass
58 Pressure meas.

★★★★ Number-Out

Shade squares so that no number appears in any row or column more than once. Shaded squares may not touch each other horizontally or vertically, and all unshaded squares must form a single continuous area.

4	3	1	5	1	6
5	1	3	2	5	3
3	3	6	5	4	1
5	4	1	6	5	3
6	5	4	5	3	5
2	6	2	1	2	4

OPPOSITE ATTRACTION

Unscramble the letters in the phrase PROPER TOT MIX to form two common words that are opposites of each other.

_____   _____

★★★★ Line Drawing

Draw a straight line from the top of the square to the bottom, so that all the letters in the "right" area have a certain characteristic that none of the letters in the "left" area have.

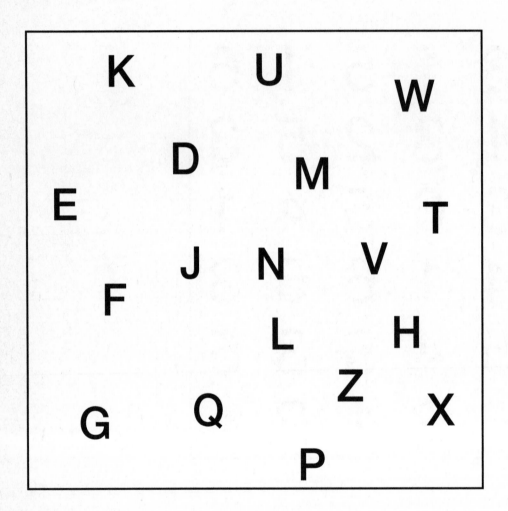

TWO-BY-FOUR

The eight letters in the word ABUNDANT can be rearranged to form a pair of common four-letter words in only one way, if no four-letter word is repeated. Can you find the two words?

— — — —   — — — —

★★★★★ Themeless Toughie by Anna Stiga

ACROSS

1 Headliners
11 Aces' spots
15 Hood associate
16 About
17 Boxing legend?
18 Branch of biol.
19 Busy times
20 Develop
22 Goal
23 Suspension subjects
26 Savage, for one
27 Tune (in)
28 Phrase of resignation
30 Film fan
34 Cost
35 Most likely to be called
36 Sounded disappointed
39 Jeremy Irons voice role
40 One bit
42 Theme-park rides, often
44 Pardons
47 Put forward
48 Long beginning
49 Some ties
51 Shakes: Abbr.
54 Lindbergh Field locale
56 Appropriate
58 Muse of history
59 Source of gossip
62 Beethoven's first?
63 Image on the Oregon state quarter
64 Marinade ingredient
65 Good judgment

DOWN

1 Dusky color
2 '60s *Action Comics* regular
3 Appeal
4 Elevator arrangement
5 Inability to smell
6 "I'm gonna pass!"
7 Bother
8 She had Fay's role in the newest *King Kong*
9 Basic
10 Sonnet section
11 Fishing spot
12 Rhythmically
13 Concept in cosmology
14 Knobs on old TVs
21 SALT signatory
24 Brewery device
25 Crunchy lunches
27 Passes out
29 Butter up, perhaps
30 Unites
31 Among others
32 Putting straight
33 Scratch (out)
37 Convention-center show
38 Mousetrap maker
41 Focal points
43 Stock origins
45 Chase's detective
46 *Pinocchio* kitten
50 __ bear
51 '80s middleweight champ
52 Odysseys
53 Big fling
55 How much you can take
57 Tent event
60 Outworlders of fiction
61 Mockingbird snack

★★ Triad Split Decisions

In this clueless crossword puzzle, each answer consists of two words whose spellings are the same, except for the consecutive letters given. All answers are common words; no phrases or hyphenated or capitalized words are used. Some of the clues may have more than one solution, but there is only one word pair that will correctly link up with all the other word pairs.

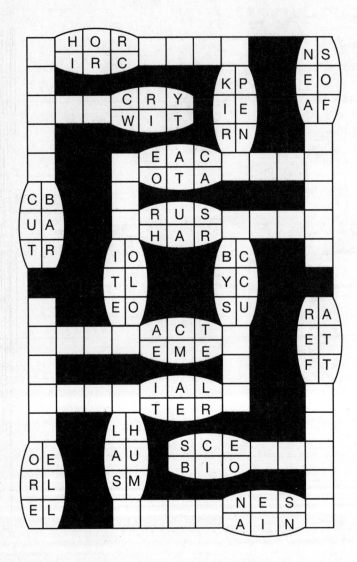

TRANSDELETION

Delete one letter from the word FOSTERABLE and rearrange the rest, to get a two-word term for a dinner entrée.

_____

★★★ Piece It Together

Fill in the blue design using pieces with the same shape outlined in black. Some pieces are "mirror-image" versions of the shape shown.

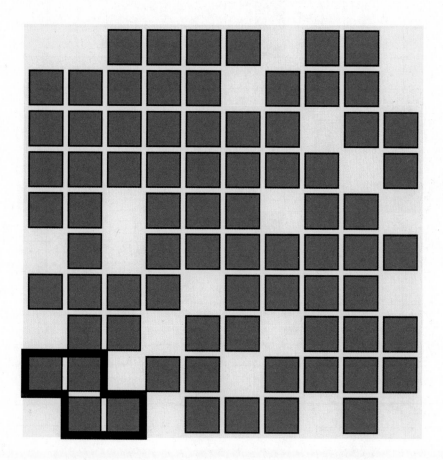

THREE AT A RHYME

Rearrange these letters to form three one-syllable words that rhyme.

A C C C E E H H H L P R R R S U

_____   _____   _____

★★★★★ Themeless Toughie by Daniel R. Stark

ACROSS

1 Biting work
7 Lotion ingredient
15 Part of an ear
16 Went off the track
17 Orchid-like flowers
18 Got past
19 Duty
20 Steel-plow inventor
22 High land
23 Excessive interest
25 Sings gaily
27 Hindu title
28 Speck of dust
29 Fidgety
30 European capital
31 Court statement
33 Decorate, as a tee
35 Fruit in a mixed drink
36 Arthur Miller title characters
37 Gauge
40 "Gateway to the West"
44 Put the pedal to the metal
45 Touches up
47 Fleming fiend
48 Jabba adversary
49 Finely contoured
50 Look after
51 Godzilla: Save the Earth maker
53 Nash creature
55 Clock numeral
56 Arose
58 Latest news
60 Stretch out
61 Turns
62 Approached sunset
63 Small hole

DOWN

1 Vail feature
2 Product delivery system
3 Compliment
4 Connections
5 Woodwindlike
6 Choice introducer
7 Like some fans
8 Pulls down
9 Nickel source
10 Pulls down
11 Bad habit
12 Slipped by
13 Tie a new knot
14 "The flower of my heart"
21 Uncle Vanya character
24 Enjoyed, as benefits
26 Wyoming range
29 December purchase
30 Next to
32 Bad-mouth
34 Lodge
36 Alaska's first capital
37 Far from proud
38 Kitchen helper
39 Impeachment juror
40 Exercised
41 Triumph
42 Give the right
43 50 Down to the max
46 Erase
49 Burn slightly
50 Sentimental
52 Penguins' milieu
54 Reflect
57 Glasgow prename
59 Hammerstein female

PAGE 17

Off-White

S	W	A	P	S		S	N	A	P		C	R	A	B
H	A	D	A	T		H	E	R	O		R	A	C	E
I	V	O	R	Y	T	O	W	E	R		E	I	R	E
P	E	R		L	E	O	S		T	R	A	D	E	R
	R	E	P	E	N	T		S	I	A	M			
		E	S	E		S	L	O	T	C	A	R		
S	O	D	A		T	A	L	O	N		H	A	U	L
C	H	E	R			L	I	P			E	R	L	E
H	I	L	L		T	O	N	E	R		E	P	E	E
	O	L	D	S	O	N	G		A	D	S			
		I	S	L	E		S	N	E	E	R	S		
S	H	O	V	E	L		S	E	C	T		A	P	E
T	A	P	E		B	O	N	E	H	E	A	D	E	D
O	V	E	R		A	L	U	M		S	L	A	N	G
P	E	N	S		R	E	B	S		T	A	R	D	Y

PAGE 18

Minty

CENTURY MARKS
52 + 12 − 1 + 39 + 4 − 6 = 100

PAGE 19

Stress-Free

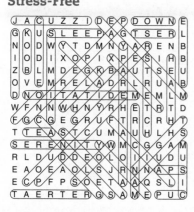

INITIAL REACTION
Love Is Blind

PAGE 20

Sudoku

6	2	5	9	8	4	3	1	7
3	7	8	2	6	1	4	5	9
4	9	1	5	7	3	6	8	2
2	6	3	8	9	5	7	4	1
7	8	4	3	1	2	5	9	6
5	1	9	7	4	6	8	2	3
1	3	2	4	5	7	9	6	8
8	5	7	6	2	9	1	3	4
9	4	6	1	3	8	2	7	5

MIXAGRAMS

C A R A T   S I T E
A G I L E   C U R B
H O N O R   O P U S
R I G I D   L I E N

PAGE 21

Sign Here

G	R	I	M	M		L	A	N	D		P	A	S	T
H	E	N	C	E		A	L	A	I		H	O	P	E
I	N	C	A	S		W	E	T	S		D	R	O	P
J	O	H	N	H	A	N	C	O	C	K		T	O	E
			E	T	S			U	N	S	A	F	E	
H	A	I	R	D	O		V	I	S	I	T			
A	C	R	E		M	A	I	N		F	O	U	L	S
T	H	O	M	A	S	J	E	F	F	E	R	S	O	N
S	E	N	O	R		A	W	O	L		E	S	S	O
			V	E	E	R	S		A	N	D	R	E	W
A	P	P	E	A	R		D	I	E					
V	I	E		S	A	M	U	E	L	A	D	A	M	S
O	A	R	S		S	A	K	E		R	O	B	O	T
I	N	I	T		E	Y	E	D		E	V	I	T	A
D	O	L	L		R	O	S	S		D	E	T	E	R

PAGE 22

Fences

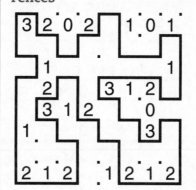

ADDITION SWITCH
3 4 8 + 2 9 3 = 6 4 1

PAGE 23

Line Drawing

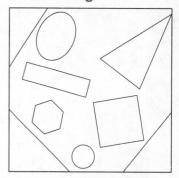

THREE OF A KIND
YELLOW HATS ARE CONSIDERED STYLISH IN WEST VIRGINIA.

PAGE 24

Sporting Chance

WHO'S WHAT WHERE?
Beiruti

PAGE 25

Woodwork

R	A	D	A	R		B	O	O	M		A	R	E	A
E	R	O	D	E		A	L	M	A		T	E	M	P
A	L	O	O	F		T	E	A	R		L	A	C	E
P	O	R		F	L	O	O	R	T	R	A	D	E	R
		P	R	E	E	N			Y	E	S	Y	E	S
S	T	R	I	D	E		P	A	R	E				
A	R	I	D		K	N	O	B		D	I	T	T	O
G	A	Z	E		S	A	L	E	S		S	A	I	L
E	M	E	R	Y		M	O	T	E		A	B	L	E
			O	R	E	S		W	H	A	L	E	S	
A	L	A	S	K	A		P	E	A	C	E			
D	E	C	K	O	F	C	A	R	D	S		L	O	U
M	A	R	E		T	O	N	E		S	P	A	N	S
I	S	E	E		E	A	T	S		L	A	N	C	E
T	E	S	T		R	T	E	S		E	L	D	E	R

PAGE 26
Number-Out

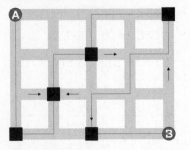

OPPOSITE ATTRACTION
FAR, NEAR

PAGE 27
Sequence Maze

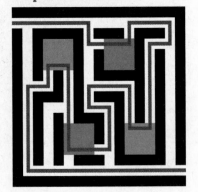

THREE AT A RHYME
SO, DOE, KNOW

PAGE 28
Celebrities of the Month

S	U	M	S		S	L	U	M		S	A	J	A	K
T	R	E	E		C	A	N	E		E	X	U	D	E
I	S	N	T		O	D	D	S		A	L	L	A	Y
R	A	U	L	J	U	L	I	A		S	E	E	M	S
		O	A	R	E	D		H	I	S	S			
M	A	J	O	R			S	O	D		V	E	G	
O	N	U	S		E	L	A	P	S	E		E	V	E
O	G	L	E		J	U	L	I	E		F	R	E	E
E	L	I		L	E	G	E	N	D		I	N	N	S
D	O	O		A	C	E			C	R	E	T	E	
	G	U	S	T		C	A	R	D	S				
S	W	A	N	S		J	U	L	E	S	T	Y	N	E
H	E	L	L	O		U	R	G	E		A	M	E	R
O	L	L	I	E		L	I	E	S		I	C	E	R
P	L	O	T	S		Y	O	R	E		D	A	D	S

PAGE 29
One-Way Streets

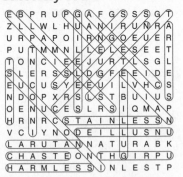

SOUND THINKING
EUPHORIA

PAGE 30
Split Decisions

TRANSDELETION
SUPERIOR

PAGE 31
Star Search

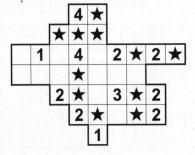

TELEPHONE TRIOS
AFFABLE, AMIABLE, CORDIAL

PAGE 32
Sincerely Yours

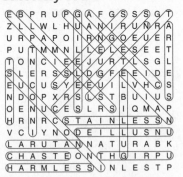

Unlisted word is HARMLESS

IN OTHER WORDS
DUMBBELL

PAGE 33
Pairs of Fives

C	O	V	E		S	T	A	T		A	S	S	E	T
O	V	A	L		A	U	R	A		S	I	L	L	S
M	E	N	U		G	R	I	N		C	L	A	M	P
B	R	I	D	E	A	N	D	G	R	O	O	M		
E	D	S	E	L			L	O	T			B	O	O
D	O	H		P	E	R	M	E	D		L	A	K	E
		W	A	Y	N	E			S	O	N	A	R	
H	O	R	S	E	A	N	D	B	U	G	G	Y		
M	I	N	E	O		S	A	Y	N	O				
E	V	E	N		T	R	A	D	E	D		G	A	B
L	E	S		L	E	E			A	B	A	T	E	
	T	R	I	A	L	A	N	D	E	R	R	O	R	
O	L	E	O	S		I	S	E	E		A	N	N	E
D	E	P	O	T		C	I	T	E		S	E	C	T
D	I	S	K	S		S	A	S	S		S	T	E	S

PAGE 34
Hyper-Sudoku

8	4	1	3	6	9	2	5	7
7	3	9	2	8	5	1	4	6
2	6	5	4	1	7	8	3	9
3	1	8	7	4	6	9	2	5
5	9	6	8	2	1	4	7	3
4	2	7	9	5	3	6	8	1
9	5	4	6	3	2	7	1	8
6	8	3	1	7	4	5	9	2
1	7	2	5	9	8	3	6	4

MIXAGRAMS

L	A	R	G	E		C	U	B	E
I	R	K	E	D		S	T	U	B
F	L	O	R	A		A	G	O	G
E	L	U	D	E		B	U	Y	S

PAGE 35

You're Booked

Don & *Dracula's Dilemma*, Jen & *Climb That Career Ladder*, Steve & *Knights of Passion*, Vanessa & *Darcy the Divine*

BETWEENER
CAR

PAGE 36

123

SUDOKU SUM
4 2 9 + 1 0 8 = 5 3 7

PAGE 37

Soon Enough

C	L	U	E		C	U	F	F		S	P	O	T	S
H	I	L	T		O	S	L	O		T	E	P	E	E
I	N	T	H	E	N	E	A	R	F	U	T	U	R	E
M	E	R	I	T	S			G	E	N	E	S	I	S
E	N	A	C	T		E	D	E	N					
			U	P	S	E	T		F	A	K	E	S	
E	R	A	S		R	P	M		S	A	T	I	R	E
B	E	F	O	R	E	Y	O	U	K	N	O	W	I	T
B	A	R	L	E	Y		T	R	I		P	I	N	S
S	P	O	O	F		S	E	N	D	S				
			E	T	D	S		O	P	A	L	S		
A	T	P	E	A	C	E			T	R	E	B	L	E
J	U	S	T	D	O	W	N	T	H	E	R	O	A	D
A	B	A	T	E		E	R	I	E		P	U	M	A
R	A	T	E	S		D	A	N	E		S	T	A	N

PAGE 38

ABC

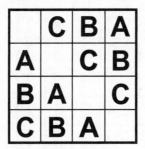

CLUELESS CROSSWORD

PAGE 39

Find the Ships

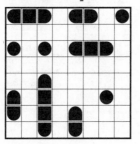

TWO-BY-FOUR
DUET, TOAD; DEAD, TOUT

PAGE 40

Ports of Call

Missing port is ROTTERDAM

INITIAL REACTION
Like Father, Like Son

PAGE 41

Out of Shape

PAGE 42

Baseball Maze

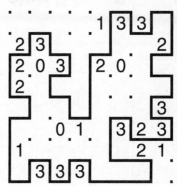

THREE AT A RHYME
GOO, RUE, WHO

PAGE 43

Fences

ADDITION SWITCH
7 0 9 + 1 1 8 = 8 2 7

PAGE 44

About Time

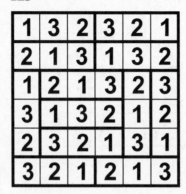

Unlisted words are TOMORROW and YESTERDAY

WHO'S WHAT WHERE?
Ivorian

PAGE 45

Business Reading

MIXAGRAMS
```
S H O W N     W A D E
S C R O D     O L E O
C O L O R     R U L E
D I O D E     K N O B
```

PAGE 46

Sudoku

7	6	2	9	3	5	8	1	4
8	3	4	1	6	7	5	2	9
1	9	5	8	4	2	7	6	3
4	7	3	5	8	1	2	9	6
9	5	1	6	2	4	3	7	8
6	2	8	7	9	3	1	4	5
3	1	6	4	7	8	9	5	2
2	4	7	3	5	9	6	8	1
5	8	9	2	1	6	4	3	7

PAGE 47

123

1	3	2	3	2	1
2	1	3	1	3	2
1	2	1	3	2	3
3	1	3	2	1	2
2	3	2	1	3	1
3	2	1	2	1	3

SUDOKU SUM
$147 + 209 = 356$

PAGE 48

Rail Journey

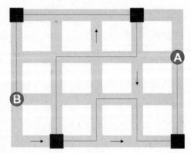

PAGE 49

One-Way Streets

SOUND THINKING
BESIEGE

PAGE 50

Maple Leaf Maze

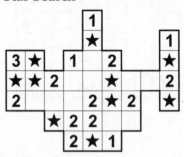

SAY IT AGAIN
TOP

PAGE 51

Star Search

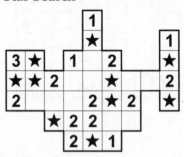

TELEPHONE TRIOS
OUTLINE, RUNDOWN, SUMMARY

PAGE 52

In the Trenches

```
P E T E R   I N F O   R E N O
A D A G E   M O A N   O L E O
P I T O F T H E S T O M A C H
A T A   W I L T   B A L K S
  G R I P   B O O N
S O B E I T   S A L E S R E P
U S I N G   C O L D   O R O
M A K E S A H O L E I N O N E
U K E   B A T S   R E M I T
P A R T N E R S   B O S S E S
  S E T A   A I N T
S H A K E   C A S T   C A P
L A S T D I T C H E F F O R T
I R I S   M E R E   A O R T A
D E S K   P R E S   D R E S S
```

PAGE 53

Airport Whodunit

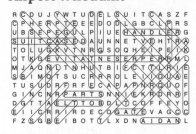

Flavia the Flight Attendant did it, with a sleep mask in the VIP area

IN OTHER WORDS
CRANKCASE

PAGE 55

Line Drawing

THREE OF A KIND
CALL AUNTIE DORIS IN FOR SUPPER.

PAGE 56

ABC

A	C	B	
B	A	C	
A	C	B	
C	B	A	

NATIONAL TREASURE
AERIAL

PAGE 57

Tabby Toys

G A S P	A R C S	A T S E A
A S T O	B U L L	S E A L S
S H I N	B E A U	T E L L S
C O R D L E S S M O U S E		
A R I S E	S P O T	S A Y
P E N	V I P	S H E L T I E
M E D I A	E A R N	
F I R S T S T R I N G		
H A L L	H E A D S	
A L A D D I N	A W E	F B I
T I M	R O A D	A A R O N
I N A U G U R A L B A L L		
H A N O I	G N A W	A N T E
E G G O N	E N C L	S C O T
P E O N S	D O E S	H E N S

PAGE 58

Five by Five

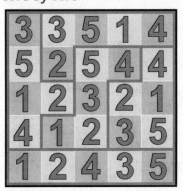

BETWEENER
WOOD

PAGE 59

???

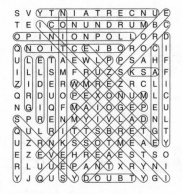

INITIAL REACTION
A Watched Pot Never Boils

PAGE 60

Find the Ships

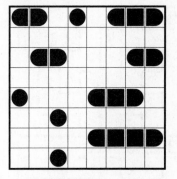

TWO-BY-FOUR
FAIR, EPIC; PICA, FIRE (or RIFE)

PAGE 61

Sudoku

7	3	4	8	6	1	9	2	5
6	1	9	5	2	7	8	4	3
8	2	5	3	4	9	7	6	1
5	9	8	6	7	3	2	1	4
3	4	7	9	1	2	5	8	6
2	6	1	4	5	8	3	9	7
9	7	3	1	8	6	4	5	2
1	5	2	7	9	4	6	3	8
4	8	6	2	3	5	1	7	9

MIXAGRAMS
S A V O R	V I E S
O M E G A	B O L T
T E M P O	S W A B
A S K E W	W A L L

PAGE 62

What's On Today?

C R O P		A G A I N		L I M A
R A K E		R A N T O		U N I V
O G L E		E N A C T		N A S A
W E A R I N G T H E P A N T S				
	M A S		C R E S T	
C U T I E S		A B E T		
O P E R A		C U E S		T W A S
L O S I N G O N E S S H I R T				
A N T S		E A T S		P E N C E
	E E L S		S A N E S T	
S A G A S			A C T	
C L O S E T O O N E S V E S T				
A T T Y		A K R O N		A R E A
R A T E		G R A D E		S I L L
F R A T		S A L E S		T E L L

PAGE 63

Fences

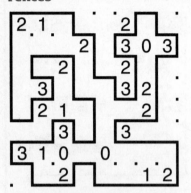

ADDITION SWITCH

5 3 5 + 2 9 6 = 8 3 1

PAGE 64

Triad Split Decisions

TRANSDELETION

WITNESS

PAGE 65

123

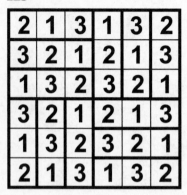

SUDOKU SUM

5 7 6 + 3 1 4 = 8 9 0

PAGE 66

Crispy

PAGE 67

Number-Out

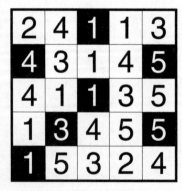

OPPOSITE ATTRACTION

ODD, EVEN

PAGE 68

Tanks A Lot

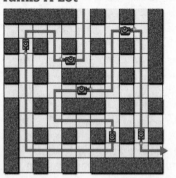

SAY IT AGAIN

BIT

PAGE 69

The Main Thing

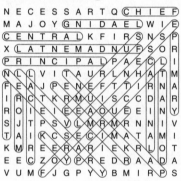

Unlisted word is ESSENTIAL

WHO'S WHAT WHERE?

Carioca

PAGE 70

At the Barber

I	D	E	A	S		L	E	N	A		A	N	N	E
T	E	L	L	A		A	G	O	G		P	O	O	L
C	L	I	P	P	I	N	G	C	O	U	P	O	N	S
H	A	S	H		V	E	S	T		P	E	K	O	E
		A	P	E	S		U	R	S	A				
S	C	U	B	A	S		I	R	E		L	E	S	S
E	A	T	E	N		I	N	N	E	R		D	N	A
C	U	T	T	I	N	G	C	A	L	O	R	I	E	S
T	S	E		C	A	N	A	L		P	A	C	E	S
S	E	R	B		S	O	S		S	E	N	T	R	Y
		O	M	A	R		C	A	S	A				
A	C	H	O	O		A	M	I	S		F	A	W	N
T	R	I	M	M	I	N	G	T	H	E	T	R	E	E
M	O	V	E		A	C	M	E		B	E	E	P	S
S	P	E	D		N	E	T	S		B	R	A	T	S

PAGE 71
One-Way Streets

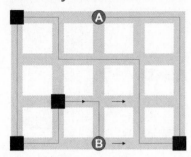

SOUND THINKING
ODDITIES

PAGE 72
Hyper-Sudoku

4	5	2	9	1	7	3	6	8
6	9	7	8	2	3	4	5	1
8	3	1	4	5	6	2	7	9
3	2	6	5	4	9	8	1	7
7	1	4	6	3	8	5	9	2
5	8	9	1	7	2	6	4	3
1	4	3	2	9	5	7	8	6
2	6	5	7	8	1	9	3	4
9	7	8	3	6	4	1	2	5

CENTURY MARKS
$11 + 8 - 3 + 61 + 14 + 9 = 100$

PAGE 73
Star Search

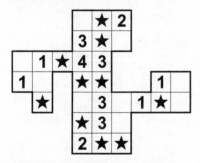

TELEPHONE TRIOS
BRING UP, MENTION, SUGGEST

PAGE 74
Flying Starts

S	A	S	H		G	A	M	E		S	T	P	A	T
A	L	M	A		A	S	E	A		C	A	I	R	O
L	O	A	N		S	T	A	R		O	T	T	E	R
T	H	R	O	W	P	I	L	L	O	W		C	A	N
S	A	T	I	R	E			B	L	A	H			
			I	D	O	T	O	O		I	D	E	A	
L	A	S	T	S		L	A	C	E		M	A	R	S
A	L	L	O	T		S	P	A		S	T	R	I	P
S	T	I	R		H	E	E	L		P	O	K	E	S
S	O	N	S		O	N	S	A	L	E				
			G	O	S	H			U	N	I	T	E	S
L	A	B		T	O	S	S	A	N	D	T	U	R	N
I	R	A	T	E		W	I	N	G		E	L	I	E
N	I	C	E	R		A	L	O	E		M	I	C	E
T	A	K	E	N		P	O	N	D		S	P	A	R

PAGE 75
ABC

CLUELESS CROSSWORD

E	M	E	R	A	L	D
Y		C		R		E
E	T	H	I	C	A	L
L		E		H		U
A	L	L	O	W	E	D
S		O		A		E
H	O	N	E	Y	E	D

PAGE 76
Dicey

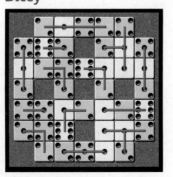

BETWEENER
TAIL

PAGE 77
Sudoku

3	5	4	9	1	2	8	6	7
6	9	1	3	7	8	4	5	2
7	8	2	4	6	5	1	9	3
1	6	8	5	3	9	2	7	4
5	7	3	2	4	6	9	8	1
2	4	9	1	8	7	6	3	5
9	3	5	8	2	4	7	1	6
8	2	7	6	5	1	3	4	9
4	1	6	7	9	3	5	2	8

MIXAGRAMS
S P O O K   G O D S
B U R S T   O V A L
A S S E T   M E L T
T H O R N   A R C S

PAGE 78
Family Viewing

B	E	S	T		W	E	E	D		A	B	H	O	R
A	U	T	O		A	X	L	E		T	I	A	R	A
T	R	U	E		R	I	S	E		E	G	R	E	T
S	O	B		S	I	S	T	E	R		O	B	E	S	E
			D	A	S			F	U	R				
T	V	S	H	O	W		T	O	R	T	O	I	S	E
H	A	L	O	S		P	I	N	E		T	R	I	P
E	L	A	L		C	A	R	E	D		H	O	N	E
T	O	N	Y		A	L	E	S		P	E	N	C	E
A	R	T	F	O	R	M	S		H	O	R	S	E	S
			A	N	T			G	A	L				
R	A	N	T	S		D	E	N	M	O	T	H	E	R
A	L	O	H	A		O	R	A	L		H	I	D	E
P	A	N	E	L		L	I	T	E		A	R	I	D
S	N	O	R	E		T	E	S	T		W	E	T	S

PAGE 79
Line Drawing

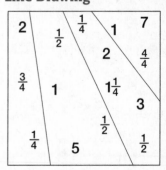

THREE OF A KIND
PAGO PA<u>GO, IN GENERAL,</u>
IS A <u>MYSTERY</u> TO PEOPLE
FROM NOR<u>WAY.</u>

PAGE 80

Find the Ships

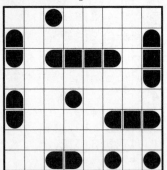

TWO-BY-FOUR
LINT, QUAY

PAGE 81

Fences

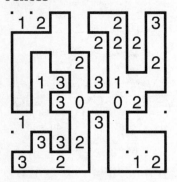

ADDITION SWITCH
309 + 276 = 585

PAGE 82

Cosmetic Counter

S H O P		S A S S Y		A P E D
H U L L		A B A T E		T O R E
A R E A		L O F A T		T W I N
G L O S S O V E R			T I D E S
	T I N E		P O R E	
A D M I T S		F A L T E R E D
T R A C E		S I L O S		B R A
W O K S		T H R O W		F L A T
A V E	C R U E T		P A U S E
R E U N I O N S		P U R E E S
	P E A T		R O S E	
P A T I O		B L U S H W I N E
O L E G		P E O N S		E D D Y
P O S H		E E R I E		L E A R
S E T S		W R E N S		L A K E

PAGE 83

Knot or Not?
Knot: 2 and 3, Not: 1 and 4

THREE AT A RHYME
BE, LEA, KNEE

PAGE 84

123

3	1	2	1	2	3	1	3	2
2	3	1	3	1	2	3	2	1
1	2	3	2	3	1	2	1	3
2	3	1	3	1	2	3	2	1
1	2	3	1	2	3	1	3	2
2	3	1	2	3	1	2	1	3
3	1	2	1	2	3	1	3	2
1	2	3	2	3	1	2	1	3
3	1	2	3	1	2	3	2	1

SUDOKU SUM
294 + 381 = 675

PAGE 85

Number-Out

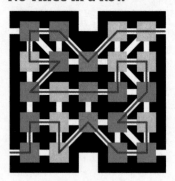

OPPOSITE ATTRACTION
FAST, SLOW

PAGE 86

By the Pound

PAGE 87

No Three in a Row

SAY IT AGAIN
HOT

PAGE 88

Split Decisions

TRANSDELETION
GRANDPA

PAGE 89

Hyper-Sudoku

8	7	4	9	1	2	5	6	3
5	9	3	8	4	6	7	1	2
6	1	2	5	7	3	4	8	9
3	4	6	7	8	5	2	9	1
9	8	5	2	6	1	3	7	4
1	2	7	3	9	4	8	5	6
7	6	8	4	2	9	1	3	5
4	5	9	1	3	7	6	2	8
2	3	1	6	5	8	9	4	7

MIXAGRAMS

TOKEN LACE
SPINE HIRE
BINGE VIAL
MOGUL RUBY

PAGE 90

What's Cooking

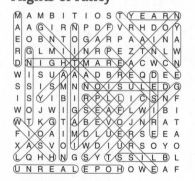

PAGE 91

Flights of Fancy

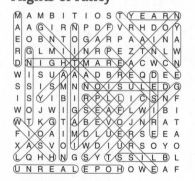

IN OTHER WORDS

HOOFPRINT

PAGE 93

One-Way Streets

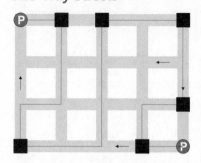

SOUND THINKING

OFFSHORE

PAGE 94

Skiing Is Believing

PAGE 95

Missing Links

THREE AT A RHYME

DIM, GYM, WHIM

PAGE 96

Star Search

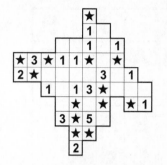

TELEPHONE TRIOS

EXAMINE, INSPECT, OBSERVE

PAGE 97

Triad Split Decisions

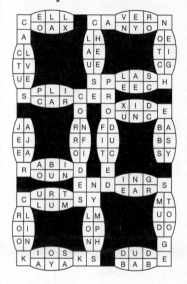

TRANSDELETION

LOCUST

PAGE 98

Speeding

L	A	F	F		G	R	I	T		A	W	A	S	H
A	R	I	A		R	E	L	O		D	E	L	T	A
T	S	E	T	S	E	F	L	Y		O	A	T	E	R
T	O	N		A	T	E			S	E	R	R	A	T	E
E	N	D	U	S	E	R	S		M	E	A			
			N	H	L		E	T	E	R	N	I	T	Y
A	S	E	A		B	A	E	R		D	R	E	D	
P	L	E	A		A	L	L	E	Y		T	A	N	S
O	P	E	R		L	E	A	N		P	E	N	T	
W	O	R	N	D	O	W	N		S	R	A			
			E	R	N		T	H	E	O	R	I	Z	E
H	O	T	D	O	G	S		O	L	A		N	E	T
A	D	O	R	N		T	W	O	E	M	D	A	S	H
S	E	G	U	E		E	V	E	N		A	N	T	I
T	R	A	N	S		M	A	Y	A		D	E	S	C

PAGE 99

ABC

A		C		B
B	A			C
C			B	A
	B	A	C	
	C	B	A	

NATIONAL TREASURE
CANDLE, DENIAL

PAGE 100

Find the Ships

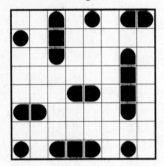

TWO-BY-FOUR
GAIN, RIOT (or TRIO); GAIT, IRON; IOTA, RING (or GRIN)

PAGE 101

On the Circuit

O	F	F		A	D	D	T	O		A	V	A	I	L
A	L	I		L	A	U	R	A		V	E	R	D	I
S	O	N		I	N	N	E	R	C	I	R	C	L	E
I	R	A		M	A	K	E		H	A	S	H	E	D
S	A	L	M	O	N	S		B	I	T	E			
		R	A	N	G		P	E	S	O		V	A	L
E	M	O	R	Y		D	I	V	E	R	S	I	F	Y
L	A	U	D		H	O	T	E	L		A	C	R	E
M	U	N	I	C	I	P	A	L		A	L	T	O	S
O	L	D		A	L	E	S		A	L	S	O		
		A	R	T	S		A	T	L	A	R	G	E	
O	V	E	R	D	O		A	L	O	E		Y	E	N
W	E	D	D	I	N	G	R	I	N	G		L	T	D
L	I	N	E	N		P	I	E	C	E		A	T	E
S	L	A	N	G		S	A	N	E	R		P	O	D

PAGE 102

Two Pairs

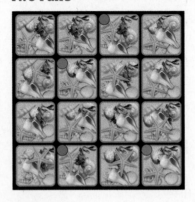

BETWEENER
HEAD

PAGE 103

Sudoku

8	2	5	3	1	6	7	9	4
7	1	4	9	5	8	3	2	6
9	6	3	7	2	4	8	5	1
1	5	9	8	6	3	4	7	2
2	7	8	1	4	9	6	3	5
3	4	6	2	7	5	9	1	8
4	3	7	5	8	1	2	6	9
5	8	2	6	9	7	1	4	3
6	9	1	4	3	2	5	8	7

MIXAGRAMS

A	B	O	U	T		R	A	F	T
V	I	S	O	R		A	K	I	N
S	K	E	I	N		C	L	O	G
N	E	E	D	Y		K	I	L	N

PAGE 104

Fences

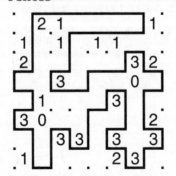

ADDITION SWITCH
2 8 3 + 3 5 9 = 6 4 2

PAGE 105

Crossing Words

PAGE 106

Number-Out

3	6	2	5	4	2
1	4	2	4	5	1
5	3	2	6	2	4
4	5	6	3	5	5
2	4	3	6	6	6
1	5	1	2	3	6

OPPOSITE ATTRACTION
BIG, SMALL

PAGE 107

Hyper-Sudoku

3	9	8	1	6	5	7	4	2
7	6	1	4	8	2	9	3	5
4	5	2	9	3	7	8	6	1
6	8	3	7	2	4	5	1	9
5	7	4	3	1	9	6	2	8
2	1	9	8	5	6	3	7	4
8	4	5	6	7	1	2	9	3
1	3	7	2	9	8	4	5	6
9	2	6	5	4	3	1	8	7

CENTURY MARKS
12 + 25 + 26 + 42 - 5 = 100

PAGE 108
Article Three

S	H	A	M		S	T	A	B		S	E	D	E	R
P	O	L	O		T	O	G	A		T	A	U	P	E
A	B	E	T		A	P	E	R		A	T	S	E	A
R	O	S	I	E	T	H	E	R	I	V	E	T	E	R
		F	L	E	A		E	D	E	N				
S	A	P		E	S	T	A	T	E	S		C	A	B
A	L	I	E	N		P	T	A		D	O	D	O	
S	I	N	B	A	D	T	H	E	S	A	I	L	O	R
S	N	U	B		U	R	I		L	E	A	R	N	
Y	E	P		F	E	U	D	I	N	G		S	E	E
			A	R	T	S		C	I	A	O			
D	E	N	N	I	S	T	H	E	M	E	N	A	C	E
E	M	O	T	E		I	A	M	B		S	I	L	L
B	I	S	O	N		E	T	A	L		E	R	A	S
T	R	E	N	D		R	E	N	E			T	Y	P	E

PAGE 109
Lily List

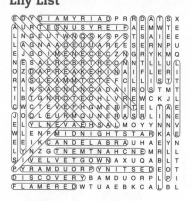

INITIAL REACTION
The Early Bird Catches The Worm

PAGE 110
Sets of Three

SAY IT AGAIN
KIND

PAGE 111
Builders' Quartet

A	R	M	S		H	E	W	S		A	Q	A	B	A
P	E	A	L		A	L	O	E		L	U	M	E	T
I	N	C	A		N	I	L	E		T	E	P	E	E
N	E	R	V	E	S	O	F	S	T	E	E	L		
G	E	O		R	O	T	E		A	R	R	I	V	E
		A	I	L		P	R	E		T	A	R		
K	N	O	C	K	O	N	W	O	O	D		U	S	A
L	O	U	T		E	A	R		O	D	E	S		
I	T	T		B	R	I	C	K	C	H	E	E	S	E
N	E	E		E	O	N		H	U	D				
E	R	R	A	T	A		S	C	A	R		F	O	E
	S	T	O	N	E	P	H	I	L	L	I	P	S	
S	T	O	R	K		G	O	O	N		A	X	E	S
O	L	L	I	E		G	O	R	E		S	E	R	A
O	C	E	A	N		S	K	E	D		T	R	A	Y

PAGE 112
One-Way Streets

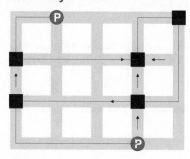

SOUND THINKING
GALLERY

PAGE 113
123

1	2	1	3	2	3	1	2	3
2	3	2	1	3	1	2	3	1
3	1	3	2	1	2	1	2	3
2	3	1	3	2	1	3	1	2
1	2	3	2	1	3	2	3	1
3	1	2	1	3	2	3	1	2
2	3	1	3	2	1	2	3	1
1	2	3	2	1	3	1	2	3
3	1	2	1	3	2	3	1	2

SUDOKU SUM
$381 + 546 = 927$

PAGE 114
Line Drawing

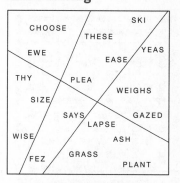

The words in each region have the same vowel sound

THREE OF A KIND
THAT PIRANHA STEAK ON A MAKESHIFT PLATTER—IT WAS TERRIBLE!

PAGE 115
How Clever

E	M	I	T	S		C	A	B	S		A	B	E	T
B	E	R	R	A		U	T	A	H		E	R	L	E
B	R	A	I	N	D	R	A	I	N		R	I	L	E
S	E	N	D	E	R		D	U	O		A	G	I	N
			E	R	O	S		L	O	A	T	H	E	S
D	A	W	N		O	L	E		K	N	O	T		
U	N	I	T		P	I	M	A		E	R	I	C	A
M	T	S		E	Y	E	B	R	O	W		D	O	S
P	I	E	T	A		R	E	N	D		T	E	N	S
	C	A	S	T		R	A	D		E	A	S	T	
C	A	R	R	Y	O	N		Z	E	T	A			
I	V	A	N		N	I	P		S	O	R	A	R	E
V	I	C	I		S	M	A	R	T	M	O	N	E	Y
I	L	K	S		I	O	W	A		B	O	N	E	R
C	A	S	H		L	Y	N	N		S	M	O	K	E

PAGE 116
Star Search

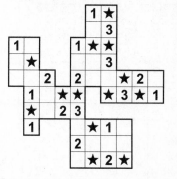

TELEPHONE TRIOS
AWESOME, STELLAR, SUBLIME

PAGE 117
Sequence Maze

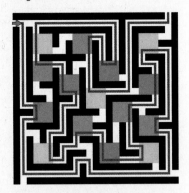

THREE AT A RHYME
IRK, LURK, PERK

PAGE 118
Women's Day

M	O	O	R		H	A	S	P		O	M	E	G	A
A	R	L	O		A	X	E	S		P	A	R	E	S
D	E	E	M		C	L	A	Y		P	L	I	N	K
	S	O	P	H	I	E	S	C	H	O	I	C	E	
		S	U	E			H	A	S				
M	S	T		E	N	D	S		M	I	S	T	E	R
A	C	H	E		D	I	A	L		T	A	R	R	Y
M	A	R	T	H	A	S	V	I	N	E	Y	A	R	D
A	R	E	N	A		H	E	R	A		S	L	O	E
S	E	W	A	R	D		D	E	M	O		A	R	R
		D	O	H			E	R	A				
	R	O	S	E	M	A	R	Y	S	B	A	B	Y	
S	E	V	E	N		S	H	E	A		R	O	O	T
A	D	E	L	E		T	E	A	K		O	L	G	A
W	O	R	L	D		E	A	S	E		N	O	I	R

PAGE 119
Hyper-Sudoku

8	6	3	5	1	2	9	7	4
5	1	7	9	6	4	8	3	2
9	4	2	3	8	7	6	5	1
4	5	8	6	3	1	2	9	7
6	7	1	2	9	5	4	8	3
2	3	9	4	7	8	5	1	6
3	2	6	1	5	9	7	4	8
1	8	5	7	4	6	3	2	9
7	9	4	8	2	3	1	6	5

MIXAGRAMS

C R A F T   H U G E
S P A R E   H E I R
S U R E R   T U F T
A C H E D   C I T E

PAGE 120
ABC

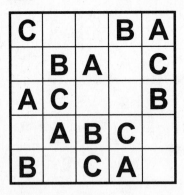

NATIONAL TREASURE
ABOARD, ABROAD, ABSORB

PAGE 121
Toy Story

A	R	C	S		N	A	M	E	S		O	H	N	O
B	E	R	T		F	R	O	D	O		E	M	U	S
O	V	E	R		L	I	V	I	N	G	D	O	L	L
M	E	D	E	A		I	T	A	L		S	L	O
B	L	O	W	S	O	N	E	S	T	O	P		
		S	I	R	E			A	B	R	O	A	D
C	S	A		A	S	S	E	T		O	K	R	A
H	A	V	E	N	O	T	R	U	C	K	W	I	T	H
A	R	E	A		S	A	L	O	N		E	S	L
P	A	R	R	O	T		S	O	O	T			
		P	L	A	Y	B	A	L	L	W	I	T	H
A	M	I		A	M	O	R		L	E	N	Y	A
G	O	F	L	Y	A	K	I	T	E		A	S	P	S
I	N	F	O		L	E	N	I	N		K	E	E	N
N	A	Y	S		E	D	G	E	D		S	T	A	T

PAGE 122
Wheels and Cogs

Tea

BETWEENER

PIPE

PAGE 123
Find the Ships

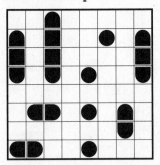

TWO-BY-FOUR
FURL, YULE

PAGE 124
Triad Split Decisions

TRANSDELETION
CANOEIST

PAGE 125
Three in a Row

PAGE 126

123

2	1	3	1	2	3	2	1	3
3	2	1	3	1	2	3	2	1
1	3	2	1	2	3	1	3	2
2	1	3	2	3	1	2	1	3
1	3	2	1	2	3	1	3	2
3	2	1	3	1	2	3	2	1
2	1	3	2	3	1	2	1	3
1	3	2	3	1	2	1	3	2
3	2	1	2	3	1	3	2	1

SUDOKU SUM

138 + 509 = 647

PAGE 127

Fences

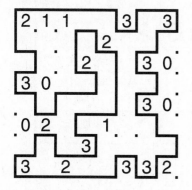

ADDITION SWITCH

653 + 284 = 937

PAGE 128

Face It

B	I	N	G		B	R	A	G	S		E	C	C	E
A	D	A	M		R	O	D	E	O		Y	A	R	D
N	O	S	E	A	R	O	U	N	D		E	R	I	E
S	L	A	N	G		F	L	E	A		O	V	E	N
			I	B	E	T		P	A	P	E	R	S
C	O	B	B	L	E	R		W	O	K	E			
A	D	O	R	E	D		J	A	P	A	N	E	S	E
D	I	N	O		F	A	X		I	D	O	S	
S	N	O	W	P	L	O	W		H	A	N	G	U	P
		B	O	E	R		L	A	R	G	E	L	Y
T	E	R	E	S	A		H	I	N	D			
A	R	E	A		F	L	O	E		O	D	D	E	R
C	A	N	T		L	I	P	S	E	R	V	I	C	E
I	S	E	E		E	V	I	T	A		D	E	R	N
T	E	E	N		T	E	N	O	R		S	T	U	D

PAGE 129

Retriever Maze

SAY IT AGAIN
ROSE

PAGE 131

Lots of Locks

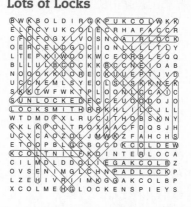

Unlisted word is GLOCKENSPIEL

WHO'S WHAT WHERE?
Kosovar

PAGE 132

Hyper-Sudoku

5	2	4	8	9	1	6	3	7
3	7	8	5	2	6	9	1	4
1	6	9	4	7	3	5	2	8
9	3	2	1	6	8	7	4	5
4	1	6	7	3	5	8	9	2
8	5	7	9	4	2	1	6	3
2	4	1	6	5	7	3	8	9
7	8	3	2	1	9	4	5	6
6	9	5	3	8	4	2	7	1

MIXAGRAMS

A L I K E   D U M P
E A R L Y   G L E N
O K A Y S   A L A S
P E N A L   R U D E

PAGE 133

Exit Lines

PAGE 134

One-Way Streets

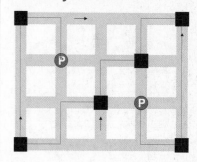

SOUND THINKING
HEROIC

PAGE 135

Star Search

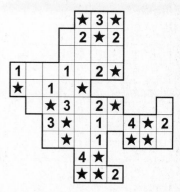

TELEPHONE TRIOS
ENDORSE, SPONSOR, SUPPORT

PAGE 136
Best Regards

D	O	L	T		R	I	N	G		O	P	T	S	
A	R	I	A		I	D	O	L		C	R	U	E	L
H	E	M	S		F	L	U	E		T	I	B	I	A
L	O	O	K	A	L	I	V	E		O	V	E	N	S
			B	E	N	E			P	A	R	E	S	
S	N	O	W	Y		G	A	M	B	I	T			
C	O	A	R	S	E		U	M	A		E	P	E	E
A	R	T	I	S	T	S		I	N	S	E	A	M	S
B	A	S	S		A	A	A		S	T	Y	L	U	S
			T	O	S	S	U	P		R	E	E	S	E
C	R	A	W	L		D	E	S	I					
H	O	D	A	D		V	I	E	W	P	O	I	N	T
A	M	A	T	I		A	B	L	E		S	C	A	R
P	E	N	C	E		S	L	E	D		L	E	I	A
	O	O	H	S		E	Y	R	E		O	R	L	Y

PAGE 139
Hugs & Kisses

W	A	S	P		C	U	B	A		P	A	S	S	
E	P	E	E		O	R	A	L		A	T	A	L	L
B	O	X	S	P	R	I	N	G		R	O	X	I	E
S	P	Y	K	I	D	S		A	L	A	M	O	D	E
			Y	E	A		R	E	A	D		P	E	R
D	I	N		T	Y	N	E		G	O	S	H		
A	M	I	T	Y		O	B	N	O	X	I	O	U	S
T	A	X	I		O	V	A	L	S		A	N	T	I
E	X	O	N	E	R	A	T	E		S	M	E	A	R
		N	E	X	T		E	R	L	E		S	H	E
F	I	T		O	H	O	S		A	T	T			
A	D	A	P	T	O	R		A	S	T	R	I	D	E
C	A	P	R	I		F	O	X	H	O	U	N	D	S
T	H	E	O	C		E	L	L	E		C	O	A	T
	O	S	S	A		O	D	E	S		E	N	Y	A

PAGE 142
All at Sea

M	E	N	U	S		E	P	P	S		A	R	C	S
O	Z	O	N	E		T	E	A	S		G	A	L	E
C	R	E	W	N	E	C	K	S	W	E	A	T	E	R
A	L	I		W	H	E	T		S	T	A	F	F	
			E	P	E	E		R	A	S	H			
S	A	I	L	O	R	S	U	I	T		A	C	C	T
A	N	O	D	E	S		N	E	O	N		O	R	E
A	T	T	Y	S		S	T	S		E	M	B	E	R
B	S	A			Y	U	R	I		S	T	A	R	E	S
S	Y	S	T			P	I	L	O	T	W	H	A	L	E
			H	A	I	L		C	A	T	O			
I	D	E	A	L		A	S	T	I		G	U	S	
C	A	P	T	A	I	N	K	A	N	G	A	R	O	O
E	R	I	C		A	K	I	N		I	N	G	O	T
T	E	C	H		N	A	M	E		N	Y	E	T	S

PAGE 137
Go With the Flow

THREE AT A RHYME
EEK, PEEK, TEAK

PAGE 138
Sudoku

5	4	3	1	9	6	2	7	8
9	7	1	8	2	5	3	4	6
6	2	8	3	4	7	9	5	1
2	3	6	5	8	1	4	9	7
4	5	9	7	6	2	1	8	3
1	8	7	9	3	4	5	6	2
3	9	2	4	7	8	6	1	5
7	1	4	6	5	3	8	2	9
8	6	5	2	1	9	7	3	4

CENTURY MARKS
23 + 47 + 7 - 10 + 33 = 100

PAGE 140
Split Decisions

TRANSDELETION
ENRAGED

PAGE 141
Number-Out

1	1	2	6	4	3
4	1	5	3	3	3
3	1	6	5	4	2
4	4	4	1	2	6
5	2	1	6	6	4
2	3	3	4	1	1

OPPOSITE ATTRACTION
BEGIN, END

PAGE 143
ABC

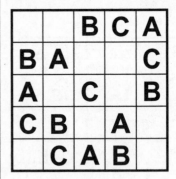

CLUELESS CROSSWORD

E	N	T	R	A	N	T
S		R		N		U
P	H	O	E	N	I	X
Y		D		E		E
I	N	D	E	X	E	D
N		E		E		O
G	E	N	E	S	I	S

PAGE 144
Piece It Together

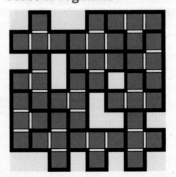

BETWEENER
PROOF

PAGE 145
Line Drawing

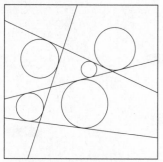

THREE OF A KIND
SERVE THE STEW OR DESSERT
WITH EIGHTY-PROOF
VERMOUTH.

PAGE 146
One-Octave Spread

M	A	L	T	A		A	P	P	L	E		C	A	B
I	L	I	A	D		C	A	R	O	N		A	V	A
C	O	M	P	A	C	T	D	I	S	C		J	A	B
S	T	E	P	P	E		S	O	S	O		U	S	E
		E	T	A	L		R	E	D	A	N	T	S	
S	E	C	T		S	A	P		S	E	E	M		
U	G	H		E	R	R	S		D	R	U	B		
R	O	O	F		S	C	O	T	T		O	S	L	O
	S	C	A	M		H	O	R	A		I	A	N	
	O	V	I	D		F	U	R		A	C	M	E	
A	D	H	E	R	E	S		T	M	A	N			
P	R	O		A	R	E	A		A	S	K	E	R	S
S	A	L		C	A	R	M	E	C	H	A	N	I	C
E	P	I		L	I	V	E	R		E	R	I	C	A
S	E	C		E	L	E	N	A		N	A	D	E	R

PAGE 147
Find the Ships

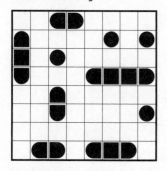

TWO-BY-FOUR
NUMB, GILT

PAGE 148
Hyper-Sudoku

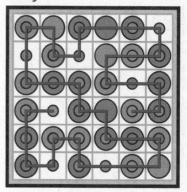

1	4	5	9	7	8	3	6	2
6	8	9	4	3	2	7	5	1
2	7	3	1	5	6	4	8	9
7	5	2	6	8	3	1	9	4
3	1	8	2	9	4	5	7	6
9	6	4	5	1	7	8	2	3
8	2	1	3	6	5	9	4	7
4	9	7	8	2	1	6	3	5
5	3	6	7	4	9	2	1	8

MIXAGRAMS

F A C E T   S T O P
A M A S S   B O D Y
P A P E R   T W I N
S T E R N   O N C E

PAGE 149
Pinnacles

L	A	M	A	S		D	E	L	L	A		P	L	Y
O	Z	A	R	K		E	V	I	A	N		E	V	A
S	U	M	M	I	T	T	A	L	K	S		A	I	R
E	R	M	A		R	A	N	T	O		S	K	I	N
R	E	A	D	M	I	T	S		T	E	C	H		
		A	A	A			F	A	D	E	O	U	T	
J	O	T		K	L	I	N	E		I	N	U	R	E
A	B	O	V	E		R	A	T		F	E	R	N	S
M	O	P	E	S		A	B	A	C	I		S	S	T
B	E	S	I	D	E	S		H	E	R				
	E	N	O	S		P	H	A	S	E	D	I	N	
A	R	C	S		C	L	A	I	M		T	O	N	E
M	A	R		C	R	O	W	N	P	R	I	N	C	E
E	V	E		D	O	M	E	D		P	R	O	U	D
N	E	T		E	W	E	R	S		M	E	R	R	Y

PAGE 150
Fences

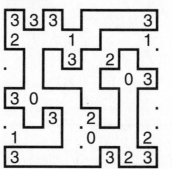

ADDITION SWITCH
3 8 7 + 4 0 4 = 7 9 1

PAGE 151
Dotty

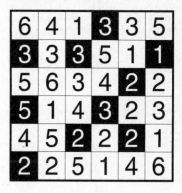

SAY IT AGAIN
BORE

PAGE 152
Number-Out

6	4	1	3	3	5
3	3	3	5	1	1
5	6	3	4	2	2
5	1	4	3	2	3
4	5	2	2	2	1
2	2	5	1	4	6

OPPOSITE ATTRACTION
WILD, TAME

PAGE 153
Looking for Help

C	U	S	P		C	A	N	S		D	E	A	L	S
A	S	I	A		A	T	O	P		R	A	N	U	P
B	A	R	S		L	I	R	A		A	R	E	N	A
			S	U	L	T	A	N	O	F	S	W	A	T
F	A	C	E	R	S		K	A	T					
O	L	A		B	O	S	S		R	E	E	V	E	S
L	E	N	D		F	O	A	M		R	H	I	N	O
S	P	O	O	N	F	U	L	O	F	S	U	G	A	R
O	P	E	R	A		P	A	P	A		D	O	M	E
M	O	S	A	I	C		D	E	N	S		D	E	S
			L	E	O			B	A	S	A	L	T	
S	E	N	S	E	O	F	S	M	E	L	L			
T	R	E	A	D		F	O	A	L		A	W	E	D
A	M	I	N	O		E	D	I	T		N	O	V	A
G	A	L	E	N		R	A	M	S		G	O	A	D

PAGE 154

123

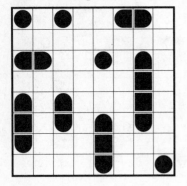

SUDOKU SUM
3 0 5 + 1 8 7 = 4 9 2

PAGE 155

Find the Ships

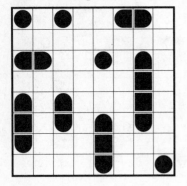

TWO-BY-FOUR
ARIA, FUND; AURA, FIND

PAGE 156

Remark-Able

T	W	I	T		O	A	R	S		B	R	U	T	E
A	I	D	E		P	L	E	A		A	N	T	I	S
S	P	E	A	K	E	A	S	Y		R	A	T	E	S
S	E	A	S	O	N		E	S	P	N		E	T	A
			E	R	A	S	E		R	O	B	R	O	Y
E	A	S	T	E	R	N		T	O	N	I	C		
A	R	T		A	M	I	N	O		E	T	H	E	R
T	E	A	R		S	P	E	N	T		S	A	L	E
S	A	T	E	S		E	D	G	E	S		O	L	E
	E	N	T	E	R		U	N	P	O	S	E	D	
S	A	V	E	U	P		P	E	T	A	L			
E	L	I		M	A	L	L		A	D	D	E	R	S
A	E	S	O	P		V	O	I	C	E	M	A	I	L
T	R	I	N	E		I	T	L	L		A	S	T	I
O	T	T	E	R		I	S	L	E		N	E	E	D

PAGE 157

B _ _ _ _ _ Time

Puzzle title is Break Time

IN OTHER WORDS
CHIPMUNK

PAGE 158

Alternating Tiles

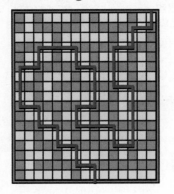

THREE AT A RHYME
COAL, ROLL, SOUL

PAGE 159

Star Search

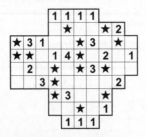

TELEPHONE TRIOS
BARGAIN, CUT-RATE, LOW-COST

PAGE 160

Success-Full

PAGE 161

Sudoku

1	8	9	7	6	4	2	5	3
2	3	7	5	1	9	8	6	4
4	6	5	2	3	8	7	1	9
6	7	4	8	2	3	5	9	1
3	1	2	9	5	6	4	7	8
9	5	8	4	7	1	6	3	2
8	4	1	6	9	5	3	2	7
5	2	3	1	4	7	9	8	6
7	9	6	3	8	2	1	4	5

MIXAGRAMS
P I L A F   J O K E
S P I E L   A S P S
P A N D A   C A S T
S U N U P   K E E N

PAGE 162

One-Way Streets

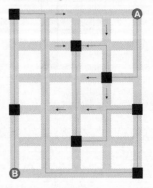

SOUND THINKING
GERANIUM

PAGE 163

ABC

B	A			C
		B	C	A
		C	A	B
C	B	A		
A	C		B	

NATIONAL TREASURE
OVERALLS

PAGE 164

Pair-O'-Docs

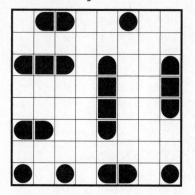

```
ATOM  BOSNS  DAFT
ROMA  OSHEA  OHIO
BLAH  ACORN  RATE
  DRIBSANDDRABS
    METRE  FIG
ASIANS    ALG  HAL
SASH    AGREE  ALE
CYLINDRICALDRUM
ONE  IOTAS    EMMA
TOT  KOS    CLASSY
    PER  COOED
  DRESSERDRAWER
PEAT  TRADE  OLES
RENT  OTTER  OMAN
EDGY  PEERS  DODO
```

PAGE 165

Ship of Fuels
A: #26, B: #3, C: #16

BETWEENER
BOOK

PAGE 166

Find the Ships

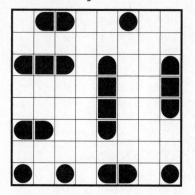

TWO-BY-FOUR
CART, LIVE (or EVIL or VEIL
or VILE)

PAGE 167

123

3	2	1	3	1	2	3	1	2
1	3	2	1	2	3	1	2	3
2	1	3	2	3	1	2	3	1
1	3	2	3	1	2	3	1	2
2	1	3	1	2	3	1	2	3
3	2	1	2	3	1	2	3	1
1	3	2	1	2	3	1	2	3
3	2	1	3	1	2	3	1	2
2	1	3	2	3	1	2	3	1

SUDOKU SUM
$158 + 309 = 467$

PAGE 169

Trifecta

```
STAB  EBBS  BEKAA
PURR  GLUT  EXITS
ELEE  GERE  RANTO
WINACCEPTANCEOF
SPOKEUP    BIT
    NAP  FLOE  ORA
ASHES  TROI  IRON
PLACETHEBLAMEON
SUNK  HERO  IPODS
ORK  FREE  SSR
    TAU  CALORIE
SHOWIMPROVEMENT
HYPER  TODO  PRAT
IDEAL  AVER  TUNA
PESKY  HEDY  UNES
```

PAGE 170

Fences

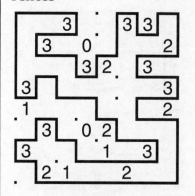

ADDITION SWITCH
$769 + 175 = 944$

PAGE 171

Number-Out

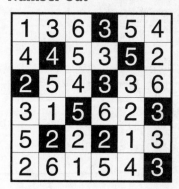

1	3	6	3	5	4
4	4	5	3	5	2
2	5	4	3	3	6
3	1	5	6	2	3
5	2	2	2	1	3
2	6	1	5	4	3

OPPOSITE ATTRACTION
START, STOP

PAGE 172

French Motto

```
SASE  PRADA  TEAK
IBAR  OILED  SANA
CRADLEOFLIBERTY
KABOOM    TOOTSIE
    COSTS  SRS
MATT  HAL  GETIT
TITO  GEMINI  RNA
ASORTOFEQUALITY
LEN  RATOUT  ACHE
CREPE  SLO  DIKE
    EBW  DROID
HOTSEAT    COILED
GREEKFRATERNITY
WENT  TETRA  TORE
YODA  SEEIN  ONES
```

PAGE 173

Liberty Bell Maze

BETWEENER

STONE

PAGE 174

Hyper-Sudoku

7	9	6	4	5	3	8	2	1
8	3	2	9	6	1	7	5	4
5	4	1	8	7	2	6	9	3
1	5	7	6	9	8	3	4	2
9	2	8	3	4	7	5	1	6
4	6	3	2	1	5	9	8	7
6	8	9	1	3	4	2	7	5
2	7	4	5	8	6	1	3	9
3	1	5	7	2	9	4	6	8

MIXAGRAMS

A L I V E	E G A D
B R O I L	B O I L
B U L G E	A L S O
A B L E R	N O U N

PAGE 175

"C" Water

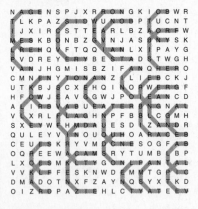

INITIAL REACTION

Home Is Where The Heart Is

PAGE 176

Risk Management

PAGE 177

Triad Split Decisions

TRANSDELETION

NUTMEG

PAGE 178

One-Way Streets

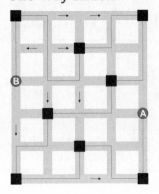

SOUND THINKING

COYOTE

PAGE 179

Promo Pieces

S	C	A	T		M	C	R	A	E		O	T	T	O
T	O	T	O		E	L	E	C	T		M	A	S	H
A	B	L	Y		M	A	C	O	N		E	X	A	M
T	R	A	C	T	O	R	T	R	A	I	L	E	R	
S	A	S	H	A		I	O	N			R	E	X	
			E	D	E	N			O	A	T	E	R	S
I	S	M	S		R	E	P	A	S	T		M	I	A
T	H	A	T	H	I	T	S	T	H	E	S	P	O	T
Z	E	N		O	N	S	I	T	E		E	T	T	E
A	S	C	O	T	S			E	A	S	E			
	H	O	E		S	I	N		U	S	A	G	E	
P	U	L	L	I	N	G	T	H	E	P	L	U	G	
H	E	R	O		N	O	L	I	E		A	I	R	Y
R	A	I	N		G	R	O	O	M		S	C	U	P
S	T	A	G		E	T	O	N	S		T	E	S	T

PAGE 180
Color Paths

SAY IT AGAIN
PLANT

PAGE 181
Star Search

TELEPHONE TRIOS
LAMPOON, MOCKERY, TAKEOFF

PAGE 182
Sudoku

1	6	8	2	9	5	3	4	7
5	9	4	7	6	3	2	8	1
3	2	7	8	4	1	6	5	9
9	8	5	3	2	4	1	7	6
7	1	3	5	8	6	4	9	2
2	4	6	1	7	9	5	3	8
8	3	9	6	5	2	7	1	4
4	5	2	9	1	7	8	6	3
6	7	1	4	3	8	9	2	5

CENTURY MARKS
41 – 17 + 48 + 29 - 1 = 100

PAGE 183
Writers' Might

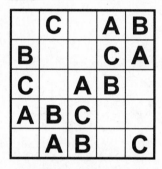

PAGE 184
ABC

C		A	B
B		C	A
C		A	B
A	B	C	
	A	B	C

CLUELESS CROSSWORD

PAGE 185
Find the Ships

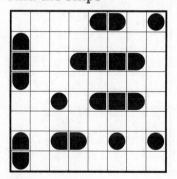

TWO-BY-FOUR
GREW, GILD

PAGE 186
Money Man

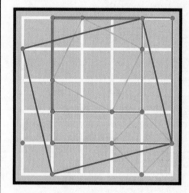

PAGE 187
Dot to Dot

THREE AT A RHYME
CODE, MOWED, TOAD

PAGE 188
123

2	3	1	2	3	1	3	1	2
3	1	2	3	1	2	1	2	3
1	2	3	1	2	3	2	3	1
3	1	2	3	1	2	3	1	2
1	2	3	1	2	3	1	2	3
2	3	1	2	3	1	2	3	1
3	1	2	3	1	2	1	2	3
2	3	1	2	3	1	3	1	2
1	2	3	1	2	3	2	3	1

SUDOKU SUM
7 4 8 + 2 0 3 = 9 5 1

PAGE 189

Fences

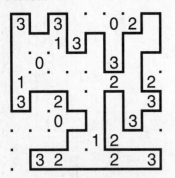

ADDITION SWITCH
$4 6 5 + 1 3 5 = 6 0 0$

PAGE 190

Assets Across

A M E S	L A N K Y	C P A S
B E N T	A D I E U	B L U E
A T T A	M O R E L	S A K E
S T A G E P R O P E R T Y	
E L I	C O N	L E V E R S
D E L P H I	A S O F	D O A
R O L L I N G S T O C K	
E S S O	O S U	I N K S
C H E M I C A L B O N D	
G O T	T O M E	B E E F U P
S E A B E E	I V A	U N E
P L A Q U E D E P O S I T	
L U A U	U T T E R	L I T E
B A R N	A N N A S	D O E R
J E T T	L E A S E	E N D S

MIXAGRAMS

```
P I T H Y   G R O W   W
P L E A D   H E R O   O
D U N C E   P E A R   R
F L A K E   B O O K   K
```

PAGE 191

Hyper-Sudoku

7	4	6	9	1	3	2	8	5
9	2	5	8	4	7	1	3	6
8	1	3	6	5	2	4	9	7
3	9	7	4	2	8	5	6	1
2	5	8	1	3	6	7	4	9
1	6	4	5	7	9	3	2	8
5	8	1	2	9	4	6	7	3
4	3	9	7	6	5	8	1	2
6	7	2	3	8	1	9	5	4

PAGE 192

Split Decisions

TRANSDELETION
PETITE

PAGE 193

Cut It Out

M A J A	S H R U G	S L A B
A B U T	P O I S E	C O R E
S A L E C O U P O N	H O L E
T S E	L U R E	E D I T O R
S E P I A S	U R I S	
D R E S S P A T T E R N	
S T A L K	W E S T S	M O O
P A N E	B O G I E	Z I N E
A C T	F A R A D	M U R A L
T H E M I D D L E M A N	
E R A S	A N I M A L
S T R E E P	S A D E	I G O
K O O K	P A P E R D O L L S
E T A L	L A U R A	F L E E
D E N Y	E U R O S	F I T S

PAGE 194

Solitaire Poker

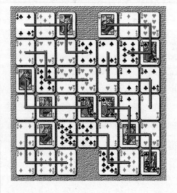

BETWEENER
BRIDGE

PAGE 195

Number-Out

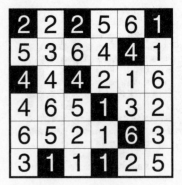

OPPOSITE ATTRACTION
BORROW, LEND

PAGE 196

One-Way Streets

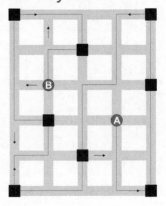

SOUND THINKING
LIKELY, LOCALE

PAGE 197

Sweet Dreams

PAGE 198

Sudoku

3	1	9	6	2	7	5	4	8
8	2	7	5	4	3	6	1	9
6	4	5	9	8	1	3	7	2
1	5	6	8	9	4	7	2	3
7	3	4	2	1	6	8	9	5
9	8	2	7	3	5	1	6	4
2	9	1	3	7	8	4	5	6
5	7	8	4	6	9	2	3	1
4	6	3	1	5	2	9	8	7

MIXAGRAMS

```
A L O N E    S H U T
R O B I N    B O N Y
S O L A R    C L U E
A P P A L    L E V Y
```

PAGE 199

Star Search

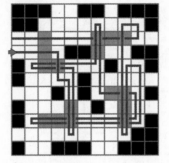

TELEPHONE TRIOS
COMPOSE, CONCOCT, DEVELOP

PAGE 200

No Resistance

R	O	T	C	■	R	A	J	A	H	■	B	U	S	T
A	B	R	A	■	B	R	O	T	H	■	E	C	H	O
G	O	E	S	W	I	T	H	T	H	E	F	L	O	W
S	E	E	T	O	■	I	N	A	■	R	O	A	D	S
■	■	A	O	K	S	■	C	R	A	G	■	■	■	■
A	V	O	W	■	I	T	C	H	E	S	■	C	S	A
L	A	M	A	■	B	R	O	■	V	E	G	A	N	S
P	L	A	Y	S	B	Y	T	H	E	R	U	L	E	S
H	O	N	S	H	U	■	T	O	R	■	A	L	E	E
A	R	I	■	A	T	B	A	T	S	■	T	A	R	T
■	■	O	R	Z	O	■	C	E	C	E	■	■	■	■
A	S	T	R	O	■	O	P	A	■	A	M	A	T	I
D	O	E	S	N	T	M	A	K	E	W	A	V	E	S
A	F	R	O	■	S	E	V	E	N	■	L	I	S	P
M	A	I	N	■	P	R	E	S	S	■	A	S	H	Y

PAGE 201

Straight Ahead

SAY IT AGAIN
CLASS

PAGE 202

Musical Spirals

```
C Y N O H A X S O L Y
K O P H X L Y O F B
E L Y P G O N G G E L
E D N Q T O T G S O W
L A A D L A R A L M O
L E M B H T N C R U
D T P M S E G A N R
I M P O X T E L E T S
T U R F L S I B A S
P M O J G C N Q O T U
R W E L A R O U G S N
E E A P R A Y N S T E
M G S T O L E D G G D
P O D N E E D U R O T
P R C E W N I L G C C
H E S C K T E R N D U
P O L A N D Z E N O T
S E O N O A A A S H W
A N T N F X O P O
S I G I B N L A R N Q
R E N X I J T O G N D
U T A C C X T E H H R
Z Z O N O A V J S K U
C V D R F A V H A R
T B R U S C Y Z E M
Y N A Y A H N M I N O
G A P P R M O P I Z F
G O M Z C T V T O Z K
M I J O U Q H A C L L
```

WHO'S WHAT WHERE?
Parmesan

PAGE 203

ABC

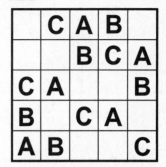

CLUELESS CROSSWORD

J	A	G	U	A	R	S
I	■	R	■	W	■	U
G	O	A	T	E	E	S
S	■	M	■	S	■	P
A	R	M	H	O	L	E
W	■	A	■	M	■	C
S	E	R	P	E	N	T

PAGE 204

Themeless Toughie

B	L	O	S	S	O	M	■	J	A	V	E	L	I	N
R	E	C	L	I	N	E	■	O	R	E	G	A	N	O
A	T	T	I	R	E	D	■	L	E	N	G	T	H	S
S	T	A	T	E	■	I	L	I	A	D	■	T	A	I
H	U	G	S	■	S	T	I	E	S	■	R	I	L	E
E	C	O	■	A	P	A	R	T	■	L	A	C	E	S
R	E	N	O	V	A	T	E	■	W	I	D	E	S	T
■	■	■	G	O	R	E	■	T	A	C	O	■	■	■
C	H	E	R	I	E	■	B	A	N	K	N	O	T	E
L	I	N	E	D	■	B	A	K	E	S	■	V	O	N
I	L	E	S	■	T	R	I	E	D	■	G	E	N	T
E	L	M	■	P	O	E	T	S	■	V	E	R	N	E
N	A	I	V	E	T	E	■	O	N	A	T	E	A	R
T	R	E	A	T	E	D	■	F	O	L	I	A	G	E
S	Y	S	T	E	M	S	■	F	R	E	T	T	E	D

PAGE 206

Find the Ships

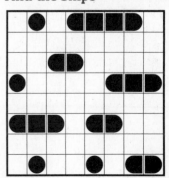

TWO-BY-FOUR
GRAY, NINE

PAGE 207

Hyper-Sudoku

3	6	5	8	4	9	1	2	7
1	9	4	6	7	2	8	3	5
2	7	8	5	3	1	9	6	4
8	2	3	1	6	7	5	4	9
5	1	9	4	8	3	6	7	2
6	4	7	2	9	5	3	8	1
7	8	6	9	5	4	2	1	3
4	5	1	3	2	6	7	9	8
9	3	2	7	1	8	4	5	6

BETWEENER
CRACKER

PAGE 208

Themeless Toughie

B	R	A	N	A	G	H	■	S	C	H	E	M	A	S
L	O	R	E	L	E	I	■	P	A	T	R	I	C	E
E	S	C	A	P	E	R	■	E	N	S	I	L	E	S
A	S	T	R	O	■	O	H	N	O	■	K	I	T	T
R	I	I	S	■	R	H	O	D	E	S	■	E	O	E
E	N	C	■	T	R	I	M	S	■	H	A	U	N	T
D	I	S	T	A	S	T	E	■	J	I	N	X	E	S
■	■	A	X	T	O	G	R	I	N	D	■	■	■	■
U	R	A	N	I	A	■	R	E	M	N	A	N	T	S
N	I	S	A	N	■	F	O	A	M	Y	■	A	O	L
C	P	O	■	G	O	A	W	R	Y	■	P	I	N	A
L	I	F	T	■	A	R	N	E	■	V	A	L	E	S
A	N	N	E	T	T	E	■	N	E	O	L	I	T	H
S	T	O	N	I	E	R	■	D	E	T	E	N	T	E
P	O	W	D	E	R	S	■	S	L	E	D	G	E	S

PAGE 209

Paper Chase
1: Square 4, 2: Square 1,
3: Square 3

THREE AT A RHYME
DIME, CHIME, CLIMB

PAGE 210

Fences

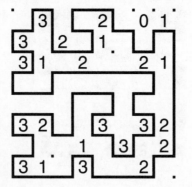

ADDITION SWITCH
1 8 7 + 7 8 5 = 9 7 2

PAGE 211

Themeless Toughie

A	M	I	A	B	L	E	■	R	E	C	O	V	E	R
B	A	N	D	I	E	S	■	E	X	A	M	I	N	E
A	R	S	E	N	I	C	■	R	I	P	S	O	F	F
S	T	O	P	S	■	A	M	U	S	E	■	L	O	U
H	I	L	T	■	B	L	U	N	T	■	B	E	R	T
E	N	E	■	D	U	A	L	■	S	C	O	N	C	E
D	I	S	S	E	C	T	E	D	■	R	A	T	E	D
■	■	E	A	S	E	■	R	O	U	T	■	■	■	■
U	T	T	E	R	■	S	T	A	N	D	S	P	A	T
P	R	I	D	E	S	■	R	I	C	E	■	R	U	E
D	I	B	S	■	I	N	A	N	E	■	M	O	R	N
A	P	E	■	S	L	U	M	P	■	L	I	M	O	S
T	O	T	A	L	E	D	■	I	R	O	N	O	R	E
E	L	A	T	I	N	G	■	P	E	S	E	T	A	S
D	I	N	E	T	T	E	■	E	V	E	R	E	S	T

PAGE 212

123

2	3	1	2	1	3	2	1	3
1	2	3	1	3	2	1	3	2
3	1	2	3	2	1	3	2	1
2	3	1	2	1	3	2	1	3
1	2	3	1	3	2	1	3	2
3	1	2	3	2	1	3	2	1
2	3	1	2	1	3	1	3	2
1	2	3	1	3	2	3	2	1
3	1	2	3	2	1	2	1	3

SUDOKU SUM
5 0 8 + 1 2 9 = 6 3 7

PAGE 213

Number-Out

2	4	5	1	6	6
1	5	1	3	6	3
6	1	3	5	3	4
4	2	3	4	4	5
4	3	3	2	5	5
4	6	4	4	1	2

OPPOSITE ATTRACTION
CLEAR, UNCLEAR

PAGE 214

Themeless Toughie

B	Y	P	A	S	S	E	D	■	S	A	T	O	R	I
E	A	R	P	H	O	N	E	■	U	P	R	O	O	T
D	R	O	P	O	U	T	S	■	G	R	I	F	T	S
E	N	D	E	A	R	S	■	G	A	I	N	S	A	Y
■	■	■	A	L	S	■	P	E	R	L	E	■	■	■
A	F	A	R	■	■	L	U	R	K	■	■	R	E	S
A	L	I	S	T	A	I	R	M	A	C	L	E	A	N
R	O	M	A	N	C	E	L	A	N	G	U	A	G	E
G	R	I	S	T	T	O	O	N	E	S	M	I	L	L
H	A	S	■	■	E	V	I	E	■	■	B	R	E	L
■	■	■	A	L	D	E	N	■	P	O	E	■	■	■
D	A	N	S	E	U	R	■	N	A	R	R	A	T	E
I	C	E	C	A	P	■	A	L	L	F	I	R	E	D
A	R	I	O	S	O	■	R	E	L	E	N	T	E	D
L	E	N	T	E	N	■	C	R	Y	O	G	E	N	Y

PAGE 215

Commonwealth Trail

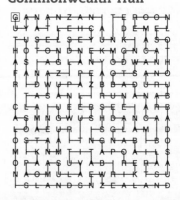

IN OTHER WORDS
AARDVARK

PAGE 216

Turn Maze

SAY IT AGAIN
GROUND

PAGE 217

Themeless Toughie

J	E	S	S	E	J	A	M	E	S		M	A	S	S
E	X	H	I	L	A	R	A	T	E		A	B	E	T
T	H	O	M	A	S	A	R	N	E		D	A	T	A
L	A	O		M	O	B		A	P	L	E	N	T	Y
A	L	T	A		N	I	P		S	A	D	D	L	E
G	E	S	T	E		A	I	D		B	O	O	E	D
			O	V	E	N	M	I	T	T		N	I	A
C	O	M	M	O	N	S	E	N	S	E	I	S	N	T
A	V	A		K	E	E	N	N	E	S	S			
M	E	R	C	I		A	T	E		T	A	T	U	M
E	R	R	A	N	D		O	R	B		K	E	N	O
T	W	I	N	G	E	D		D	A	D		N	I	T
R	O	A	N		C	A	P	A	C	I	T	A	T	E
U	R	G	E		O	R	A	T	O	R	I	C	A	L
E	K	E	S		R	E	L	E	N	T	L	E	S	S

PAGE 218

ABCD

C		B	D		A
A	C	D		B	
	D	A	B	C	
B		C	A		D
	A		C	D	B
D	B			A	C

NATIONAL TREASURE
STANZA, THANKS

PAGE 219

Sudoku

7	2	9	3	4	1	5	6	8
6	5	3	7	2	8	1	9	4
1	8	4	6	5	9	2	7	3
4	1	5	2	6	7	3	8	9
3	9	7	8	1	5	4	2	6
2	6	8	9	3	4	7	5	1
9	4	1	5	7	6	8	3	2
8	7	2	1	9	3	6	4	5
5	3	6	4	8	2	9	1	7

MIXAGRAMS

T A B O O   L O G Y
H O W D Y   S A I L
A R M E D   F O R T
T O T A L   H U L A

PAGE 220

Themeless Toughie

U	N	S	U	R	E		L	U	T	I	S	T	S
N	A	P	L	E	S		S	O	N	I	N	L	A	W
C	R	A	N	E	S		C	O	D	E	N	A	M	E
A	R	C	A	D	E	G	A	M	E		S	L	E	D
R	A	E		S	N	O	R	E	R	S		O	L	E
I	T	A			B	E	D		E	M	M	Y	S
N	O	G		E	T	A	S		G	E	M		
G	R	E	A	S	E	D		D	E	P	I	C	T	S
		L	T	D		M	O	T	S		O	R	E
R	O	M	E	O		S	U	R		M	A	N
E	M	U		P	A	U	S	I	N	G		M	I	A
B	E	T	E		D	I	S	C	O	R	D	A	N	T
U	L	T	I	M	A	T	E		B	O	R	N	E	O
T	E	E	N	A	G	E	D		L	O	A	D	E	R
S	T	R	E	W	E	D		E	M	B	O	S	S

PAGE 221

One-Way Streets

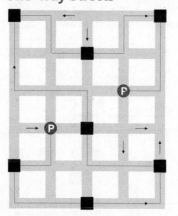

SOUND THINKING
MAESTRO

PAGE 222

Split Decisions

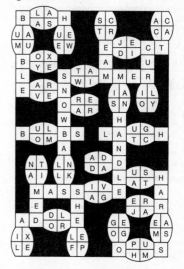

TRANSDELETION
CHRISTIE

PAGE 223

Themeless Toughie

R	I	M	S	H	O	T		S	Q	U	E	E	Z	E
U	N	A	W	A	R	E		E	U	C	H	R	E	D
M	A	R	I	L	Y	N		N	E	L	S	O	N	S
		T	E	X	A	S	T	E	A		D	D	E
S	P	I	C	Y		C	O	R	N		R	E	A	L
H	I	G	H		M	E	L	I	S	S	A		
A	L	L	E	G	E		S	E	R	E	N	A	D	E
W	O	O	D	A	R	D		S	O	A	K	S	U	P
S	T	O	O	L	I	E	S		O	R	A	T	E	S
		F	A	T	B	A	C	K		N	A	T	O
F	I	E	F		B	O	N	E		C	D	R	O	M
I	D	A		D	A	N	D	R	U	F	F		
L	A	S	O	R	D	A		E	L	L	I	P	S	E
T	H	E	M	A	G	I		A	N	A	L	Y	S	T
H	O	L	S	T	E	R		L	A	T	E	E	N	S

PAGE 224
Looped Path

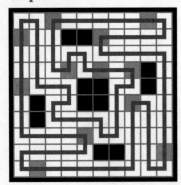

SAY IT AGAIN
DEPOSE

PAGE 225
Star Search

TELEPHONE TRIOS
COBBLER, PUDDING, SHERBET

PAGE 226
Themeless Toughie

T	H	E	A	T	E	R		S	E	T	B	A	C	K
H	O	S	T	I	L	E		P	R	A	I	R	I	E
I	N	T	E	N	S	E		L	O	I	T	E	R	S
E	K	E		T	E	N	N	I	S		T	A	C	T
V	E	E	P	S		T	I	C		R	E	C	U	R
E	R	M	A		D	E	L	E	T	E		O	L	E
		S	W	O	R	E		B	R	I	D	A	L	
	M	O	S	E	Y	S		L	O	U	D	E	R	
R	E	V	E	A	L		V	A	N	N	A			
O	D	E		R	E	L	I	V	E		H	E	R	B
S	I	R	E	S		A	B	E		C	O	Y	E	R
T	E	R	R		B	R	E	N	D	A		E	P	A
E	V	I	N	C	E	D		D	I	S	P	L	A	Y
R	A	D	I	A	T	E		E	V	A	S	I	V	E
S	L	E	E	P	E	R		R	E	S	I	D	E	D

PAGE 227
Number-Out

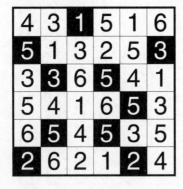

OPPOSITE ATTRACTION
IMPORT, EXPORT

PAGE 228
Line Drawing

The "right" letters all look the same when held up to a mirror

TWO-BY-FOUR
BAND, AUNT (or TUNA)

PAGE 229
Themeless Toughie

PAGE 230
Triad Split Decisions

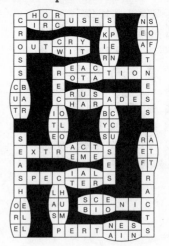

TRANSDELETION
ROAST BEEF

PAGE 231
Piece It Together

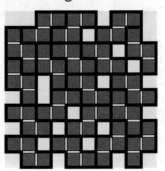

THREE AT A RHYME
LURCH, PERCH, SEARCH

PAGE 232
Themeless Toughie

S	A	T	I	R	E		A	L	O	E	V	E	R	A
K	E	R	N	E	L		D	E	R	A	I	L	E	D
I	R	I	S	E	S		O	V	E	R	C	A	M	E
J	O	B		D	E	E	R	E		N	E	P	A	L
U	S	U	R	Y		L	I	L	T	S		S	R	I
M	O	T	E		T	E	N	S	E		B	E	R	N
P	L	E	A	D	I	N	G		T	I	E	D	Y	E
			P	I	N	A		S	O	N	S			
A	S	S	E	S	S		W	I	N	N	I	P	E	G
S	P	E	D		E	D	I	T	S		D	R	N	O
H	A	N		S	L	E	E	K		S	E	E	T	O
A	T	A	R	I		L	L	A	M	A		V	I	I
M	U	T	I	N	I	E	D		U	P	D	A	T	E
E	L	O	N	G	A	T	E		S	P	O	I	L	S
D	A	R	K	E	N	E	D		E	Y	E	L	E	T